FRUSTRATED PATRIOTS

FRUSTRATED PATRIOTS

North Carolina and the War of 1812

by Sarah McCulloh Lemmon

The University of North Carolina Press
Chapel Hill

Copyright © 1973 by
The University of North Carolina Press
All rights reserved

Manufactured in the United States of America
Printed by The Seeman Printery, Inc.
Library of Congress Catalog Card Number 73-455
ISBN 0-8078-1209-9

Library of Congress Cataloging in Publication Data

Lemmon, Sarah McCulloh.
    Frustrated patriots; North Carolina and the War of 1812.
Bibliography: p.
    1. North Carolina—History—War of 1812.
2. United States—History—War of 1812. I. Title.
E359.5.N7L43   973.5′24′56   73-455
ISBN 0-8078-1209-9

TABLE OF CONTENTS

PREFACE

Previous studies of the causes and events of the War of 1812 seldom mention the state of North Carolina. The state is obliquely included in the "southern states" when causes are discussed, referred to in a phrase when the British blockade is described, but otherwise ignored. The British landing at Ocracoke rates no inclusion with Cockburn's depredations in the Chesapeake. North Carolina's heroes Forsyth, Blakeley, and Burns may be found in the histories but their native state is not given; her great dissenter Gaston does not receive his due.

Two questions then arise. First, to what degree and why did North Carolina support the war, if she did? Second, what, if anything, did she contribute to this frustrating, poorly conducted, far from unanimous war effort? It was in an effort to answer these questions that I undertook the research which has resulted in this book.

Much of the source material in the Old Military Branch of the National Archives pertaining to the southern department and in the Public Record Office in London appears never to have been examined. Should histories of other southern states in the War of 1812 be undertaken, not only will ample data be found, but, I am convinced, a reevaluation of the war effort on the southern seaboard will eventually result.

I extend my thanks to Meredith College which granted me

sabbatical leave for research on the project and other courtesies as well. Memory F. Mitchell, who first interested me in the War of 1812; Victor Sapio, Carolyn A. Wallace, and William S. Powell, who encouraged me; Leslie Syron, who aided in locating materials in the Public Record Office; Meredith Smaw of New Bern; and the helpful staffs of the North Carolina Department of Archives and History at Raleigh, the Southern Historical Collection and the North Carolina Collection at Chapel Hill, and the National Archives deserve special mention and thanks for making easier the fascinating but laborious work of research.

I am particularly grateful to the Mary Reynolds Babcock Foundation, Inc., for financial assistance in support of the publication of this volume.

ABBREVIATIONS

LC	Library of Congress, Washington, D.C.
NA	National Archives, Washington, D.C.
NC Archives	State Department of Archives and History, Raleigh, N.C.
NCC	North Carolina Collection, The University of North Carolina Library, Chapel Hill, N.C.
SHC	Southern Historical Collection, The University of North Carolina Library, Chapel Hill, N.C.

FRUSTRATED PATRIOTS

1 *NORTH CAROLINA GOES TO WAR*

The United States faced an early test of its independence when revolutionary France declared war against the First Coalition, including Great Britain, in 1793. Breaking the Alliance of 1778 with France, President George Washington issued a proclamation of neutrality in an effort to enable the new nation to develop peacefully into a strong and independent power. It was not to be accomplished that simply; first France, then France and England, and finally England ignored that neutrality in the great struggle against Napoleon. America found itself on the verge of war with France during 1797 and 1798, and with Britain when the British *Leopard* fired on the unprotected United States warship *Chesapeake;* finally war came with Britain in 1812.

When Napoleon resumed his conquest of Europe in 1803, Britain attempted to sever his supply lines through the blockade of Continental ports. Neutral ships were theoretically permitted to carry noncontraband of war to Europe provided these goods did not come directly from French colonies. American ships were quick to take advantage of this trade, and they rapidly built up a commerce between the French West Indies and American ports, reshipping goods thence to Dutch, German, Swedish, and other European ports, to the distress of the British. Attempting to enforce their blockade, the British increased the size of their navy and the rigors of their search and seizure processes, to do which called for ever larger numbers of sailors.

Sailors were difficult to find for the British navy, for working conditions were exceptionally bad in addition to wartime dangers. Press gangs therefore rounded up British subjects at home, and naval captains searched foreign merchant vessels at sea for deserters. A man who had been born a British subject was regarded as inalienably so; therefore American certificates of naturalization and seamen's certificates of home ports were ignored if a reason could be found for considering a sailor to have been once a British subject. When the *Leopard* stopped and searched the *Chesapeake* in June 1807 just beyond the territorial waters of the United States, killing three men and impressing four, the bitter cup of humiliation led the American public to cry for revenge. Several new companies including a rifle company were authorized and recruited for the regular army in 1808.

President Thomas Jefferson, however, did not desire war. Trusting in peaceful economic coercion, he attempted to force the British into abandoning impressment by a nonimportation policy in 1806 and an embargo in 1807. Both of these merely injured American shipping rather than halting British depredations and insults, so that the repeal of the embargo in 1809 was hailed with great rejoicing by Americans.

The French were striking at their enemy through Napoleon's decrees, such as those of Berlin and Milan, proclaiming that any neutral ship allowing itself to be searched by the British was fair prey for the French. Many American ships were seized under this policy and occasionally burned, some barely out to sea from their home ports, some in the West Indies, and some off the Iberian peninsula. The American response was the Non-Intercourse Act of 1809 forbidding both British and French vessels to enter American waters, but promising to restore commerce with whichever country first ceased to violate American neutral shipping rights.

In 1809 the new British minister of foreign affairs sent D. M. Erskine to Washington as minister plenipotentiary. He signed with Secretary of State Robert Smith the Erskine Agreement, which was widely hailed by the United States as a satisfactory answer to her protestations of injured dignity, especially since it was coupled with reparations for the still festering *Chesapeake-Leopard* affair. But the British government repudiated the agreement because it contained unauthorized promises. This was taken as a new insult by the Americans, and Macon's Bill No. 2 replaced the Non-Intercourse Act in 1810.

Macon's Bill No. 2 was the last major effort to maintain national pride and international respect short of war. By its provisions, commerce was resumed with both Britain and France; if either country recognized and acceded to American demands, trade would immediately cease with the other. Napoleon, quickly perceiving an opportunity, caused an ambiguous note to be sent to the American minister in Paris which President James Madison promptly seized upon as a satisfactory pledge and a last means to resist war pressures. He thereupon declared trade with Britain to be prohibited. The British finally repealed their Orders in Council on 23 June 1812 but it was too late to avoid war.

At the same time persistent Indian troubles were threatening the frontiers. The steady westward movement of settlers, accelerated after the treaty of independence in 1783, had instigated a coalition of Indians against the newcomers only to be crushed by General Anthony Wayne in 1794. The Jay Treaty of 1795 finally removed British military units from the northwest fur trading posts and peaceful coexistence between Indians and whites for a time seemed possible. By 1805, however, the spirit of resistance again flamed among the Indians. In Ohio the Prophet and a devoted band of lesser prophets preached a return to the purity of former Indian ways. His brother Tecumseh, a war chieftain, attempted to form a confederacy embracing all the frontier tribes in order to drive back the white man. In the latter movement the British in Canada took great interest. Although the backbone of Indian resistance was broken in 1811 at the battle of Tippecanoe by troops under the command of William Henry Harrison, trouble was still brewing among the southern tribes, especially among the Creeks in Alabama. Tecumseh himself fled to Canada where he eventually was killed in battle while fighting on the British side during the War of 1812.

Much has been made of western ambitions to acquire Canada and southern desires to annex Spanish Florida as the true causes of the American declaration of war. With the exception of Georgia, which passionately desired Florida, most of the early discussion of the acquisition of new territory centered on Canada and pertained to its temporary conquest for use as a hostage by which to force Britain's acknowledgment of American honor and position among the nations of the Western world.

When the Twelfth Congress assembled in Washington at the end of November 1811, it was still uncertain whether or not war would be deemed necessary. Bills for military preparations were introduced, debated, and passed; yet one last attempt at an effective nonimportation policy was also made. The peace advocates tried to secure an adjournment of Congress while waiting for a message from the British government that might show a conciliatory attitude. The move for adjournment failed; the nonimportation effort failed; the British message was not forthcoming. On 1 June 1812 Madison sent a war message to Congress, enumerating American grievances against Britain since 1803. Impressment, the hovering of British vessels off American ports, illegal blockades, British intransigence over negotiations, and a brief mention of the revival of Indian warfare constituted the list. In the House on 4 June, and in the Senate on 17 June, the bill declaring war was passed. On 18 June Madison signed it and war had begun.

Although the major reasons offered as causes of the War of 1812 have included expansionism, the Indian menace, disruption of trade, and the impressment of seamen, North Carolina supported the declaration of war against Great Britain less for any of these reasons than because of old resentments from the era of the Revolution and because of what she regarded as insults to the national honor. Until January 1812 she hoped that means short of war could be found to maintain the nation's honor, but finding that this was impossible, her congressional delegation more regretfully than otherwise cast the majority of its votes for war.

Expansionist sentiment was weak in North Carolina. Agreement was rather with statements of Henry Clay and James Monroe. Clay wrote to Thomas Bodley that "when the War was commenced Canada was not the end but the means; the object of the War being the redress of injuries, and Canada being the instrument by which that redress was to be obtained." Monroe told John Taylor that "in case of war it might be necessary to invade Canada, not as an object of war but as a means to bring it to a satisfactory conclusion."[1] William R. King of Wilmington, later vice-president of the United States, firmly stated that the invasion of Canada was only a means of bringing Britain to terms. Israel Pickens, representative to Congress from Burke County, called an invasion of Canada merely an offensive tactic, not an offensive war. Richard Stanford, member of Congress from Orange County, violently opposed an invasion of Canada, and he gave notice that should this occur he would oppose the entire war. When William Gaston of New Bern offered a resolution that "it is inexpedient to prosecute military operations against the Canadas," four of the North Carolina delegation in the House voted in favor.[2] Senator Jesse Franklin of North Carolina wrote to Major General William Lenoir that "as for territory God knows we [have] enough already. More than we can cultivate or sell." The Raleigh *Minerva* agreed, saying, "We have little desire here to march a thousand miles to conquer frozen deserts and bring away for our pains a knap sack full of snow-balls. . . . notwithstanding the rage which has been kindled in their bosoms against Great Britain, they hate no nation so fervently as to make foreign conquests and to spill the blood of neighboring brethren." Although James A. Bayard once surmised that the "Southern Gentlemen" disliked the "frightful" idea of annexing Canada because it would be "divided into States and inalienably incorporated into the Union,"[3] no expression by a North Carolinian to this effect has

1. Henry Clay to Thomas Bodley, 18 Dec. 1813, *The Papers of Henry Clay*, ed. James F. Hopkins (Lexington, 1959), 1:842; James Monroe to Colonel John Taylor, 13 June 1812, *The Writings of James Monroe*, ed. Stanislaus Murray Hamilton (New York, 1901), 5:207 (hereafter cited as *Monroe Writings*).

2. *National Intelligencer* (Washington, D.C.), 4, 18 Jan. 1812; U.S., Congress, *Annals of Congress*, 13th Cong., 2d sess., 1814, p. 1,054.

3. Jesse Franklin to William Lenoir, 15 Feb. 1812, Lenoir Family Papers, SHC (hereafter cited as Lenoir Papers); Raleigh *Minerva*, 31 Jan. 1811 [1812]; James A. Bayard to Andrew Bayard, 2 May 1812, "Papers of James A. Bayard, 1796-1815," ed. Elizabeth Donnan, *Annual Report of the Amer-*

been found. During the months of debate preceding the declaration of war, Congress was torn between two techniques for bringing Britain to terms: conquest of Canada or building a navy. None of the North Carolina delegation spoke in favor of conquering Canada prior to June 1812, but several promoted either the building of a navy or the passage of another embargo. There was more interest expressed in the acquisition of Florida than of Canada, although this too was relatively little. The annexation of West Florida was approved by Representative Archibald McBryde; Senator James Turner voted for the bill authorizing the president to take control of West Florida south of the Mississippi River, a bill that passed the Senate but not the House. The *Minerva*, however, continued its opposition to foreign conquest by declaring that attempts to take East Florida were "greedy of corrupt spoil." Only after two years of war did Nathaniel Macon, representative from Warren County, who had initially also opposed the annexation of West Florida as a warlike gesture, shift his position and approve the acquisition of both Canada and Florida as necessary means for maintaining a peaceful and stable frontier.[4] By no means can it be held that there was any strong sentiment for territorial expansion in North Carolina.

Nor was there a strong desire for war against Britain because she gave arms and encouragement to the Indians. The Cherokee Indians on the North Carolina frontier were friendly to the United States and had become farmers and cattle raisers rather than tribal hunters. It is true that some expression was made of resentment against the British for stirring up the Indians. In a Fourth of July address in 1812 Pickens referred to "the savage warfare against the peaceful inhabitants of our frontier, which is clearly proved to proceed from British arms and influence." Macon thought that "probably" the British had helped to stir up the Prophet. "Whenever we come near a point with Great Britain, do not the Indians move?" he

ican *Historical Association for the Year 1913* (Washington, D.C., 1915), 2: 196-97.

4. Archibald McBryde to Archibald Debow Murphey, 20 Jan. 1811, Archibald Debow Murphey Papers, NC Archives; *National Intelligencer*, 5 Oct. 1813; Raleigh *Minerva*, 22 Jan. 1813; *National Intelligencer*, 15 June 1814. In 1812 Macon had opposed the annexation of West Florida since it was claimed by a friendly power, Spain (*National Intelligencer*, 24 Mar. 1812).

asked. He also explained that the mountain people supported the war because they equated the troubles of impressed sailors with their own Indian troubles. Yet, for the most part, the white inhabitants of the frontier were calm. Although frightening stories about Indians were being circulated near Asheville in May 1812, Thomas Lenoir wrote to his father that reports of new British muskets in the hands of the Cherokees were "groundless" and statements of the theft of one hundred horses from Georgia were exaggerated. "I apprehend no danger from those savages," he concluded. His brother, William B. Lenoir, a resident of eastern Tennessee, also told his father that "I have no reason to think the Cherokees unfriendly." Frontiersmen who asked the governor for military aid to defend their land against the Indians put it that if war came, the Indians would attack; Indian attacks were not causes, but results, of a declaration of war.[5] It must be concluded that had there been no Indian problem, North Carolina would still have voted for war.[6]

Much more complex as a cause of war was the restriction of American trade by Great Britain and France. It has been maintained that suppression of this trade was the basic cause of the war, that the South and the West strongly desired freedom of trade. When this freedom could not be obtained by economic coercion, then these regions supported war. The thesis has been advanced that, because of the need to export her cotton, South Carolina was a leader in the movement for war, and that she was supported in this movement by Georgia, Virginia, and North Carolina.[7] This does not, however, appear

5. Israel Pickens, *Circular to the Citizens of Burke, Rutherford, Lincoln, Buncombe, and Haywood* (Washington, D.C., 1812), 4 July 1812; *National Intelligencer*, 12 Mar. 1812, 16 June 1814; Thomas Lenoir to William Lenoir, 11 May 1812; William B. Lenoir to William Lenoir, 23 Sept. 1813, Lenoir Papers; N.C., Executive, Letterbooks of Governor William Hawkins, Letterbook 18, 16 Apr. 1812, p. 147, NC Archives (hereafter cited as Hawkins Letterbook).

6. Reginald Horsman, *The Causes of the War of 1812* (Philadelphia, 1962), p. 267, believes that the Indian menace has been exaggerated as a cause for war.

7. Horsman, *Causes of the War of 1812*, p. 225, maintains that suppression of American trade was the cause of the war. When freedom of the seas, desired by the South and West, could not be secured by economic coercion, war resulted and was supported by the same regions. Margaret Kinard Latimer had earlier suggested that such was the case in South

to have been a strong motivation for war as far as North Carolina is concerned. Only two public statements seem to support the thesis; Nathaniel Macon in 1812 told the Congress that "we must either prepare to maintain the right to carry our produce to what market we please, or to be content without a market: to attempt another negociation, would be useless." Macon was a large planter who marketed his tobacco abroad, through the ports of Virginia; but there were very few Macons in the state. The second statement was made by Stanford, who charged France with depriving the southern states of markets for cotton and tobacco.[8] But North Carolina's chief exports at this period were naval stores; it would be decades before she was an important producer of cotton and tobacco. Basically, North Carolina was not a major exporter and was hardly affected by the British and French restrictions. The complexity of the question, however, is illustrated by the fact that much North Carolina produce was exported from Norfolk and from Charleston rather than from Wilmington, New Bern, or Edenton; therefore statistics cannot clarify the entire picture. But, as far as statistics reveal, North Carolina did not lose enough foreign trade to cause her to support war in an effort to regain it. The state's exports between 1802 and 1812 averaged 1.67 percent of the annual national total. She ranked sixth from the bottom nationally, and exported the least of all the southern states. Rather than losing trade, indeed, during the European wars, her exports of lumber and naval stores increased greatly in value between 1809 and 1811; exportation of oak bark continued to increase through 1813.[9] There is no record of any North Carolina vessel having been seized in the cases of such vessels brought before the British admiralty between 1808 and 1812.[10] Most of her vessels were small ones employed in the coasting trade. She ranked variously between eighth and tenth nationally in tonnage employed in foreign trade, but fifth in vessels under twenty tons used in

Carolina in her article, "South Carolina—A Protagonist of the War of 1812," *American Historical Review* 61 (1955-56):927.

8. *National Intelligencer*, 2 Jan., 20 Feb. 1812.

9. Adam Seybert, *Statistical Annals . . . of the United States of America* (Philadelphia, 1818), pp. 88, 142-45; Timothy Pitkin, *A Statistical View of the Commerce of the United States* (New Haven, 1835), p. 49.

10. *Reports of Cases Argued and Determined in the High Court of Admiralty . . . 1798-1815*, 3 vols. (London, 1806-15), *passim*.

the coasting trade. Such vessels, of course, were seldom liable to seizure. Importations likewise showed very little variation because of French and British restrictions. From 1808 to 1812 revenue from customs duties paid in North Carolina ports changed almost none. In 1813 and 1814, however, there was a great increase, an indication of greater use of North Carolina ports due to the strict blockade of New England and New York.[11] One might almost surmise that North Carolina went to war in order to increase her import business! Since her geographical handicaps prevented her from being a great commercial state, the restrictions on her commerce could not have been a major cause for her support of the war. One merchant family of the state was indeed prowar and appears to fit the analysis of war causes suggested by those who see trade restrictions as the chief causes. This was the Blount family of Washington, North Carolina, owners of perhaps the largest single business firm in the state. Yet even here the motivation goes back to pre-Revolutionary days and is less economic than might appear on the surface.[12]

The impressment of seamen was another cause of the war. Here again, since North Carolina was not a great commercial state, she suffered very little from impressments. In the first place, she had very few seamen in comparison with other states. Although statistics for the years involved are extremely incomplete, those that have survived are revealing and indicative of the situation. Under the Act for the Relief and Protection of American Seamen passed in 1796, sailors registered

11. Pitkin, *Statistical View*, p. 52; Seybert, *Statistical Annals*, pp. 322, 324, 330; Charles Jared Ingersoll, *Historical Sketch of the Second War between the United States of America, and Great Britain . . .* , 3 vols. (Philadelphia, 1845), 1:257. Names of coasting vessels from Edenton may be found in William Rombough's Account Book, 1793-1810, NC Archives. The increase in import receipts in 1813 rose from 1.16 percent to 6 percent of the national total, and in 1814 it rose still further to nearly 9 percent (Seybert, *Statistical Annals*, pp. 394, 433-37). John Heritage Bryan, congressman from New Bern, N.C., in 1826, cited information from the Treasury indicating the extensive commerce carried on at Beaufort and at Wilmington during the war. Federal revenues collected at Beaufort in both 1813 and 1814 approached $100,000, while at Wilmington there were collected in 1813 revenues of $184,000; in 1814, $182,000; and in 1815, $256,000 (*Annals of Congress*, 19th Cong., 1st sess., 1825-26, p. 1,234).

12. William H. Masterson, *William Blount* (Baton Rouge, 1954), pp. 19-35, has explained that the Blounts became anti-British for political reasons following the Regulator outbreaks.

at their home ports in order to have evidence of their citizenship. Samples indicate that in 1796, for example, whereas 4,849 seamen were registered in the nation, only 55 registered from North Carolina; in 1805, with 10,722 registered nationally, 101 were from North Carolina. The proportions were usually the same from 1796 through 1806, the years for which these particular statistics are available. Where seamen were identified by citizenship, figures reveal that some 96 percent of those in North Carolina were native born. For the years 1808 to 1815, the Seamen's Register has listed all certified seamen, of whom only 28 were from North Carolina, all native born. Thus there were few men to be impressed. In the second place, of this small number, even fewer found their way into the hands of Great Britain. The total number of impressed seamen whose release had been requested up to June 1814 was 5,987. Again, from the lists that are extant, it can be ascertained that a total of 25 North Carolina seamen were impressed. It is possible that five more belong in this category because their names matched those of known North Carolina seamen although their home states were not given. The grand total that can be identified is thus 30 out of the 5,987 reported,[13] hardly a large enough number to justify a declaration of war.

It was not Great Britain alone who ravaged commerce, but France as well. Although it was largely a political maneuver, some congressmen tried to involve France in the war debate, perhaps merely to becloud the issue but to a certain extent because they believed the nation had at least as much griev-

13. Records of Impressed Seamen, Miscellaneous Lists and Papers, 1796-1814; Seamen's Register of Certificates, 1808-16, Record Group 59, NA. A letter from P. Irving to Albert Gallatin, 3 June 1814, Record Group 59, is a report on the total number of seamen whose release had been requested by the United States. An example of an impressment from the Miscellaneous Lists was the case of one William Blount, born near Edenton, who was taken from on board the brig *Defiance* on 11 March 1796 by the British sloop of war *Scorpion*. Blount was described as twenty-five years old, of small size, formerly a shipwright. In an undated list of citizens of the United States who were impressed, Thomas King of Edenton, brother-in-law of the merchant John Little, was taken on board the *Merlin*, while the mate of the ship *Patty* of Wilmington was seized by the *Drake*. Thomas Trotter of Washington, N.C., believed that many British subjects were serving on board American ships in spite of protests to the contrary. There were at Washington, he said, "some Gun Boats here that there is not 6 native Americans on Board of them, they are all nearly British Man or warsmen. . . ." Thomas Trotter to Ebenezer Pettigrew, 8 July 1812, Pettigrew Papers, NC Archives.

ance against one country as against the other. A few, all Federalists, thought France and Napoleon were the enemies and Great Britain was America's friend. During the enforcement of the Berlin and Milan decrees, France had seized 307 American vessels, a far greater number than were seized by the British during the same period. Both in 1808 and 1812, considerable excitement occurred over the French burning of American vessels which they had stopped on the high seas, especially the incident of the *Asia* off the harbor of Lisbon, Portugal. The Federalists also encouraged a suspicion that Napoleon and Madison had arranged for France to invade Russia at the time that the United States declared war against Britain.[14] To a degree, this attitude was reflected in the statements of certain North Carolinians. The Federalist *Minerva* pointed out in 1808 that several ships and impressed seamen had been released by the British in an effort to appease the country, while Jefferson was endeavoring "to bring about hostilities with Britain, in order to throw us into the arms of France." If this were not true, then Jefferson must be "afraid of Bonaparte." The embargo, continued the *Minerva*, was helping Bonaparte to hurt friendly Britain. Upon the repeal of the Non-Intercourse Act in 1812, the *Minerva* charged that Congress seemed to believe "that the moon must be made of green cheese." The same newspaper in 1813 called attention to two vessels sunk by the French, adding, "Yet such is the friendship for which we have undertaken to fight England." The editor urged the electorate to vote against the Republicans because they had led the country into war against the wrong enemy.[15] Gleefully the *Minerva* reported that two French frigates had stopped a schooner between the Bahamas and Wilmington, and had bragged of recently capturing thirteen American ships.[16] Stanford maintained that the quarrel was actually with Napoleon's Continental system, not with Britain. It was

14. Seybert, *Statistical Annals*, pp. 79-80; Henry Adams, *History of the United States during the Administrations of Jefferson and Madison*, 9 vols. (New York, 1918), 4:313, 6:193, 198; William Barlow, "Congress during the War of 1812" (Ph.D. diss., Ohio State University, 1961), p. 246.

15. The term Republican will be used consistently throughout rather than Democratic-Republican or Democratic party. The terms as used by contemporaries of the war should be regarded as interchangeable.

16. Raleigh *Minerva*, 8 Jan. 1808; 14 Feb., 24 Apr., 1812; 26 Mar., 9 Apr. 1813.

France, he insisted, who was depriving the southern states of their market for cotton and tobacco. Representative Joseph Pearson of Salisbury spoke at length on the floor of Congress, pointing out France's depredations against America.[17] Continuously during the war, the North Carolina Federalists attempted to shift attention to France in an effort to embarrass the administration. When Daniel Webster attacked the administration in 1813, charging collusion with France, William Gaston of New Bern supported him in a lengthy speech. France, he stated, had instigated the war and the administration had betrayed America by allowing itself to be inveigled into it.[18] Since there were many fewer Federalists in North Carolina than Republicans, however, this view was not influential. Some persons, on the other hand, thought that both European countries should have been included in the declaration of war. To Wood Jones Hamlin of Halifax a friend wrote, "Bona. is a Dog also. I most sincerely wish we possess the means of flogging both the English & French rascals untill they were honest but It would take all the Timber between this and Roanoke." Macon himself, as late as March of 1812, wrote to a friend that "the Devil himself could not tell, which govt England or France is the most wicked."[19] In spite of these charges, in actuality the Republican policy was to regard the war with Britain as an entirely separate event from Napoleon's war with the same country. There was no subserviency to the French, although there was opportunism and recognition that it was decidedly a help to have Britain occupied with another war while the United States was fighting her. With this view, most North Carolinians probably agreed.

The real quarrel was, and undoubtedly had to be, with Britain. In the first place, she was the old enemy of 1776 and France was the former ally. Throughout all the North Carolina discussion of war runs the thread of the events of the Revolutionary War, equating opposition to Britain at that time with loyalty to the United States in 1812. In accepting

17. *National Intelligencer,* 20 Feb., 27 June 1812.
18. Ingersoll, *Historical Sketch of the Second War,* 1:487-90; *Annals of Congress,* 13th Cong., 1st sess., 1813, p. 240.
19. John Penistorn to Wood Jones Hamlin, 19 June 1812, Wood Jones Hamlin Papers, NC Archives; Nathaniel Macon to Joseph Nicholson, 24 Mar. 1812, Joseph Nicholson Papers, LC.

a sword from the state legislature, Colonel Joseph Winston of Stokes County, who had fought at Kings Mountain, wrote that his country was now fighting "the same proud, austere and oppressive nation." He urged soldiers to fight as had General George Washington and gain "immortal honor." When Joseph Carson wrote to Major General Lenoir offering his services in the war, he gave as his reasons for so doing his "zeal for my countrys welfare a warm attachment for that freedom and Indipendence which you and our old patriots have purchased for us through blood and toil." Nathaniel Macon regarded the causes of the two wars as the same, that is, "to prevent oppression & to maintain our rights." Great Britain, said Macon, was like a highwayman whom one tried to avoid but if necessary fought in self-defense. Britain, he said, had "a great hatred" for the former colonies and would continue to have as long as the Revolutionary generation still lived in America. The Revolutionary patriots who fought Britain over a tax on tea, he declared in another speech, would never have submitted to impressment.[20] The war was to promote the "independence" of the country, declared the Senate of North Carolina in a resolution to President James Madison. Independence was also the theme of Governor William Hawkins's proclamation that war had been declared; peace was to be sought "compatible with the honor, dignity, and independence of the United States."[21] Representative William Blackledge retorted to those who said America was too weak to undertake such a war, that their ancestors with one-third the population had forced Britain to give America justice and it could be done again. "Why then should we now despond?" he asked. Charges were instigated concerning militia officers who were alleged to have been pro-British during the Revolution in attempts to prevent their securing appointments. An advertisement in one newspaper was published by a man who felt he was falsely accused of having been pro-British. The "Patriotic Fathers" of Mecklenburg County, all veterans of

20. Joseph Winston to William Hawkins, 20 Oct. 1813, reprinted in *National Intelligencer*, 9 Nov. 1813; Joseph Carson to William Lenoir, 13 June 1812, Lenoir Papers; *National Intelligencer*, 15 June 1814, 21 Jan. 1812.

21. N.C., General Assembly, Senate, *Journals of the Senate of the State of North Carolina, 1811*, p. 45 (hereafter cited as *N.C. Senate Journal*); *Niles' Weekly Register* (Baltimore), 18 July 1812.

the Revolution, organized themselves for home service. Five members of the North Carolina delegation to the United States Congress between 1811 and 1815 had served in the war, three as officers and two as privates. Great Britain was charged with jealousy for growing American maritime power by Blackledge and Jesse Franklin, and British atrocities were the lengthy subject of a report by a congressional committee chaired by Macon, in which he elaborated on bad treatment of prisoners, destruction and pillage of private property, atrocities at Hampton, Virginia, and encouragement of massacre and burning by Indian allies.[22]

The second reason for deciding to declare war against Britain instead of France was the emotional feeling that America's national honor was being trodden under foot by haughty Albion. Speeches, letters, newspapers, all proclaim this fact. On only two occasions were any references made in acceptance of so-called offenses to the national honor. In 1810 Macon and Stanford joined the Old Republicans in a vote against a resolution that British Minister Francis James Jackson had insulted American honor. In the second instance the Raleigh *Minerva* accused Madison of attempting to inflame and irritate the "sore" instead of healing it.[23] The vast majority of vocal Carolinians felt that everything short of war had been tried, and that the national honor admitted of no other recourse. As early as 1809, the Raleigh *Star* foresaw "an ultimate resort to hostile measures on the part of the American government; and by a great many it is supposed, that the day is *near at hand* when our right to navigate the ocean, and to export our surplus produce, without licenses from others, will be defended at the mouth of the cannon." The British disavowal of the Erskine Agreement was "base, dishonorable, and faithless conduct," said the *Star*. "We deprecate war. We look upon it as the worst of human evils, but there are periods beyond which concessions cannot be made. We must at some time, on some occasions defend our rights, or we shall soon be left without any thing worth defending." Said Blackledge,

22. *National Intelligencer,* 21 Mar. 1812; *Raleigh Register,* 8 Oct. 1813; Hawkins Letterbook 19, 25 Nov. 1812, pp. 13-14; U.S., Congress, *American State Papers* (Washington, D.C.: Gales & Seaton, 1832-61), *Military,* 1:339-82.

23. Adams, *History of the United States,* 5:182-83; Raleigh *Minerva,* 31 Jan. 1811 [1812].

"Rather than submit to pretensions so degrading to our national honor, and which, if submitted to, must lead to consequences so destructive both to the agricultural and commercial interests of the nation, I do not hesitate to prefer war." Macon believed that the administration had done all possible "to avoid the present crisis, and to keep the nation at peace." All Britain had to do to avoid war, he said, was to cease to violate neutral and national rights. Then, "if we cannot fight by paper restrictions, we must meet force by force. If we cannot do this, it is time we put ourselves under the protection of some other power." It was a war, Macon said in 1814, "for the rights of the poor and not for the property of the rich." A "begging nation cannot maintain her rights," he continued, "nor prevent injustice by begging." King spoke of southern "love of country" which "burns with unextinguished ardor." Submission to Britain's demands would be too degrading. King was not, he said, voting for war to support the "carrying trade," but the right to sail where we will "I will never yield." Of course, he agreed, North Carolina would suffer from a war, but loss of national honor could never be found wanting in the scale with pecuniary loss. As to impressment, he concluded, "I had rather that fast anchored isle . . . should be swept from the catalog of nations than submit that one American . . . should at her will be torn from his family, his country" and be imprisoned in "the most horrid slavery." Pickens, who with King was the nearest to a "war hawk" in the state, also agreed that the money value of rights should not be weighed against the principle. America was aspiring to "equal and honorable rank" among the nations of the world, and she must not give up any rights. Do not, he pleaded, calculate the dollars and cents of national defense. If this had been the Spirit of Seventy-six, he added, "you and I would not have been here." He referred to "indignities to our flag," and called for "the defence of the civil and religious liberties, the honor, the independence handed us from our brave ancestors." He concluded his circular of July Fourth, 1812, "Let us rise together—our cause is just—the God of our fathers, who has heretofore blessed our exertions, will again be our guardian and our shield."[24] Gov-

24. Raleigh *Star*, 19 Jan., 3 Aug. 1809; *National Intelligencer*, 21 Mar., 21 Jan., 2 Jan. 1812; 16 June 1814; 4 Jan., 18 Jan. 1812; Pickens, *Circular*, 4 July 1812.

ernor Hawkins, a strong supporter of the Madison administration, called upon every citizen "to unite in repelling those aggressions, insults, and injuries, with which we have been and yet are assailed." Following the declaration of war, he added that war had been "so justly declared against a power who has . . . long since been waging War against the United States, by actual and positive aggressions."[25] Nathan Tisdale of Beaufort volunteered his services "in so just a war." Andrew Joyner of Hamilton, also volunteering, preferred war; "[R]ather than submit any longer to the injuries and indignities which have been heaped upon us by Great Britain and France, without a hope of their being redressed by friendly means, let War with all its calamities be encountered by the Nation." Brigadier General Alexander Gray of the militia likewise believed that every effort had been made "comportable with our national dignity" to keep peace, "without effect" and he therefore approved the declaration of war.[26] The cessation of war could only be brought about at the impossible price of being at the feet of Great Britain, said the *Raleigh Register*. Citizens of Rowan County, although it was heavily Federalist, at a meeting charged that "vile submission" was the only way to peace on Britain's terms, and the nation therefore had to go to war "in support of our liberty and national honor." The expression of "rights" may be found in almost every address on the subject, among them such remarks as the "sacred cause of defending our country's rights," the "defense of the rights of his country," refusal to agree to "the surrender of any of our essential rights," war as the "only possible means of maintaining our rights," the necessity to "compel the enemy to respect our rights" and so on.[27]

When the war vote was taken in Congress, North Carolina's two senators voted yea in a vote of 19 to 13; while Willis Alston, Blackledge, James Cochran, King, Macon, and Pickens voted yea in the House with Archibald McBryde, Pearson, and Stan-

25. Hawkins Letterbook 18, 26 Dec. 1811, p. 17; 30 June 1812, p. 210.
26. Hawkins Letterbook 19, 16 Mar. 1813, pp. 130-31; Hawkins Letterbook 18, 2 June 1812, p. 177, 3 July 1812, p. 231.
27. *Raleigh Register*, 7 May 1813; Raleigh *Minerva*, 11 Dec. 1812; Niles' *Weekly Register*, 14 Dec. 1811, supplement; *National Intelligencer*, 2 Jan. 1812; Alexander Gray, *To the Free Citizens of Rowan, Chatham, and Randolph* (Salisbury, N.C., 1813); Raleigh *Minerva*, 25 Sept. 1812.

ford in the negative in a vote of 79 to 49, with four not voting.[28]

Stanford, an Old Republican along with John Randolph of Roanoke and Edwin Gray of Virginia, gave Congress in 1812 as Randolph reported it, "an old fashioned & most admirable discourse." His opposition to the war was based on the thesis that a republic was supposed "to cherish peace, and to avoid war and its evils as the last of the alternatives before us." More cause for war had existed in 1798 than in 1812, in his opinion, yet war was avoided. Impressment, although a just complaint, had existed since the days of President Washington without war being declared; indeed, rather than go to war, President Thomas Jefferson had resisted popular feeling for it after the *Chesapeake-Leopard* affair and substituted an embargo in place of hostilities. A defensive war he would support, but this was obviously an offensive war. Yet, although he voted against the war, he declared that he would vote for the means to support it if the war bill carried. Basically his was an ideological opposition: he would let others "reconcile the old republican policy with the new in their own way. It was not in his power to do it." In a letter to George Logan, Stanford elaborated on this ideology. The war, especially if territories were annexed, would ruin the nation by changing the character of its government and its civil institutions; "for a republic, the very apparatus of war is enough to destroy it—essentially at any rate," he told Logan. "We may well implore heaven to forgive us, for it seems literally true, that we know not what we do." For such a stand as this, Stanford was praised by the *Carolina Federal Republican* because he adhered wisely to the country's rather than the party's interest.[29] Pearson and McBryde were both signers of a lengthy pamphlet setting forth the minority report against the declaration of war, written by Josiah Quincy of Massachusetts with the aid of James A. Bayard. In the pamphlet the war was castigated as not "necessary, or required by

28. *National Intelligencer*, 20 June 1812.
29. John Randolph to James Garnett, 13 Dec. 1811, Garnett-Randolph Manuscripts, University of Virginia, Charlottesville, Va., quoted in Roger H. Brown, *The Republic in Peril: 1812* (New York, 1964), p. 225, n. 33; *Annals of Congress*, 12th Cong., 1st sess., 1811-12, pp. 511-16; *National Intelligencer*, 20 Feb. 1812; Richard Stanford to George Logan, 4 Jan. and 12 June 1812, George Logan Manuscripts, Historical Society of Pennsylvania, Philadelphia, Pa., quoted in Brown, *Republic in Peril*, pp. 155-56; *Carolina Federal Republican* (New Bern, N.C.), 10 Apr. 1813.

any moral duty, or any political expediency." Federalist Pearson was linked by Henry Clay with Timothy Pitkin of Connecticut and Harmanus Bleecker of New York in their opposition to the war.[30] McBryde was, like Stanford, a Republican who, after casting his vote against war, retired from Congress to serve in the state legislature.

Leading the affirmative vote for war was the senior representative, Nathaniel Macon, who had originally opposed it but had gradually shifted his views until he sacrificed his oldest and truest friendship, that with John Randolph, for his belief. In 1808 Macon had written to his friend Joseph Nicholson, "I am as much against war as [Albert] Gallatin is in favor of it, thus I have continued in Congress till there is not one of my old fellow laborers, that agrees with me in opinion." Two years later he still supported an embargo as "the only measure which would bring G. Britain to terms, there is no chance for that." At this same date he favored reducing the army and navy, "or rather for putting them altogether down, and if we have any military take a new start," because the officers who opposed Madison so hated those who supported him that the services were emasculated. When the Twelfth Congress met in November 1811, Macon had once more become a "sound party man prepared to support war," noted Henry Adams, but he still attempted to find means other than war to resolve the difficulties with Britain. Convinced that the national honor must be preserved, he was not yet quite ready to solidify his opinion, as he told Nicholson. "I see you are for war," he wrote to him, "and must observe to you, that it seems much easier to form opinions, at home than here at this place [Washington]. [Congress] are nearly all too wise or too mysterious to form hasty conclusions." As late as April he was still hoping that a limited maritime war would prove to be all that was necessary. Convinced at last that a strong embargo could not be obtained and that defense of national honor left no other alternative, he voted for war.[31] His nephew Willis Alston re-

30. *An Address of Members of the House of Representatives of the Congress of the United States on the Subject of War with Great Britain* (Raleigh, 1812), p. 28; *National Intelligencer,* 5 Feb. 1813.

31. Nathaniel Macon to Joseph Nicholson, 4 Dec. 1808, 3 Apr. 1810, Nicholson Papers; Adams, *History of the United States,* 6:123-24; Macon to Nicholson, 21 Nov. 1811, 30 Apr. 1812, Nicholson Papers. Macon spoke for

flected the same change. Initially Alston hoped that Congress would have "taken another Course, now too late. [I]t would have been better to protest against the belligerents & let Commerce thrive, this should have been done from the Beginning."[32] Yet when the time came, Alston voted affirmatively on every war measure. Senator Jesse Franklin likewise asserted that "there is not a man in the nation would be more rejoiced than myself to see some event that Shoud render our Military preparations unnecessary but we must make the best of a bad Bargain." To Lenoir, his old comrade in arms, he explained that the French let American ships go if they had no contraband of war, but that Britain declared a whole continent under blockade and confiscated everything. Israel Pickens, whose wife was the daughter of Major General Lenoir, told a constituent that "I could not have come [to Congress] in a more serious & critical moment."[33] Pickens's strongly hawkish views may well have been influenced by those of his father-in-law.

An analysis of the twenty-one different men who served in the Congress from November 1811 to January 1815 may be revealing.[34] Of these twenty-one, most were exceptionally well qualified for the times. Seven had attended college; four either had been or later became governors of states; three later became United States senators; one was to be elected vice-president of the country; one had been Speaker of the House; one became an outstanding jurist. Lawyers were the most numerous of the professions represented; three were farmers and only one a merchant; however, this data is incomplete since the occupations of all are not known. Support for the war came from five who were veterans of the Revolutionary War, from two of the state's seaports (Wilmington and Edenton), and

two hours in the House in support of the war during the 1813 debate on the bill to increase the army (*National Intelligencer*, 13 Jan. 1813).

32. Journal of Augustus John Foster, 18 Mar. 1812, Augustus John Foster Manuscripts, LC, quoted in Bradford Perkins, *Prologue to War: England and the United States, 1805-1812* (Berkeley, 1961), p. 433.

33. Jesse Franklin to William Lenoir, 15 Feb. 1812, Lenoir Papers; Israel Pickens to———, 6 Mar. 1812, Personal Miscellany Manuscripts, LC, quoted in Brown, *Republic in Peril*, p. 60.

34. Brief basic data may be found in U.S., Congress, House, *Biographical Directory of the American Congress, 1774-1949*, H. Doc. 607, 81st Cong., 2d sess., 1950; R. D. W. Connor, ed., *A Manual of North Carolina* (Raleigh, 1913); Samuel A'Court Ashe, Stephen B. Weeks, and Charles L. Van Noppen, eds., *Biographical History of North Carolina*, 8 vols. (Greensboro, 1908).

from the geographical center and the extreme western parts of the state. Opposition to the war came from the other two seaports (New Bern and Washington), from Rowan County in the west, and from the one teacher and the one clergyman in the delegation. The seaports provided a mixed picture: while the representatives in Congress voted one way, in actuality at home the feeling was almost equally divided between support for and opposition to the war. Federalist newspapers like the *Minerva* and the *Carolina Federal Republican* opposed the war; Republican papers like the *Raleigh Register* strongly supported it. Both support and opposition crossed party lines. One Federalist supported all the war measures; two Republicans opposed all the war measures; and two Republicans changed views, Macon becoming a supporter and Senator David Stone an opponent of the war. The matter of their ages seems irrelevant to the way in which they voted, except that all those who were old enough to have served in the Revolution were prowar. In considering all factors, it appears that each man's position on the war was based more on his personal beliefs than it was on party measures and popular attitudes. Both Pearson and Senator David Stone, for example, were punished at the polls for their opposition to the war, but they persisted. Macon gave up his old friend Randolph whom he loved like a brother rather than oppose the war. The high caliber and integrity of such men as Macon, King, Stanford, McBryde, Gaston, and Stone seems above question; they were not demagogues. There were, it is true, a few seekers after popularity like Alston and Blackledge; a few nonentities like Meshack Franklin, Lemuel Sawyer, whose ill health prevented his regular participation, James Cochran, who did not live to complete his term, and Peter Forney, the oldest member in point of years. For the most part, however, it was a strong delegation.

It has been maintained that the election of 1810 was a revolution which brought a group of young war hawks to Congress and thus precipitated the war. North Carolina had four war hawks. Of these, Alston had already served several terms prior to 1810; Pickens, elected in 1810, replaced a strong administration man who declined to run for another term. Two men, Blackledge and King, out of eleven representatives elected, may correctly be counted toward the change in the former pattern of representation from the state and therefore as evidence of a war hawk "revolution." Blackledge was not a great addition to the strength of the war party, but King, together with Pickens, provided much leadership and strength. North Carolina's swing toward support for war depended less, however, on the fact that two additional war hawks had been elected than it did on Macon's break with Randolph and the Quids and his final conversion to support for the war. It was Macon who was the dean of the delegation and the wielder of great influence in the state, not the newcomers Blackledge, King, or Pickens.

The War of 1812 may be considered a dividing line between men like Stanford who were old constitutionalists and frontiersmen, and a new emotional younger generation that was beginning to feel a growing spirit of nationalism and that foreshadowed the Manifest Destiny spirit of the next several decades. Stanford was on one side of the dividing line, Pickens and King on the other, while Macon moved from the former to the latter. North Carolina may be viewed as an excellent example of a past not yet cast off for a future that could not be held in check. For her, the War of 1812 was truly the second war for independence.

2 ORGANIZING FOR NATIONAL DEFENSE

When the United States began its preparations for war, it "not only showed inefficiency and errors but indicated that nothing had been learned from the lessons of the Revolutionary War and the campaigns in the Northwest Territory." It was indeed, as Charles Jared Ingersoll bitingly phrased it, "the experiment . . . of making war without soldiers or officers, money, taxes, or manufactures."[1]

Beginning in November 1811, Congress passed legislation to provide for the national defense. In spite of having created an army in 1799 and again in 1808, in 1810 the regular army had only 5,788 men. To this number Congress first added six companies of rangers; then, on 11 January 1812, it created ten additional infantry regiments, two of artillery, and one of light dragoons, to be enlisted for five years. Money was appropriated for bounties to be paid for 30,000 volunteers for these new regiments, as well as for bringing the old regiments up to full strength. To secure these volunteers, Congress increased the pay, eventually changed the five year enlistment term to the "duration of the war," and gave a bonus of four dollars to each man enlisting. Since this did not raise a sufficient number

1. Marvin A. Kreidberg and Merton G. Henry, *History of Military Mobilization in the United States Army, 1775-1945* (Washington, D.C., 1955), p. 59; Ingersoll, *Historical Sketch of the Second War*, 1:67.

of troops, in 1813 twenty regiments of infantry, ten of rangers, one corps of engineers, and one corps of sea fencibles were authorized, to be enlisted for one year, with a bonus of sixteen dollars, land in the amount of 160 acres, and an additional three months' pay upon honorable discharge. By 1814, the need still not having been met, Congress authorized three regiments of riflemen, called for 50,000 volunteers, and increased the land bounty to 320 acres. Secretary of War James Monroe thought this a hopeless plan; he had suggested three others, the first two of which foreshadowed the selective service of the twentieth century, but none of which was adopted.[2]

Supplies for the new army were most inadequately provided for. Both a purveyor and a quartermaster general were appointed, with resulting confusion as to their separate duties. Contracts for food were let to civilians who supplied troops that were stationed in their areas or that marched through en route to other points. Emergency purchases were allowed by commanding officers, deputy quartermasters, and others, most of whom kept poor records; such purchases, while indeed necessary because of slow communications with the seat of government, nevertheless added to the confusion. By the middle of the war, it became necessary to name a superintendent general of military supplies to keep track. Purchasing of supplies other than food was centralized at Philadelphia, from whence supplies were shipped by water or by land to distribution points, sometimes becoming lost on the way.[3]

The money with which to finance the war was likewise hard to come by. War loans and taxes were the two sources resorted to by Congress. In all, four loans were authorized, totaling some $75 million, plus treasury notes worth an additional $40 million, less than half the value of which was subscribed. The Bank of New Bern subscribed $25,000 to the 1812 loan, while the State Bank at Raleigh subscribed $50,000 to the 1813 loan.[4] Taxation was more successful. Taxes were

2. Seybert, *Statistical Annals,* pp. 561-63; Kreidberg and Henry, *History of Military Mobilization,* pp. 43, 47, 55-56.
3. Kreidberg and Henry, *History of Military Mobilization,* p. 58.
4. Seybert, *Statistical Annals,* pp. 534-36; Ingersoll, *Historical Sketch of the Second War,* 1:249; James McKinlay to Major General Thomas Pinckney, records of the Office of the Secretary of War: Letters Received by the

levied on stills, retail licenses, sales at auction, sugar, carriages, bank notes, and salt. North Carolina in 1814 ranked fifth among the twenty-two states and territories in the amount of taxes paid on stills; sixth on carriages; ninth on retail licenses; and tenth on bank notes and stamped paper. By comparison, North Carolina paid taxes of $175,922.07 on distilled spirits but only $23,270.60 on manufactured goods. A direct tax was levied in 1813 apportioned according to population, and another in 1815 apportioned on the valuation of property. North Carolina in the 1810 census had 1/13 of the population of the United States, with a resulting assessment of some $220,000 in taxes to be paid for 1813. A proadministration newspaper claimed that the tax was being paid "with the greatest promptness, and without a murmur." Indeed, North Carolina collectors received $117,000, the third highest amount from any state. The 1815 levy found North Carolina at the bottom of the list in value per acre of her land, but the increase in slaves had offset this to the extent that the state ranked eighth in total property value during 1814-15. Assessed $440,000 in 1815, the state levied forty-six cents per $100 valuation and collected the fourth highest amount from any state.[5] North Carolina's record ranks her as above average in financial support for the war.

The national government had turned its attention to military strategy even before it considered the necessary finances. The defense plan called for the division of the United States into six military districts, later expanded into nine, each one operating under a major general and all theoretically coordinated by the secretary of war. Most believed that a holding action along the coast would probably be all that would be required for defense, since Great Britain was busily occupied against Napoleon in Europe. Monroe proposed one hundred men for the defense of North Carolina, three hundred each for Charleston and Norfolk, and larger numbers for the greater ports of the north. Each significant seaport, recommended Monroe, should be supplied with an engineer. To the chairman

Secretary of War, Main Series, 1801-70, Record Group 107, Microcopy 221, NA (hereafter cited as RG 107, M 221); *National Intelligencer*, 8 Sept. 1813.

5. Ingersoll, *Historical Sketch of the Second War*, 1:229, 231, 232-35, 236-38; Seybert, *Statistical Annals*, pp. 39, 502-3; *Raleigh Register*, 1 July 1814; Seybert, *Statistical Annals*, p. 507; Pitkin, *Statistical Review*, pp. 311, 313-14.

of the Military Committee of the Senate, Monroe wrote: "It may be said that it is not probable that the enemy will attempt an invasion of any part of the coast described with a view to retain it, and less so for the purpose of desolation. It is nevertheless possible, and being so provision ought to be made against the danger."[6] A half-million dollar appropriation was passed by Congress for the defense of the coast, the smallness of the sum indicating that congressmen did not really believe the enemy would attempt an invasion. Even less money would Congress grant for the navy. After defeating an attempt by pronavy advocates to provide funds for building new frigates, Congress finally approved the sum of $480,000 to repair existing ships.[7] Because military strategy became a political question in Congress, and because in many cases the ranking military officers were either political strategists or the objects of such, no clear plan of action was ever devised or acted upon.

When the new army was authorized in January 1812, a scramble began to obtain commissions. Congressmen, cabinet members, and even the president were pursued by those desiring their influence. For major general of the Sixth District, which included Virginia, North and South Carolina, and Georgia, both William R. Davie and Thomas Pinckney were at first rumored to be strong candidates. Both men had served in the Revolutionary War, and both were Federalists. Although President Madison was Republican, he was desirous of uniting all parties behind the war effort and was anxious to name a Federalist to a high post of command. Since Davie indicated that he was not interested, the field was cleared for Pinckney, a South Carolinian. Macon disapproved heartily of Pinckney, stating that he did not "possess the talents necessary for his station." His selection would be a "cause of grief to all men, who wish proper men appointed." On the other hand, William Lowndes of South Carolina wrote to his wife that only one or two men in Washington did not approve.[8] While many were

6. *Monroe Writings*, 5:229.

7. *National Intelligencer*, 6 Feb. 1812, 5 Mar. 1812, 28 Jan. 1812, 25 Jan. 1812.

8. John C. Calhoun to Patrick Calhoun, 24 Jan. 1812; Calhoun to Patrick Noble, 22 Mar. 1812, *The Papers of John C. Calhoun*, ed. Robert L. Meriwether (Columbia, 1959), 1:90, 96 (hereafter cited as *Calhoun Papers*); J. G. de Roulhac Hamilton, *William Richardson Davie: A Memoir*, James

surprised because of his politics, his military ability was generally not questioned. Pinckney was appointed and accepted.

William Polk of North Carolina, also a Federalist and a noted Revolutionary War hero, was named a brigadier general to serve under Pinckney in the Sixth District, in charge of recruiting. For three months Polk, initially taken by surprise, deliberated over his acceptance, creating problems for the army and invoking criticism from those of opposite political beliefs. Seeking advice from his friend John Steele, Polk indicated that he was "distressed and embarressed [sic]" over the decision. If he accepted, his business affairs "would be all but ruined." A lesser rank would not affect his business as much but would be personally unacceptable. If he declined, he would be charged with "party motives." Polk had analyzed the situation correctly, for Congressman Blackledge sneered that Polk would accept the post only if he could have his headquarters at Raleigh where he could continue simultaneously to be president of the State Bank. Finally when Adjutant General Alexander Smyth lost patience and demanded a decision by return mail, declaring that Polk had had sufficient time to deliberate, and that "the public service requires your decision," Polk declined.[9] When no other North Carolinian was offered the rank of a general officer, Calvin Jones of Wake County, physician and adjutant general of the state, aspired to a military career. Although both Polk and Governor Hawkins recommended him, he was not commissioned; probably A. G. Glynn was correct in telling his friend Jones that appointments were obtained by intrigue and political influence.[10]

Sprunt Historical Monograph, no. 7 (Chapel Hill, 1907), p. 20; Nathaniel Macon to Joseph H. Nicholson, 25 Mar. 1812, Nicholson Papers; William Lowndes to wife, 28 Mar. 1812, quoted in Harriott Horry Rutledge Ravenel, *Life and Times of William Lowndes of South Carolina, 1782-1822* (Boston, 1901), pp. 103-4.

9. *National Intelligencer*, 28 Mar. 1812; William Polk to William Eustis, 4 Apr. 1812, RG 107, M 221; Polk to John Steele, 4 Apr. 1812, *The Papers of John Steele*, ed. H. M. Wagstaff, 2 vols. (Raleigh, 1924), 2:672 (hereafter cited as *Steele Papers*); William Blackledge to John Gray Blount, 13 May 1812, John Gray Blount Papers, NC Archives; Alexander Smyth to Polk, 12 May 1812, Records of the Adjutant General's Office: Letters Sent by the Office of the Adjutant General, Main Series, 1800-90, Record Group 94, Microcopy 565, NA (hereafter cited as RG 94, M 565).

10. Calvin Jones to Major William S. Hamilton, 4 Apr. 1813; A. G[J?]. Glynn to Jones, 6 Sept. 1813, Calvin Jones Family Papers, microfilm, SHC.

General Pinckney left his plantation for Charleston and took charge immediately and competently. Under his command were placed the Eighth, Tenth, and Eighteenth Infantry, the Second Artillery, and the Second Light Dragoons, all new units. Later the Forty-third Infantry was authorized for the southern department. These regiments were to be recruited in southern states and organized as speedily as possible into companies, regiments, and battalions. Recruiting reports were to go directly to the War Department and from thence would be forwarded to the general. The War Department would try not to interfere with his troops, it informed Pinckney, but reserved the right to do so in case of emergency.[11]

In the face of exceedingly difficult problems, Pinckney performed well, disproving Macon's disparagement of him. In the first place he faced the problem of a formidable territory under his command. Some six hundred miles of seacoast had to be put into a state of defense, from the North Carolina–Virginia border on the north to St. Mary's River on the Florida-Georgia border in the south. In pursuit of his duties, he campaigned to the Alabama River, visited St. Mary's several times, traveled up the coast of Georgia, South Carolina, and North Carolina. Even the fact that Norfolk was shortly taken over directly from Washington did little to reduce his responsibilities. He had fortifications to erect and maintain, transportation lines of great length to protect, Indians on the west, British and Spanish on the south, unhealthful conditions along the marshy coasts, and scattered troops only too few in number.

Pinckney also suffered for the want of officers of field grade. Following Polk's decision not to accept the appointment as brigadier general, it was some time before a replacement was found in the person of John Thomas Flournoy of Georgia. But Flournoy did not serve under Pinckney for long; he was sent to the southwest where he took part in the Creek Indian War and the defense of New Orleans until his resignation. The same thing happened to Major General Wade Hampton who, although originally scheduled for a southern post, was transferred to the Canadian front. In fact, Pinckney

11. Thomas Cushing to Thomas Pinckney, 5 Sept. 1812, RG 94, M 565; William Eustis to Pinckney, copy, 29 Apr. 1812, Records of the Adjutant General's Office: Letters Received by the Office of Adjutant General, 1805-21, Record Group 94, Microcopy 566, NA (hereafter cited as RG 94, M 566).

never had a permanent brigadier general for the Sixth District. Not only was his staff weak on this score, but it also was short of colonels. In 1813, for example, the colonels of the Eighth and Tenth regiments had been assigned to the recruiting service; the lieutenant colonel of the Eighth was mentally deranged; there was no field officer available to station anywhere along the coast. When the dragoons came back from the Creek War, they had no captain and lacked several other officers. Unless he could have some officers, Pinckney complained in 1814, every post would be left under the command of militia officers, which he thought inadvisable because of their lack of experience. He begged the secretary of war to recognize southern defense needs instead of transferring every capable officer to Canada.[12]

Worse than the lack of officers, and in fact perhaps the greatest problem that Pinckney had to face, was the lack of supplies. For his three regiments, Pinckney estimated that he needed 10,300 shirts, 2,998 blankets, 2,136 pairs of trousers, 2,872 coats, 444 camp kettles, 500 tents, and 120 spades, among other items. Nearly five months after he had assumed command, he had received only 1,450 shirts, 1,080 blankets, 804 pairs of trousers, 8 coats, 69 camp kettles, 13 tents, and no spades. This continued to be the story throughout the entire war. Blankets, wrote Colonel James Wellborn of the Tenth Regiment from Salisbury, North Carolina, were hard to get and would "come high." Recruits were frequently reported by Wellborn as being "quite bare and marching about in that condition will discourage others from enlisting."[13] An unusually severe winter during 1812-13 further aggravated the lack of warm clothing and blankets. Winter clothing had not arrived at Salisbury by 12 November 1812; nor had it appeared a month later. In January 1813, Pinckney learned that the clothing had reached Norfolk and was on its way to Wellborn's troops under the care of a Lieutenant Vashon. He himself ordered uniforms made by seamstresses in Charleston and

12. Thomas Pinckney to Major J. R. Bell, 14 Aug. 1814, RG 94, M 566; Pinckney to Secretary of War, 22 May 1813, RG 107, M 221; Pinckney to Secretary of War, 14 July 1814, RG 94, M 566; Pinckney to Secretary of War, 1 Nov. 1814, RG 107, M 221.

13. Thomas Pinckney to Secretary of War, 26 Aug. 1812, RG 107, M 221; James Wellborn to Adjutant General, 28 May 1812, 4 June 1812, RG 94, M 566.

other nearby points for the remaining regiments under the assumption that Wellborn's regiment was provided for. March came, but still no clothing. The troops at Salisbury were "froze up here for the want of winter cloathing. Our nakedness in so inclement a season has had a tendency to through [*sic*] a damp in the young men of the Country who inclined to join us," Wellborn told the adjutant general. After Pinckney suggested tracing the lost supplies, clothing finally arrived at Salisbury in April when winter was over; yet even then the count was woefully short. Out of 600 suits needed, only 150 arrived. Said Wellborn, "It is folly to complain of being neglected but it is honest to say that my Regiment both here and at the different posts has been entirely neglected." For almost a year some of the recruits had been waiting, until they had "lost all hope." The lost clothing had simply evaporated, for it was traced as far as Kempville, Virginia, and never heard of again.[14] Supplies other than clothing were fortunately not as difficult to obtain. Pinckney named deputy assistant quartermasters, two for North Carolina and three each for Virginia, South Carolina, and Georgia, who for the most part appear to have been reasonably competent in their positions. Wellborn did, however, upon one occasion complain that Lieutenant Samuel Champlin in Charleston was holding too many offices and therefore not performing efficiently. In Wilmington, North Carolina, Hanson Kelly served satisfactorily throughout the war as deputy commissary of purchases, to whom the North Carolina recruiting officers applied for their needs.[15] The problems seemed chiefly those of transportation, resulting in

14. James Wellborn to Thomas Cushing, 15 Dec. 1812, RG 94, M 566; Thomas Pinckney to Secretary of War, 22 Dec. 1812, 5, 28 Jan. 1813, RG 107, M 221; Wellborn to Cushing, 22 Feb. 1813, RG 94, M 566; Pinckney to Secretary of War, 15 Mar. 1813, RG 107, M 221; Wellborn to Cushing, 19 Apr. 1813, RG 94, M 566; Pinckney to Secretary of War, 11 June 1813, RG 107, M 221; Wellborn to Charles R. Gardner, 27 Sept. 1813, RG 94, M 566. While Wellborn's men suffered, officers seem to have fared better. Captain John Gray Blount, Jr., purchased for himself on 15 Nov. 1813, 1 pair blue cassemere pantaloons, 2 pairs flannel drawers, 1 pair quarter shingvalies [?], 1 pair trowsers and 1 coat for his servant, totaling $63.00 (receipt in Blount Papers).

15. Alexander Macomb to Thomas Pinckney, 16 June 1812, RG 94, M 565; James Wellborn to Thomas Cushing, 10 Aug. 1812, RG 94, M 566; Cushing to Hanson Kelly, 10 Oct. 1812; Cushing to D. M. Forney, 31 Oct. 1812, RG 94, M 565.

delays but not in the complete absence of supplies. No arms had been received in Salisbury in August 1812; no blankets from either Charleston or Columbia had reached Salisbury; arms needed for coastal defense had not reached the south even as late as October 1814. Supplies for North Carolina, instead of being sent to Wilmington, were sent to Charleston, creating additional delays and expenses. When the Third Rifle Regiment was being recruited at Charlotte, North Carolina, the lack of arms, although there was a plentiful supply at the Richmond armory, was a serious hindrance to the inculcation of discipline and of training. When the Third Rifle Regiment marched north and camped near Richmond, so few tents were available that Lieutenant Colonel William S. Hamilton thought it best not to use any lest jealousies arise. Isolated problems did, however, occur. The civilian contractor serving the Tenth Regiment during the winter of 1814 was roundly taken to task for failure to furnish fuel and vinegar rations, for short rationing soap, salt, and whiskey, and for giving the troops the poorest quality of meat. Furthermore, the bread was so miserable that it was "insufferable."[16] Fortunately for the southern states, no battles were fought there between opposing armies and no sieges were conducted, so that the deficiencies in supplies did not materially affect the course of the war.

Lack of money was at the root of the problems of supply and transportation. Congress seemed desirous of running the war at the least possible expense, and such money as was voted was spent on the attacks on Canada rather than on the defense of the seaboard and the south. Pinckney warned the secretary of war that wars, if they are to be won, must be prosecuted with vigor. Therefore, he wrote, "it appears to me that sparing any expense which may place our military service upon an efficient footing is not true economy."[17] Yet pay for many troops was constantly in arrears, two months so or more in June 1813, as much as fifteen months in September 1814. The mutiny at Carlisle, Pennsylvania, in 1815 was due to the

16. James Wellborn to Thomas Cushing, 13 Aug. 1812; Wellborn to Alexander Smyth, undated; Wellborn to Smyth, 5 July 1812, RG 94, M 566; William S. Hamilton to J. R. Bell, 2 Sept. 1814; Hamilton to Daniel Parker, 15 Dec. 1814, ibid.; Henry Cansou to Hamilton, 5 February 1814, ibid.
17. Thomas Pinckney to Secretary of War, 12 Dec. 1812, RG 107, M 221.

great arrearage in pay. The situation had become "deplorable" by 1814. Treasury notes were available but they had to be converted into money, and Pinckney's paymaster refused to sell them below par. Since all notes were selling below par by 1814, this meant that the paymaster was holding $150,000 while the troops received nothing. Pinckney pleaded for instructions that would relieve his suffering troops. Two months after his appeal, having received no aid, Pinckney personally took matters into his own hands and drew on the State Bank at Raleigh for $10,000 in favor of the quartermaster's department, without knowing if his draft would be honored. He secured a loan of $25,000 from the Bank of New Bern, which apologized for the smallness of the sum but assured Pinckney that it was a small bank and could not manage more. The Charleston banks refused to lend money unless it were used to defend their city; the Savannah banks refused unconditionally; not much was hoped for from the banks at Augusta. Considering pay for the troops, a price of $500 for a first-rate wagon and team, and such sums as an inadequate $15,000 personally ordered spent by Pinckney for clothing for the troops,[18] it is obvious that a steady flow of money was essential—a flow that did not exist.

Not only was Pinckney short of men, money and supplies, but when a company was recruited and trained, or when an officer showed ability and promise, such company, regiment, or officer was usually sent elsewhere by the general government. All rifle and light dragoon companies were ordered to the northern front in November 1812, following General Isaac Hull's surrender at Detroit. Major General Wade Hampton, who was to command the coastal defense of North and South Carolina, was detached to sit on Hull's court-martial, and then placed in command at Burlington, Vermont. The Tenth Regiment, which had been recruited chiefly in North Carolina, was ordered to the northern front in the fall of 1813. Most of the junior officers of ability were on recruiting duty. Desperately, in the spring of 1814, Pinckney appealed to the secretary of war for proper defense measures. The coast had not

18. Thomas Pinckney to Secretary of War, 24 Sept. 1814, 30 Nov. 1814, RG 107, M 221; James McKinlay to Pinckney, copy, 7 Nov. 1814, ibid.; Pinckney to Secretary of War, 26 Oct. 1814, 11 June 1813, ibid.; James Wellborn to Major W. R. Bootes, 20 Jan. 1813, RG 94, M 566.

received the supplies needed, he informed Monroe; the officers had been sent to recruit elsewhere; the companies were not as full as they should be. If the British would be kind enough not to attack for a month or six weeks, he hoped to be in better shape and able to offer respectable resistance in case they should come.[19] In view of the capabilities of the United States if properly organized, this was a pitiful cry for help.

The health of the troops was a grave problem both during the "sickly season" in the southern climate and during bitter winter months in the piedmont and in the north. Efforts to meet these needs were made by naming a surgeon or physician for each regiment, together with two surgeon's mates or assistants. For North Carolina's Tenth Regiment, Dr. Egbert H. Bell of Wilmington and Dr. William Southall of Richmond were named surgeon's mates, and Dr. James Norcom of Edenton was named surgeon. If medical aid were needed and there was no surgeon available, a private physician might be employed; such a physician made his account and sent it to the accountant of the War Department for settlement, accompanied by an officer's certificate that he had performed the services itemized therein. Yet every surgeon's mate in the army was expected to attend all troops whether of his own regiment or not. When Dr. Bell attempted to collect extra pay for attending men other than those in the Tenth Regiment, he was admonished by the adjutant general. "It is the duty of every officer in the Army," he was told, "to devote his whole time and attention to the public service at the Post or place at which he is stationed, and although your duties may have been arduous for a time you certainly have done no more than the public has a right to exact from you."[20] Bell evidently learned from this incident, for a year later at Green Leaf Point near Washington City, he was recommended by Colonel Wellborn for the post of surgeon, as "a well educated young man & could take charge of the health of a Regt. to his own credit, & to its advantage." At the same time, Wellborn certi-

19. Thomas Cushing to Thomas Pinckney, 12 Nov. 1812, RG 94, M 565; Pinckney to Secretary of War, 29 June 1813, 5 Sept. 1813, 8 Apr. 1814, RG 107, M 221.

20. Thomas Cushing to Dr. James Norcom, 3 Sept. 1812; Cushing to D. M. Forney, 22 Oct. 1812; Cushing to Dr. Egbert Bell, 15 Mar. 1813, RG 94, M 565.

fied that his surgeon, Dr. Isaac Forster, was incompetent to perform his duties. Major (later colonel) Hamilton, then serving in the Tenth Regiment, also recommended Bell as "a skillful young man, & very attentive to his duties. He merits advancement." Forster, he added, "holds a place beyond his merits. He is not learned in his profession, not industrious, and not sufficiently sober." Some of the medical reports sent in to superior officers were distressing indeed. In December 1813, the Tenth Regiment had more than one hundred men ill at the same time. There were deaths, reported their colonel, every day: one the preceding day, one today, and two more dying. Twenty-four men had to share one fireplace, there was only one blanket per man, and no medical attention outside of the hospital. The surgeon was lame and not very active. Not enough plank was available for the necessary coffins. If another physician were not provided for them, "we shall bury the greater part of this Detachment, without seeing the enemy." As another example, the Third Rifle Regiment, encamped at Bottom's Bridge near Richmond in December 1814, had twenty-one men in the hospital and fifty-eight sick in their quarters. Having just marched three hundred miles from Charlotte in bitter weather, the troops needed rest, warm clothes, and good quarters to restore their health.[21]

The final problem with which Pinckney as well as others in command had to cope was the lack of authority. He was given a task to do, without proper delineation of lines of authority, with the secretary of war constantly being replaced, with Congress attempting to plan campaigns and keep control over events. The resulting confusion showed at every level. After Pinckney was informed of his appointment as major general and had accepted, he heard nothing further about his duties, his officers, his staff, or his equipment, for months. First notified in March 1812, he inquired in June and again in July for further information. He did not even have the authority to repel a "hostile aggression" if one should be launched, without first consulting the secretary of war. Pinckney often complained that many of his questions on important matters went unanswered. He read orders from the adjutant

21. James Wellborn to Secretary of War, 11 Mar. 1814; William S. Hamilton to Daniel Parker, 15 Dec. 1814; Wellborn to ———, 31 Dec. 1813, RG 94, M 566.

general and the inspector general in the *National Intelligencer* before he had received them. Were these news articles, he demanded to know, to be considered as official?[22] In March 1813, Colonel Wellborn did not know who was the commissary general. Lieutenant Colonel Hamilton received orders from the Sixth District adjutant general to do one thing and the adjutant general in Washington to do another. Colonel Wellborn received orders from the adjutant general to march to Norfolk, and contradictory orders from Pinckney to march instead to St. Mary's River. Although Wellborn was required to make returns for all men of his regiment serving at coastal points, the local commanding officers had been directed instead to send their reports directly to Pinckney. The adjutant general in Washington had never heard of the troops which rendezvoused at Tarboro, North Carolina: how many men were there, to what regiment they belonged, or who was in command. Just prior to the end of the war, fortifications at Charleston which had been recommended two years earlier by Major (later general) Joseph G. Swift, and plans for which had been drawn by Major William McRee and a Colonel Armistead, had not even been begun. When Swift tried to have two forts constructed for the Beaufort, North Carolina, area, he was unable to get labor and materials. Although Governor Hawkins suggested calling out a regiment of militia to secure the necessary labor, Swift could not authorize this plan. Communication by mail was at a snail's pace; a letter to Captain John Nicks at Fort Hampton, North Carolina, mailed in Charleston on 4 September did not reach him until 1 October.[23] Indeed the task of Pinckney and all other general officers was a formidable one—to organize an army from nothing in the face of

22. Thomas Pinckney to Adjutant General, 3 June 1812; Pinckney to Inspector General, 21 July 1812, RG 94, M 566; Pinckney to Secretary of War, 18 May 1812, 20 Feb. 1813, 9 Mar. 1814, RG 107, M 221; Pinckney to Secretary of War, 17 Aug. 1813, RG 94, M 566.

23. James Wellborn to Thomas Cushing, 9 Mar. 1813; William S. Hamilton to Francis R. Huger, 10 Nov. 1814, RG 94, M 566; Cushing to Wellborn, 4 May 1813, RG 94, M 565; Wellborn to Adjutant General, 18 May 1813, RG 94, M 566; Cushing to Dr. James Norcom, 16 Oct. 1812, RG 94, M 565; Thomas Pinckney to Secretary of War, 30 Aug. 1814, RG 107, M 221; Joseph Swift to War Department, 4 Apr. 1814, cited in Edward James Wagner II, "State-Federal Relations during the War of 1812" (Ph.D. diss., Ohio State University, 1963), p. 151; Pinckney to Secretary of War, 27 Oct. 1812, RG 107, M 221.

indecision and inefficiency from above. Even with the best of intentions and cooperation, as Pinckney knew, miracles would not be wrought. To Thomas Cushing he wrote, "Where the whole army is inexperienced and ignorant, you are aware how slow must be the progress to discipline and efficiency."[24]

Although beset with many problems, Pinckney prepared his defense plans and attempted to implement them. Coastal defenses were to be put in the best possible order, especially those of Charleston and Savannah. As recruits were raised, they were to be brought to man the defenses; meantime, militia was to be used. Arms were sent by the general government to Charleston in the amount of five thousand stand; to Savannah, one thousand; to Fort Johnston, North Carolina, sixteen hundred. Of accoutrements, Charleston received three thousand; Savannah, eight hundred; Fort Johnston, eleven hundred. Tents to the number of 230 to Charleston, 135 to Savannah, and 310 to Fort Johnston were gotten under way by the War Department, and a medicine chest to each of the above places. Pinckney's plans were to garrison all the coastal forts with artillerists, hoping to be allocated twelve hundred men out of the national quota of 5,920. Fort Hampton, North Carolina, should have fifty; Fort Johnston also fifty; Charleston harbor, which had several forts, five hundred; and so on down the remainder of the coast. As infantry was needed, it could be added. All other troops he planned to assemble in a position where they could be marched to the "most exposed part of our frontier" upon any major threat; until such need arose, these troops could be instructed and drilled. He was counting on the mild southern climate to allow outdoor drill in the winter. Actual war games, or "maneuvres of the line," could be carried out, he thought, if he were given one more infantry regiment and some mounted dragoons and field artillerists.[25] The general's evaluation of the state of defense of each major post relied heavily upon a survey made by Major Joseph G. Swift, chief engineer of the regular army at the outbreak of the war. Although Swift had visited Charleston twice in 1811 and pointed out that the coast was unprepared for war,

24. Thomas Pinckney to Thomas Cushing, 23 Sept. 1812, RG 94, M 566.
25. William Eustis to Thomas Pinckney, copy, 21 May 1812, RG 94, M 566; Alexander Smyth to Pinckney, 15 June 1812, RG 94, M 565; Pinckney to Thomas Cushing, 23 Sept. 1812, RG 94, M 566.

nothing had been done to follow up. Pinckney in 1812 found Port Royal, South Carolina, defenseless, although it was the only harbor between the Chesapeake and the Florida border deep enough for heavy frigates.[26] Assigned to the southern department in command of engineering was Major William McRee of North Carolina, on whose excellent judgment Pinckney learned to rely. McRee at the outbreak of war was busy completing the defense works at Fort Jackson near Savannah, Georgia, with orders to follow that project by rebuilding Fort Wayne in the same area. Pinckney instructed him to build at Fort Wayne an earth fortification with a revetment of turf, which would be inexpensive yet adequately secure while more permanent plans were being developed. McRee also planned the construction of a military hospital at Charleston. When it was thought that Florida might be invaded and St. Augustine besieged, McRee made a survey of the ordnance necessary for the undertaking. Pinckney thought enough of McRee's abilities to support him above a Colonel Wadsworth whose estimate of the force necessary for attacking St. Augustine was, in the major's opinion, an underestimation. Pinckney forwarded McRee's detailed critique to the secretary of war. When McRee was transferred to New York, Pinckney, although reluctantly, permitted him to go, because he "thought it a pity that a young gentleman of his talents should remain here idle when his services may be usefully employed elsewhere." If an attack should come in the southern department, he asked to have McRee returned, or some other engineer of "talents and experience."[27] As recruits were raised and trained for the regular army, Pinckney disposed them around his district to the best advantage possible, considering their lack of experience and numbers. An artillery unit was sent to Fort Johnston; men from the Tenth Regiment garrisoned all the posts north of Charleston. All but one troop of dragoons were placed on duty in Georgia. In Charleston harbor, the Eighteenth Infantry and two companies of the First Artillery were stationed in its several forts. On the Flor-

26. Wagner, "State-Federal Relations during the War of 1812," p. 9; Thomas Pinckney to Secretary of War, 6 June 1812, RG 107, M 221.

27. Thomas Pinckney to Secretary of War, 25 June 1812, 9 July 1812, 22 Dec. 1812, 30 July 1813; William McRee to Pinckney, 25 Jan. 1813, RG 107, M 221.

ida border was the largest part of the Eighth Regiment, other detachments having been sent to Fort Hawkins on the Creek Indian frontier and to Beaufort, South Carolina.[28] Pinckney never had at his disposal more troops than these, and sometimes fewer.

Apparently Pinckney was instructed to be more concerned over attacking East Florida than any other matter of the war in the South for approximately the first year. Once he had placed minimal protection at the major forts already established on the seaboard, he was constantly involved in plans for invading Florida. At times he even acted as a diplomatic envoy under directions from the secretary of state and the secretary of war. By July 1813, however, the decision not to attack East Florida had been reached by the general government, and Pinckney abandoned Point Petre and the St. Mary's River area leaving it for the navy to defend.[29]

Entirely unanticipated at the outbreak of the war was the war with the Creek Indians. Although trouble had been brewing and was expected in the Old Northwest, and although the prophets had come seeking allies among the Creeks, it was generally held at Washington that there would not be Indian hostilities in the South. Colonel Benjamin Hawkins, the Indian agent at Fort Hawkins, was thought to have matters well under control. And so he did until the massacre at Fort Mims, Alabama. At that point, Pinckney was directed to take over the Indian campaign, even though it was not in his territory, and conduct it to a successful finish.[30] This provided a heavy drain on the manpower available for defense of the seaboard, and distracted the general's full attention from his regular duties. By the summer of 1814, however, the Indian war was over.

It was fortunate that the Creek War ended when it did, for Napoleon had been defeated at the Battle of the Nations and sent into exile on Elba, thus permitting Great Britain to turn her attention to the war in North America. Although as early as the fall of 1813 word had been received of great prep-

28. Thomas Pinckney to Secretary of War, 4 July 1812, 6 Aug. 1812, 3 Aug. 1812, enclosures; 11 Feb. 1813, RG 107, M 221.

29. Thomas Pinckney to Secretary of War, Dec. 1812, *passim*; 31 July 1813, RG 107, M 221.

30. Thomas Pinckney to Secretary of War, 30 Oct. 1813, RG 107, M 221.

arations in Halifax, Nova Scotia, for some sort of southern invasion, it was not until the spring of 1814 that alarm began to spread. Pinckney had always been aware of the lack of defense; in November 1813, he had asked for recruits from the new Forty-third Regiment and had urged additional fortifications at Fort Johnston. Upon his return from the Creek War in 1814 he visited Savannah, Beaufort, South Carolina, and Charleston to inspect their defenses, going from thence up the North Carolina coast and inland to confer with Governor Hawkins at Raleigh. Following a warning that the British were raising an army large enough for the protection of Canada and at least fifteen to twenty thousand additional men for landing on the Atlantic coast, Pinckney, with only the equivalent of four companies of artillery to protect the South against what Gallatin called an intention to inflict a "chastisement that will teach [America] that war is not to be declared against Great Britain with impunity," begged for more artillery. Pinckney wrote the governors of the three southern states that while the South was probably safe during the fall hurricane season, southern cities should emulate New York and Philadelphia by raising their own defensive militia companies in preparation for the period thereafter. Although he knew that the southern cities were not wealthy, they had Negro labor which would compensate to some extent for lack of funds. He called on the southerners "to make equal exertions with our brethren of the north." After the British captured Washington on 24 August, Pinckney ordered his colonels in North Carolina and Georgia, under authority proclaimed by the president, to call on the state governors for militia when deemed necessary. North Carolina, he felt, was perhaps safer than the other two because she had "natural strength of the maritime frontier" and a large population, for which reasons he was more hopeful that "a small immediate force" would suffice to insure its protection.[31] It is difficult to see what more Pinckney could have done; the South was fortunate that the

31. Thomas Pinckney to Secretary of War, 4 Nov. 1813, 6 May 1814, RG 107, M 221; *Raleigh Register*, 17 June 1814; *The Writings of Albert Gallatin*, ed. Henry Adams (1872; reprint ed., New York, 1960), 1:627 (hereafter cited as *Gallatin Writings*); Pinckney to Secretary of War, 14 July 1814; Pinckney to Governor of South Carolina, 30 Aug., 1814; Pinckney to Secretary of War, 13 Sept. 1814, 26 Sept. 1814, RG 107, M 221.

British decided to attack New Orleans instead of the Atlantic coast.

Although the navy would today be expected to take a major share of the responsibility for coastal defense, in 1812 there was practically no navy. A few gunboats constituted the entire fleet for the southern department. In 1808 Wilmington was protected by Gunboat Number 7, under the command of Sailing Master Thomas N. Gautier. Authorized because of the importunities of the citizens to construct three new gunboats, he spent four years getting Numbers 166, 167, and 168 launched. The same problems of lack of money for officers' pay, lack of money for bills incurred in boat building, lack of response to important letters to Secretary of the Navy Paul Hamilton, were experienced at Gautier's level as at Pinckney's. To a navy friend he wrote, "Sans an article of military equipment, sans money, sans officers or men, I have done as much . . . as in some places would have been done having everything at hand." He spoke sharply of "these economical times," for indeed Congress was parsimonious in its naval appropriations. Eventually, however, all was ready; the navy promptly ordered the best gunboat to St. Mary's, another of the new ones to Beaufort, while Wilmington was left with only two. Gautier pleaded for more; Wilmington needed five plus a heavy brig for proper defenses, he urged. Without these, Bald Head could be a rendezvous for the enemy even as it had been during the Revolutionary War. Yet Gautier, as a loyal officer, promised to try to "ease the Wilmingtonians of their fears" with the remaining two boats. In response to his plea, Gautier received three more boats and was placed in command, not only of Wilmington but also of Beaufort and Ocracoke. Even this protection, however, was taken away in 1813 when orders were issued calling in all gunboats in North Carolina waters and directing them to be laid up and crews discharged. Bitterly, Gautier inquired if they should be shedded over and protected with varnish, or "suffered to die a natural death." To his friend and commanding officer he wrote: "I then shall sit down in sullen retirement and view the Boats in the mud and to reflect on the situation of my state not a single armed vessel allotted for her defense." Following Napoleon's defeat and with the anticipation of a large scale British attack, in October 1814 a flotilla under the command of newly commissioned Lieutenant Gautier was finally sent to the defense of Wilmington.[32] Meanwhile, suggestions for improving coastal defense included one for building and equipping row galleys, with twenty oars and muskets on each side, at a cost of $50,000 or $60,000 each, which would be able to stop raids by small British vessels and could perhaps even attack larger ones in the night. Although the suggestion was handed on by President Madison to the secretary of the navy in 1813, nothing seems to have come of it.[33] Attempts to organize companies of men called sea fencibles were more successful than efforts to obtain naval vessels. Congress authorized the raising of ten companies of sea fencibles under act of 26 July 1813, but no field officers were allowed. Six North Carolinians received commissions in the sea fencibles, including Captain Frederick Brooks of Washington, who was sent full instructions for organizing a company. The men were to serve only when the state was actually invaded; they received no enlistment bounties and were allowed no musicians. Brooks was told, "Your corps is a nondescript force and its efficiency and use will depend in a very great degree on your own arrangements and personal exertions." The pilots at Wilmington, some forty or fifty, were willing to form a company to serve either in boats or on land in case of an invasion. Marines were used on board vessels; Gautier had sixteen marines and four officers for his gunboats.[34] Again, it was fortunate for the state that these meager defenses were never tested in battle.

North Carolina's response to the measures taken for its

32. Thomas N. Gautier, 23 Jan. 1809, 1810-11, *passim*, 19 Oct. 1811, 22 Apr. 1812, 21 Aug. 1812, 23 Sept. 1812, 30 Nov. 1812, 2 Dec. 1812, 10 Mar. 1813, 29 Mar. 1813, Thomas N. Gautier Letterbook, 1808-13, SHC; *Raleigh Register*, 9 July 1813, 21 Oct. 1814.

33. James Madison to Thomas Jefferson, 6 June 1813, *Letters and Other Writings of James Madison* (Philadelphia, 1867), 2:564-65 (hereafter cited as *Madison Writings*).

34. The six were: Richard Bayner, 1st lieutenant; John Bonner, 3d lieutenant; Frederick Brooks, captain; Robert Lytle, 1st lieutenant; Byrd B. Mitchell, 2d lieutenant; and John Nicholson, captain. Francis J. Heitman, *His torical Register and Dictionary of the United States Army . . .* (Washington, D.C., 1903), 1:143, 201, 230, 249, 651, 716, 747; Thomas Cushing to Frederick Brooks, 10 Jan. 1814, RG 94, M 565; Hawkins Letterbook 18, no date, p. 232; Gautier Letterbook, 18 Feb. 1812, 14 Mar. 1812.

defense was one of dissatisfaction, of anger, and finally of hopelessness. When the state legislature convened in December 1811, a resolution was addressed to Congress requesting adequate coastal defenses. "Whereas the warlike attitude assumed by Congress is calculated to awaken in the Citizens of North Carolina an anxious solicitude for their safety and protection," the legislature declared, an appropriation "commensurate with our rights" was sought. Governor Hawkins inquired of General Pinckney why more was not done in 1812 in preparation for the war, to which Pinckney was forced to reply that he had so much coast to defend and so little money that he had to choose the most vulnerable and significant ports and could not protect all. North Carolina had only two places "deemed of sufficient importance, or so exposed, as to require the support of fortifications," the Cape Fear and Beaufort. Even the valuable Sea Islands, Pinckney explained, had only a few gunboats and armed barges. North Carolina would be forced to fall back upon its own resources, the general indicated, and he thereupon authorized the governor to call out the militia of the state when an attack was made or "obviously threatened." He suggested that Wilmington and Edenton could have companies ready to be called in time of need. However, he assured the governor, he had submitted to the War Department the defense needs of the coast, and hoped Congress would authorize the necessary funds to build fortifications.[35] The following session the legislature became so distressed that it addressed letters to the secretary of war, to its congressmen and senators, and to the president asking for greater protection. The response from the War Department was that measures for coastal defenses were being prepared and would be submitted to Congress within a few days. Senator Stone, when asked to use his influence on Capitol Hill, was astounded that no troops were guarding the North Carolina coast, while North Carolina troops were at New Orleans, Savannah, Charleston, and Norfolk, and were distinguishing themselves on the northwestern frontier. He obtained promises from the navy of five gunboats, and from the War Department of ammunition for three companies of militia. John Gray Blount, prominent eastern North Carolina business man,

35. Hawkins Letterbook 18, 23 Dec. 1811, p. 12; 6 Oct. 1812, pp. 334-36.

also used his influence to try to obtain gunboats for Beaufort and Swansboro.[36] Following a British landing on the North Carolina coast, another legislative memorial was addressed to the president in November 1813. The memorial expressed humiliation that the state's plea for help had been treated with "indifference and neglect." Although the state had furnished nearly as many regulars as any state, not one had been employed in her defense. Governor Hawkins sent Calvin Jones to Washington carrying the memorial. After a journey of several days by the "accommodation stage," Jones dined with Madison, but brought no more help back to North Carolina than had any of the previous efforts. Madison merely repeated the original views expressed by Pinckney eighteen months earlier. Trying to protect everything, he said, was almost an impossibility; the government could only do its best. As soon as possible, he promised, an inspection would be made of the coast. Additional gunboats would be allotted "as soon as they can be made ready for service," but meanwhile North Carolina should continue to supply its own defenses.[37] North Carolina's Select Committee on Claims in 1833 summed up the feeling of the state by saying, "The first great object which led to the formation of the Union was to provide for the common defense. The defense of North Carolina had been overlooked by the public authorities. Our sea coast was blockaded, and our defenceless towns threatened with destruction." After citing the fact that the militia of the state was called away to protect the frontiers of Georgia and to garrison Norfolk, the committee expostulated that "half the whole number who were stationed at the latter point, died in the service, and those who returned, brought with them a pestilence, which spread disease and death throughout a large portion of the State."[38]

36. Hawkins Letterbook 19, 25 May 1813, p. 221; 11 June 1813, pp. 260-62; 22 June 1813, pp. 267-69; George Evans to John Gray Blount, 29 Mar. 1813; James Taylor to John Gray Blount, 6 June 1813, Blount Papers.

37. *N.C. Senate Journal, 1813*, pp. 11-12; Calvin Jones to William Hawkins, 3 Dec. 1813, Governor William Hawkins Papers, NC Archives; James Madison to the Senate and House of Commons of the General Assembly of the State of North Carolina, 11 Dec. 1813, *Madison Writings*, 2:577-78; Niles' *Weekly Register*, 29 Jan. 1814.

38. N.C., General Assembly, *Report of the Select Committee on the Claims of the State upon the General Government* (Raleigh, 1833), pp. 3, 4 (hereafter cited as *Select Committee on Claims*).

North Carolina felt abandoned, even betrayed, throughout the war.

The furnishing of recruits was the major military activity and the major contribution of the southern district. North Carolina led the three southern states in this area of activity.

William Polk, who had been appointed brigadier general in March 1812, was directed by the war office to go to Columbia, South Carolina, for recruiting duty. Under him was placed Colonel James Wellborn of Wilkesboro. When Wellborn went to Raleigh to confer with Polk, however, he found that the general had not decided on accepting the appointment, so that nothing had been done on the public business. Upon Polk's decision not to serve, Wellborn was placed in command of the recruiting for the southern department, and forthwith went to Columbia to organize. Technically, Brigadier General John Thomas Flournoy was later placed in charge, but since he was assigned first to Georgia and then to Mississippi Territory under Pinckney's orders to watch for the Spanish and Indian menaces, Wellborn handled all the recruiting for the first several months.[39]

Three regiments of infantry were to be raised, one of artillery, and one of light dragoons, to come from North and South Carolina and Georgia, with part of the Tenth Regiment to come from Virginia. Volunteer companies were also authorized in 1815. Officers were dispatched to various towns and centers with money for paying enlistment bounties, Lieutenant Colonel Archibald Macneill to Wilmington for the dragoons, and Major Daniel M. Forney to Salisbury for the artillery. Others, not North Carolinians, went to other posts, but all reported to Wellborn at Columbia. In the fall of 1812, the adjutant general reorganized the recruiting service and assigned to the commanding officer of each regiment the responsibility for recruiting his own men. Stress was to be placed on obtaining entire companies, if possible, from the same vicinity so that the men could serve with their friends. Flournoy was technically in command, Wellborn in charge of North Carolina, Lieutenant Colonel Andrew Pickens in South

39. *National Intelligencer,* 23 Apr. 1812; James Wellborn to William Eustis, 7 May 1812, RG 94, M 566; Alexander Smyth to Thomas Pinckney, 15 June 1812, RG 94, M 565; Pinckney to Secretary of War, 21 July 1812, RG 107, M 221.

Carolina, and a Colonel Jack in Georgia. In September, when Flournoy made a report to the secretary of war, 300 recruits had been obtained in Georgia, 350 in South Carolina, and 500 in North Carolina. Virginia recruits were not separated in the report from North Carolina recruits, as they were all to report to Wellborn at Salisbury. Under the new plan, Wellborn arrived in September at Salisbury, his "principle rendezvous," and vigorously prosecuted his task. Even when one battalion of the Tenth Regiment was ordered north, the best recruiting officers were left behind to continue until full strength was reached. As each company was completed, it was to be sent north to join the first battalion.[40]

In January 1813, the regimental recruiting plan was abolished and a district plan adopted, with men being assigned to various regiments although recruited from the same district. North Carolina was one such district, with Salisbury as the principal rendezvous. Wellborn was still in charge. "I am willing," he wrote to the adjutant general, "to travel from one end of the state to the other to get men—as that in my opinion is of the most importance. We cannot fight without them." Wellborn disposed his best men at strategic locations for recruiting: Oxford, Charlotte, Rutherfordton, Wilkesboro, Raleigh, Duplin Court House, Lincolnton, Salisbury, and one at large. Seven officers were recruiting for the Tenth Infantry, and one each for artillery and dragoons.[41] In May, once again the organization was changed, with all three southern states being placed in the same district; once again Wellborn was in command, returning to Columbia, South Carolina, to prosecute his duties. Although Wellborn would have preferred a combat command, he made every effort to contribute all in his power to "the public good." It was hard work: "the recruiting service if well attended to requires more labour and difficulty than can well be performed by any two men," he informed the adjutant general. In addition to the above re-

40. Thomas Cushing to Thomas Pinckney, 8 Aug. 1812; Cushing to Archibald Macneill, 5 Sept. 1812; Cushing to Pinckney, 5 Sept. 1812, RG 94, M 565; Pinckney to Secretary of War, 7 Sept. 1812, RG 107, M 221; Cushing to James Wellborn, 9 Sept. 1812, RG 94, M 565; Wellborn to Cushing, 13 Sept. 1812, RG 94, M 566; Cushing to Wellborn, 30 Dec. 1812, RG 94, M 565.

41. Thomas Cushing to Thomas Pinckney, 19 Jan. 1813, RG 94, M 565; James Wellborn to Cushing, 22 Feb. 1813, RG 94, M 566.

cruiting, in 1814 William S. Hamilton was sent to North Carolina to recruit for the Third Rifle Regiment; and a new regiment, the Forty-third, was created with Colonel Nicholas Long in charge, headquartered at Raleigh, concentrating on Georgia for enlistments.[42]

Recruiting duties required money, clothing, and arms to be at the disposal of the officers for distribution among the new troops. Money for bounties and premiums came from the paymaster, and contingent expenses for officers from the secretary of war. The contingent fund was to be used for "quarters, fuel, transportation, straw, stationery, tin pans, kettles, & medical aid." Wellborn was given $10,000 initially which he divided among the districts in proportion to the number of men to be raised in each. When all the money first allocated for North Carolina was spent by June, Wellborn asked the paymaster general for an additional $10,000, which was remitted. In a report to the adjutant general, he accounted for his recruiting money thus: Of the first $10,000, he had spent $4,500 in North Carolina, $3,440 in South Carolina, and $1,999.97 in Georgia. He drew a bill of exchange for $5,000 more for North Carolina, received $10,000 for contingencies, and also received a draft for $10,000 on a South Carolina bank. He and the adjutant general did not agree on the sums he had received. This Wellborn regretted. "I confess I am at a loss to know how & what I ought to charge the United States with. Please inform me. My inexperience in this kind of business is I hope a sufficient apology for the trouble I give you."[43] For the year 1814, some idea of the number of recruits may be obtained from the bounties paid. Recruiting officers paid out in North Carolina $60,000 in bounties and premiums, which was twelfth in rank of the twenty-two states and territories, New York ranking first with $495,320. Each officer on recruiting duty started off with $180 for bounties and premiums, $180 for pay in advance, and $100 for contingencies, then asking his superior officer for additional funds when these

42. Thomas Pinckney to Secretary of War, 29 May 1813, RG 107, M 221; James Wellborn to ———, 2 July 1813; Wellborn to Charles R. Gardner, 5 Aug. 1813, RG 94, M 566; *Raleigh Register*, 11 Mar. 1814.

43. Alexander Smyth to James Wellborn, 13 June 1812, 25 June 1812, RG 94, M 565; Wellborn to ———, 27 June 1812; Wellborn to Paymaster General, 29 June 1812; Wellborn to Smyth, 31 July 1812; Wellborn to Smyth, undated [June 1812?], RG 94, M 566.

were used. A receipt to Captain John Gray Blount of the
Third Rifle Regiment shows $900 being sent to him by Lieu-
tenant Colonel Hamilton for bounties and premiums. "Hard
money" was preferred in the "up country" because of the
lack of banks. The land bounty certainly appealed to men in
the western counties, because in 1835 several veterans who
had served only nineteen days appeared in Buncombe County
Court to claim their land. Although money was supplied, and
although four hundred suits of clothing were sent for the
exclusive use of troops at Salisbury, Fayetteville, and Tarboro,
besides clothing to the other southern states, recruiting suffered from lack of money and clothing throughout the entire
war. "Injurious reports" about lack of pay and clothing constantly hindered the recruiters' appeals to enlist. Hamilton,
who was without a paymaster in 1814, wrote four times to the
adjutant general asking to have one appointed. At Plattsburg,
New York, when the enlistment terms of men in the Tenth
Regiment were due to expire, recruiting money was not available to induce them to reenlist.[44]

Recruiting techniques used the old-fashioned methods
reminiscent of the Revolutionary War and the army of 1799.
Although the earlier armies had specified that recruits must be
able bodied, over 5 feet 6 inches tall, and between 18 and
45 years of age, by 1814 the size specification was dropped,
and any "free, effective able bodied man" up to the age of
fifty was accepted. A copy of *A New Useful & Complete System of Drum Beating Etc.* was sent to Wellborn for his regiment. Wellborn was also allowed to use his old drummer
and a fifer at his recruiting station, as they were deemed more
useful there than in the field. Fife and drum, appeals to
patriotism and self-interest, plus "the judicious application of
rum," brought in the men. Advertising circulars proclaimed
such sentiments as, "Where is the spirit of seventy-six? Arouse

44. *American State Papers: Military*, 1:511; Report of the Paymaster of
the Army to Secretary of War, 26 Oct. 1814, RG 107, M 221; James Well-
born to Francis R. Huger, 7 Sept. 1813, RG 94, M 566; Receipt, 1 Sept.
1814; Blount Papers; Thomas Pinckney to Secretary of War, 26 Nov. 1812,
RG 107, M 221; War of 1812 Claims of Service, Clerk of Superior Court,
Buncombe County, N.C., Apr. 1855, pp. 1-19, NC Archives; Pinckney to
Secretary of War, 13 Sept. 1814, RG 107, M 221; William S. Hamilton to
Adjutant General, 27 July 1814; Hamilton to John B. Walbach, 5 Jan. 1814,
RG 94, M 566.

ye sons of freedom!" Another one proclaimed, "Free yourselves from that dull and lethargic state in which you are
plunged. . . . Panegyrics will be written on your heroic characters and your deeds memorialized and registered among
those of the heroes of 76." Appealing to the spirit of the rifleman, Hamilton declared that the war provided a "GOLDEN
OPPORTUNITY" to those with "a pure spirit and a sacred impulse"
to join the army. He promised to "equip you in the RIFLE
DRESS and give you your FAVORITE WEAPON, and . . . you will
cover yourselves with glory."[45] As recruits were gathered in,
they were collected at the rendezvous where training began.
For every fifty men, one platoon officer was assigned as in-
structor, Duane's *Handbook for Infantry* being the principal
manual used for instruction. The primitive methods of han-
dling firearms at that time are well illustrated by this example
of Duane's orders to load a gun. Thirteen steps were involved
in loading and firing: open pan, handle cartridge, prime, shut
pan, cast about, load, draw ramrod, ram down, return ramrod,
shoulder arms, make ready, aim, fire.[46]

Recruiting progress in North Carolina occurred in two
particular waves, the first one during 1812 and the second one
in 1814 after the burning of Washington. Initially *"considerable"* progress was made. About 800 men had been raised
in the state by August 1812. Paymaster A. G. Glynn, who was
in a good position to know, estimated that by September 1813,
between 1,700 and 2,000 recruits had been raised, including
the "loan of 400 men to South Carolina's 18th Regiment."
Henderson and Fayetteville were regarded as good recruiting
districts, in spite of the fact that Fayetteville was the seat of
much discord about the conduct of the war. Hamilton had to
warn Captain Thomas J. Robeson not to let this discord disturb him, and to remember that his business was recruiting.
Glynn called the men of Fayetteville except for one or two,
"mere plodders" with no taste for "War, Politics, or Pleasure."

45. Seybert, *Statistical Annals,* 591; Thomas Cushing to James Wellborn,
12 Nov. 1812, 15 Mar. 1814, RG 94, M 565; Kreidberg and Henry, *Military
Mobilization,* 49n; *Raleigh Register,* 17 June 1814; Raleigh *Minerva,* 8 July
1814; "A Rendezvous for the Third Regiment of Riflemen," *Circular* (n.p.,
1815).

46. Thomas Pinckney to Thomas Cushing, 23 Sept. 1812, RG 94, M 566;
William Duane, *Handbook for Infantry* (Philadelphia, 1812), p. 100.

Asheville was also a successful place for recruiting, as Captain Robert Love and Lieutenant Archibald Bigby of the Forty-third Regiment found. Captain George Dabney, on the other hand, wrote that Hillsborough was a bad place, and asked to be sent to Person Courthouse where he knew more people.[47] The second wave of recruiting came in 1814, when the Tenth Regiment was trying to fill its second battalion and when Congress had created three rifle regiments. Hamilton and Wellborn both reported successes at this time. Wellborn raised 130 men near Wilkesboro; by June he had 178 who were ready for marching orders as soon as their camp equipage arrived. Hamilton, based in Charlotte, had 500 riflemen within a few months' time.[48] Newspapers in the state frequently carried articles describing small groups of men going to their rendezvous, calling them "active enterprizing young men" or something similar. When 52 men left Washington, North Carolina, for the rendezvous at Tarboro, they were given a royal send-off. Three volunteer militia companies escorted them two miles out of town, halted, opened to right and left, and presented arms as the recruits marched through. Refreshments were then offered them. After a patriotic address by a veteran of the Revolutionary War, the recruits pledged to do their duty. Three cheers were given by their escort and the spectators, after which they set off "in high spirits" for their destination.[49]

In spite of numbers of enlistments, the successes of recruiting did not measure up to the optimistic hopes of Congress. Regiments did not fill up and when, by 1814, there were too many officers for the number of privates, a consolidation was conducted that eliminated many of the original regiments and surplus officers. Reasons for the failure of recruiting are

47. James Wellborn to ———, 13 June 1812; Wellborn to Thomas Cushing, 13 Aug. 1812, RG 94, M 566; A. G. Glynn to Calvin Jones, 6 Sept. 1813, Calvin Jones Family Papers, microfilm; Wellborn to Francis R. Huger, 7 Sept. 1813, RG 94, M 566; William S. Hamilton to T. J. Robeson, 9 Sept. 1814, William S. Hamilton Papers, SHC; Glynn to Jones, 20 April 1812, Calvin Jones Family Papers, microfilm; Israel Pickens to Adjutant General, 5 Jan. 1813, RG 94, M 566; Captain Geo. Dabney to Recruiting Office, 19 Jan. 1814, Hawkins Papers.

48. James Wellborn to John B. Walbach, 19 May 1814, 16 June 1814; William S. Hamilton to Adjutant General, 17 Sept. 1814, RG 94, M 566.

49. *Raleigh Register*, 21 Aug. 1812, two articles.

not hard to find. In the southern district, Polk's indecision on accepting his commission caused so much delay in recruiting that by the time it was started "the young men of the country had . . . made their engagements for the summer" as Pinckney explained. The confusion in Washington over the officers of inspector general, adjutant general, and others, in charge of organizing the new levies, contributed to the problem. Lack of pay and lack of uniforms hindered enlistments. A regimental coat was an inducement to those "not so well or handsomely clad," as the general pointed out. For 300 men at Columbia, no supplies were available. The men were, declared Wellborn, "as fine looking men as any, but all partly naked, without blankets, shoes, shirts, or anything else." When 285 men were ordered to march to the coast from Salisbury without uniforms, it depressed the chances of recruiting others into the service. It was essential that recruits be dressed in uniform to attract others. Illnesses such as pleurisy that developed from lack of clothing and protection from the winter weather did not encourage men to offer their services. Indeed, the bad condition of the recruits at Tarboro became so notorious that Adjutant General Cushing intervened to direct Deputy Commissary Hanson Kelly at Wilmington to purchase clothing "for their comfortable accommodations."[50]

Another difficulty with recruiting in the South was the climate of the coast where all the fortifications were located. Men did not want to serve at these posts during the summer months. William A. Blount pointedly described the hardships of coastal service in a letter to his brother from Fort Johnson, South Carolina. He deplored his "misfortunes. I mean in my unenviable situation as a military man—shut up in an obscured garrison but dialy [sic] exposed to iminent [sic] danger—threatened sometimes with immediate dissolution by the all powerful sand flies and blood thirsty musquitoes [sic]." Fort Hampton was regarded as a bad place to serve because of the topography of the surrounding country. The "insular position of this post, and the peculiar topography of the neigh-

50. Thomas Pinckney to Secretary of War, 27 Aug. 1812, RG 107, M 221; Pinckney to Thomas Cushing, 23 Sept. 1812; James Wellborn to Cushing, 10 Aug. 1812, 13 Nov. 1812; Wellborn to Alexander Smyth, no date [June 1812?]; Wellborn to Cushing, 15 Dec. 1812, RG 94, M 566; Cushing to Pinckney, 29 Sept. 1812, RG 94, M 565.

boring country" so discouraged Captain John W. McClelland that he was hourly hoping for the arrival of a relief officer. While recruiting went fairly well in the interior parts of the country, the men declined to enlist if they suspected that they would have to serve on the coast. Wellborn suggested at one time that if the recruits could be promised that they would not be marched to the coast until fall or winter, he could secure 700 or 800 men without any difficulty. There was also a lack of good officers for recruiting and for instruction and drill. The better ones rebelled at the "lazy, useless life to which, as officers, we are here subjected," and they asked for transfers. McClelland was mortified that he appeared to be confined to the recruiting service; "if there is danger to be encounter'd, give me leave to share it," he begged. Others were inadequate. Captain A. H. Brandon was an absolute failure at recruiting, getting none from March through June 1814, and only five in July. He was charged with being unwilling to work as hard as others, some of whom undertook "heavy rides at night," swimming rivers, struggling all day to get recruits. Pinckney deplored the lack of regular officers to mix with the new levies, but he was told that none was available for that purpose.[51]

There was also rivalry between branches of the service. The states and the federal government were competing with each other, many men preferring to serve six months in the militia instead of a longer time in the regulars, and preferring to fight Indians in Alabama instead of Indians and Canadians in the cold north. Infantry and rifle corps competed for the same men, with most young men preferring the rifle regiments. Wellborn and Hamilton feuded over which one was to have the recruits raised by Lieutenant Willie I. Gordon; Wellborn even appealed to the secretary of war on the matter. Hamilton tried to have fifteen dragoons reassigned to the riflemen, because they were "too stout" for dragoons. Distances created problems: although the Second Regiment of artillery was

51. William A. Blount to Thomas H. Blount, 31 Aug. 1814, Blount Papers; John W. McClelland to William Eustis, 28 Dec. 1811, RG 107, M 221; James Wellborn to Alexander Smyth, 27 July 1812; Wellborn to Adjutant General, 17 June 1813, RG 94, M 566; Edward Tattnall to Recruiting Officer, 10 Feb. 1814, Hawkins Papers; William S. Hamilton to John Armstrong, 2 Sept. 1814; Thomas Pinckney to Thomas Cushing, 23 Sept. 1812, RG 94, M 566.

supposed to recruit its men from Virginia, Pennsylvania, and the western states, the recruiting headquarters was Charleston, South Carolina. Wellborn, ordered to visit each post in his district, informed the adjutant general that there was a distance of three hundred miles between Salisbury and some of his posts. He could not possibly make regular trips and keep up with his weekly returns. On the home front there was sometimes animosity. Local merchants who profited from the presence of troops became angry when they were marched away. As Wellborn reported, "everybody is not influenced by patriotic motives, but a proportion from self interest, & I find whenever we get fifteen or twenty together, we have the assistance of the merchants & others who can get a cent from the soldiers, but move them away, they get angry & do all they can to injure the service." Gautier remarked several times that the Wilmingtonians detested the crews of the gunboats, necessary though they were, and would have enjoyed seeing them in trouble or aground on the bar.[52] The paper work connected with recruiting was also a headache both to Washington and to the officers in the field. A constant correspondence went on demanding accurate returns on the one hand, and explaining the problems on the other. It is understandable that no audit of the men who served has ever been possible. In 1815 after the war was over, Colonel Hamilton was still trying to get the records straight on a man who was reported erroneously as belonging to another regiment.

Even after troops were recruited, there was the problem of keeping them in the army. While it would not appear that desertion should be a problem in a volunteer army, one must remember the lack of clothing, shelter, arms, and other supplies that faced the recruits, the cold winter marches, and the lack of medical attention. These undoubtedly were the main causes for desertion. Wellborn expressed it exactly when he told the adjutant general that it was because the men had not been paid and clothed: "their rights were not attended to."

52. Wagner, "State-Federal Relations during the War of 1812," p. 21; James Wellborn to Adjutant General, 30 Aug. 1814, 7 Nov. 1814; Wellborn to Francis R. Huger, 30 Dec. 1814; William S. Hamilton to Adjutant General, 27 June 1814; Thomas Pinckney to Secretary of War, 20 Aug. 1813; Wellborn to Thomas Cushing, 22 Feb. 1813, 17 June 1813, RG 94, M 566; Gautier Letterbook, *passim.*

Rewards were offered for the capture and return of deserters, and every effort was made to apprehend them. Wellborn reported that it had cost $500 "recently" to apprehend deserters from the Tenth Regiment. Ten dollars per deserter was the usual sum rewarded. Newspapers carried lists and names of those being sought; 35 names with full descriptions in the Raleigh *Minerva* of 10 February 1815; eight deserters from the Tenth Regiment in the *Raleigh Register* of 4 June 1813, and others. Occasionally additional details would be given. Four men were pursued one hundred miles through the Sorrowtown [Sauratown] Mountains and brought back to Salisbury within six days. One James Carmichael of Guilford deserted from the dragoons, and was reported to be working around the area, harbored by "some of those disaffected persons that are inimical to the cause which he has sworn to support." A deserter named Britt "had the impudence to address the Secretary of War," reported Hamilton. A mulatto from Charleston, serving on Gunboat Number 150 at Wilmington, and a Frenchman named Joseph Flewry from Number 146 were both navy deserters. A reward of $25 was offered by Gautier for four deserters known to pass and repass in the neighborhood of Lockwoods Folly. He also captured four deserters from the New York rendezvous for the *President*, and held them in "durance vile." Five men in Captain Benjamin Forsyth's rifle company deserted to the British in Canada carrying their rifles with them, three of whom had recently joined the company claiming to have deserted from the British.[53] There were times too when officers were reported absent without leave and were cashiered from the army. Usually courts-martial were held when several deserters had been apprehended and returned to stand trial. The situation was so bad in Salisbury in October 1813 that Wellborn, in asking for a general court-martial of twelve deserters and four mu-

53. James Wellborn to Charles R. Gardner, 8 Oct. 1813; Wellborn to Adjutant General, 7 Nov. 1814, RG 94, M 566; Receipt for returning a deserter, 12 Dec. 1812, Blount Papers; Raleigh *Minerva*, 10 Feb. 1815; *Raleigh Register*, 4 June 1813, 25 Dec. 1812, 16 July 1813, 30 July 1813; Wellborn to Thomas Pinckney, 3 Mar. 1813, RG 94, M 566; Raleigh *Star*, 5 Feb. 1813; William S. Hamilton to Daniel Parker, 19 Dec. 1814, RG 94, M 566; *Wilmington* (N.C.) *Gazette*, 2 Oct. 1813; *Carolina Federal Republican*, 13 Feb. 1813; Gautier Letterbook, 27 Apr. 1813, 11 Nov. 1811; Raleigh *Star*, 12 Feb. 1813.

tineers, groaned "I long to leave this place it is a den of dis-
organizers." An occasional report has been found of an execution for desertion. In an effort to keep the rolls of the regiments filled, President Madison twice issued blanket pardons
for those who would return to their military posts, once in
December 1812 and again in July 1814. A long list of names
followed in each case.[54]

Such was the organization of the army that was to fight
America's first war since independence. Even by the end of
the war it was still poorly organized, with weak supply sys-
tems, inadequate training, a volunteer system that did not
function, lack of direction from above, and much political
interference. This army, however, was supplemented by the
state militia system, which was jealously guarded by the
states yet even less organized than was the regular army.

54. James Wellborn to Charles R. Gardner, 19 Oct. 1813, RG 94, M
566; Raleigh *Minerva*, 19 Nov. 1813, 18 Dec. 1812; *Raleigh Register*, 29
July 1814.

3 *NORTH CAROLINIANS*
IN FEDERAL SERVICE

Although before the war North Carolina was "but a feather in the political balance" as A. G. Glynn wrote to Calvin Jones, her record of support for the war by 1813 caused her "to rank high" among the other states.[1] Between 4 percent and 6 percent of the additional men in the regular army came from North Carolina whose population was some 7 percent of the national total.[2] To command these men were 120 commissioned officers from the state, including three West Point graduates, but the highest ranking officers were not North Carolinians. By the end of the war, only three men had attained the rank of colonel, six men that of lieutenant colonel, nine men that of major, and twenty-five men that of captain; the remainder were subalterns. Following the war, two of these men, Duncan Lamont Clinch and Henry Atkinson, became brigadier

1. A. G. Glynn to Calvin Jones, 6 Sept. 1813, Calvin Jones Family Papers, microfilm.

2. A. G. Glynn to Calvin Jones, 6 Sept. 1813, Calvin Jones Family Papers, microfilm. Glynn, paymaster, estimated between 1,700 and 2,000 recruits from North Carolina. Seybert, *Statistical Annals*, pp. 562-63, states that the national troops totaled 32,160 in 1815, an increase of some 26,000 over the prewar figure. North Carolina's percentage is based on this, allowing for inaccuracies in estimates. Also according to Seybert, ibid., p. 39, North Carolina's population was 1/13 that of the United States in 1810.

generals. Most of the officers were in the infantry, 88 of them, for that branch of the service was the most numerous. In the Artillery and Engineer Corps there were fifteen; in the Rifle Corps, ten; in the Dragoons, only four; and three were in miscellaneous positions such as ordnance and paymaster. Not all of these officers served for the duration of the war, for in that day and age one could resign his commission and some did so. Eighty officers were either honorably discharged on 15 June 1815 or elected to make a career in the army; nine were cashiered in one way or another, as is indicated by such euphemisms as "struck from the rolls," "dismissed," or "discontinued"; five died in service from either hostile action, duelling, or illness; the remainder resigned before 1815.[3]

The largest number of North Carolinians in a single unit served in the Tenth Regiment of Infantry, which was created on 11 January 1812 and combined with the Fourth Regiment on 17 May 1815. James Wellborn of Wilkesboro resigned his militia commission as a brigadier general and was appointed colonel of the Tenth. The lieutenant colonels were William Drayton and Andrew Pickens, Jr., of South Carolina; majors were Laurence Manning and William Strother; Anthony J. Glynn was paymaster.[4] Wellborn had a long background of military experience, having served as a captain in the state troops of Georgia from 1789 until he moved to North Carolina, during which time he had commanded the line of forts on the Indian frontier with 150 men under him. After moving to North Carolina in the 1790s he was elected a brigadier general of militia, which post he held until the outbreak of war. At every requisition for troops, that is, in 1799 and 1808, he had volunteered his services. His term of service as colonel in the War of 1812 ran from 12 March 1812 to 15 June 1815, at which time he was honorably discharged. Wellborn's experience must have been the chief reason for Pinckney's appointment of him to head the recruiting service when Polk declined a commission. Although Wellborn was "neighbor and friend" to militia general Montfort Stokes before the war, he was

3. Heitman, *Historical Register*, vol. 1, *passim*.
4. Ibid., 1:100, 1,016; *Raleigh Register*, 19 June 1812; James Wellborn to Adjutant General, 28 May 1812, RG 94, M 566. Wellborn praised Glynn "as he is said to be a young man of Sober Habits & good moral character . . . ," Wellborn to Adjutant General, 4 June 1812, ibid.

apparently not so well liked by others of his neighbors in the mountain counties of North Carolina, since Major General Lenoir informed Governor Hawkins that if Wellborn should remain in the militia, he, Lenoir, would resign because "it would be very disagreeable and improper for us to be together in the same service."[5]

Recruiting began immediately so that men of the Tenth could replace the militia who had been called out to man the coastal fortifications following the declaration of war. By August 1812, enough men were enlisted for one company to go from Tarboro to Fort Hampton, and one company from Fayetteville to Fort Johnston; but because of the unhealthy season of the year in the coastal lowlands, orders to send a battalion to Charleston with detachments to Savannah and St. Mary's were postponed until the end of October. Because recruiting for the Tenth was also being conducted in Virginia, the first of four companies raised there was sent to Norfolk for duty. In December, General Pinckney gave orders for all elements of the Tenth not on garrison duty to be gathered at Salisbury and marched either to the southern frontier or to a more central place as directed. By 15 December, Wellborn had all of his men except one party in Salisbury and preparations to move were being made. Before the troops departed, the ladies of the town offered to make the colors for the regiment, which Wellborn much appreciated, praising their spirit of patriotism. To the adjutant general he wrote: "The spirit of patriotism begins to dawn in this neighborhood, opposition begins to subside to the Government more especially amongst the ladies." Cushing was highly gratified, trusting that the ladies would produce "as flattering a specimen of taste as they have already done of patriotism."[6]

The men and officers were ready, except for winter clothing; housed in huts under strict discipline, well fed, but ignorant of where they would be going. Rumors indicated Florida, and indeed General Pinckney sent orders to Wellborn to

5. James Wellborn to Alexander Smyth, 5 July 1812; Wellborn to William Eustis, 7 May 1812, RG 94, M 566; William Lenoir to William Hawkins, 22 May 1812, Hawkins Letterbook 18, pp. 199-200.

6. Thomas Pinckney to Secretary of War, 27 Aug. 1812, 3 Dec. 1812, 4 Dec. 1812, RG 107, M 211; James Wellborn to Thomas Cushing, 15 Dec. 1812, 9 Mar. 1813, RG 94, M 566; Cushing to Wellborn, 26 Mar. 1813, RG 94, M 565.

march to St. Mary's. But before receiving those orders, Wellborn had received orders from Cushing to march to Norfolk;
he therefore followed the prior directions. By the end of April
1813 Major Taylor and three complete companies had gone to
Norfolk. Reinforced there by Virginia recruits, a battalion left
in June for Sackett's Harbor on Lake Ontario. "They are hearty,
robust young men," said the Raleigh *Minerva,* "and for the
short time they have been in training, very well disciplined."
This group, under Pickens, reached Annapolis, Maryland, at
the end of August, and after the British left the Chesapeake
Bay continued northward to join Major General Wade Hampton on the Canadian front.[7] Meanwhile, Wellborn was recruiting for the second battalion, and getting these men ready to
march south. On 16 August 1813, however, came orders for
this battalion also to march north, halting at Washington,
D.C., for further orders. Not until September did an officer
arrive to relieve Wellborn of his recruiting command, so that
Wellborn was unable to march until long after that. At Salisbury he had 324 men, with 120 coming up from Charleston to
join him. Glynn admired the recruits, calling them very respectable young men, mostly farmers, and of higher caliber
than the earlier enlistees. By October the Tenth had still not
moved, provoking the secretary of war to exclaim that he had
"expected you would before this time be at the head of your
regiment on Lake Champlain. You should march with all your
recruits without a moments delay." Delay there still was,
however. Wellborn's young officers, never having received
any pay, were all in debt and could not leave Salisbury without
settling their accounts. The men from the South Carolina
garrisons at Charleston, Mt. Dearborn, and Georgetown were
slow in arriving; Wellborn owed $1,442 for their transporta-
tion and did not have the money on hand. When Paymaster
Glynn arrived with the money, Wellborn notified the adjutant
general that "I shall move with all possible dispatch, which will

7. Raleigh *Minerva,* 1 Jan. 1813; *Hornet's Nest* (Murfreesboro, N.C.), 7
Jan. 1813; James Wellborn to Thomas Cushing, 22 Apr. 1813, RG 94, M
566; *Raleigh Register,* 23 Apr. 1813, 18 June 1813; Raleigh *Minerva,* 18
June 1813; G. Cano [?] to James Turner, 30 Dec. 1813, RG 94, M 566;
Secretary of War to Wade Hampton, 28 Sept. 1813, quoted in E. Cruik-
shank, ed., *Documentary History of the Campaign on the Niagara Frontier
in 1814,* 9 vols. (Welland, Ontario, 1896-1908), 7:175 (hereafter cited as
Documentary History of the Niagara Campaign).

not exceed ten or twelve days." Yet not until 11 November did the troops begin their trek to Washington.[8]

Wellborn, meanwhile, underwent a crisis. He had frequently expressed his ardent desire for a combat command rather than recruiting duty, yet each time that the troops left for action, he was ordered back to recruiting and the active command devolved on someone else. Additionally, in July 1813 two men who had entered the service as lieutenant colonels at the same time he was commissioned had not only been promoted but placed in rank ahead of him. "It would be improper for me to state my impressions on this subject," he told the adjutant general, "and it would be equally so to state my feelings." He had "left a comfortable home, and a numerous family, with an expectation of distinguishing myself as a patriot and soldier." Even his "bitterest political enemies" must admit that he had worked hard and had kept his troops in proper subordination. He felt that his resentment at being passed over was justifiable. "If I had no resentment I should be unworthy of an appointment in any army." He indicated later that when his accounts were settled, he would resign. Resignation would be very painful for him, a genuine regret, but he felt it to be his only alternative, since he appeared to have lost the confidence of the War Department. He changed his mind, however, because he found "all the officers unwilling to stay in the army if I should leave it," although he continued to maintain that justice had not been done him. Cushing reassured him that "your conduct, I am directed by the Secretary for the War Department to assure you has always been approved."[9]

The battalion of the Tenth that left Salisbury under Wellborn's command in November reached Green Leaf Point outside Washington and spent the winter there. During these

8. James Wellborn to Charles R. Gardner, 5 Aug. 1813; Gardner to Wellborn, copy, 16 Aug. 1813; Wellborn to Gardner, 2 Sept. 1813, 21 Sept. 1813, 27 Sept. 1813, RG 94, M 566; A. G. Glynn to Calvin Jones, 6 Sept. 1813, Calvin Jones Family Papers, microfilm; Thomas Cushing to Wellborn, 7 Oct. 1813, RG 94, M 565; Wellborn to Gardner, 8 Oct. 1813, 19 Oct. 1813, 26 Oct. 1813, RG 94, M 566; Raleigh *Minerva,* 19 Nov. 1813; *Raleigh Register,* 19 Nov. 1813.

9. James Wellborn to Charles R. Gardner, 2 July 1813; Wellborn to John Armstrong, 27 July 1813; Wellborn to Gardner, 16 Aug. 1813, RG 94, M 566; Thomas Cushing to Wellborn, 16 Aug. 1813, RG 94, M 565.

weeks at Green Leaf Point, some dissatisfaction developed concerning Wellborn, and rumors were rife that Major William S. Hamilton was going to be placed in command. To prevent complaint from supporters of Wellborn, Hamilton requested an extended furlough in order to remove himself from the spot. Yet there must have been a degree of truth to the rumors, for Hamilton inquired of the adjutant general "what disposition you have made of Wellborn. So soon as he shall get off to see his family, I shall desire to take charge of the battalion." Wellborn was sent back to recruiting duty, Hamilton was transferred to the rifle corps, and Lieutenant Colonel Duncan L. Clinch took command of the Tenth. He found the battalion in "the most wretched want of discipline & everything else that could make men respectable or comfortable" but the materials were good, the men and officers anxious to do their duty. He expressed the hope that they could leave for Plattsburg in ten or twelve days. In June they indeed marched, being escorted through Baltimore by the Volunteer Band of Baltimore Yagers. The men were praised by the editor of Niles' *Weekly Register* as being "as likely as any we have seen to do credit to themselves and the southern country."[10]

Upon Wellborn's return to Wilkesboro for recruiting, his "political enemies" took full advantage of the situation to chastise him for leaving his troops to suffer at Green Leaf Point during the winter while he was snug and warm at home. With bitter sarcasm they pointed out that it was very convenient for him to "have his quarters at his own dwelling, and attend to his still-houses and his hogs, receive returns and make out despatches, all at the same time!" Some months later Wellborn's former friend Montfort Stokes wrote to Pickens urging that Wellborn be removed. According to Stokes, he was "robbing the public without rendering any services to Government." His salary as an officer was $3,000 per year, he had the privilege of naming the commissary, and he padded the accounts for $1,000 more. He sold to the commissary "his own stinking whiskey and damaged flour . . . at an ex-

10. William S. Hamilton to John B. Walbach, 4 Jan. 1814, 11 Jan. 1814, RG 94, M 566; Thomas Cushing to James Wellborn, 6 Jan. 1814, 6 Mar. 1814, RG 94, M 565; Duncan L. Clinch to Nicholas Long, 9 Apr. 1814, Hawkins Papers; *Raleigh Register*, 24 June 1814; Raleigh *Minerva*, 24 June 1814.

horbitant price, besides furnishing beef & other provisions."
As an officer he had allowances for two servants and room
rent, so that he rented out his officer's quarters to a Dr. Martin
and himself lived at home. He was also accused by Stokes of
speculating with the government's money. His name was
held in such contempt that "no honorable man will serve
either with him, or under him, if he can help it." Stokes further
charged that he was "too illiterate to write three lines of common sense." He called him a nightmare—a canker—and asserted
that any administration that permitted "such a scandalous and
profligate expenditure of public money" would not get Stokes's
vote. A similar letter to Pickens was written by A. R. Ruffin
of Salem, who maintained that Wellborn would never move
from Wilkesboro of his own accord while he could draw a
colonel's pay and still attend to business at home.[11] Obviously
some of these charges were false. Wellborn was certainly not
illiterate, as his letters readily show; and just as certainly he
pleaded to be sent to the field of action instead of being left
on recruiting duty.[12] As Wellborn wrote in March 1815, when
he discovered the criticisms levied against him, "I regard
them not so long as I know myself to be innocent of any neglect of duty knowingly." He had not entered the army "to procure my Bread, thank Heaven I have a competency"; instead,
his only object had been to serve his country.[13] Yet there must
have been some reason that he was passed over and never
allowed to command the Tenth Regiment in the field. It may
have been that he was so good at recruiting that an apprecia-
tive government left him in that occupation. It may have
been that political enemies were responsible. On the other
hand, he nearly always went home to the mountains in the
sickly season, whether from Columbia, South Carolina or
Green Leaf Point.[14] It may also be that he too much impor-

11. Raleigh *Minerva*, 25 Mar. 1814; Montfort Stokes to Israel Pickens,
12 Dec. 1814; A. R. Ruffin to Pickens, 18 Dec. 1814, RG 94, M 566.
12. In August 1813 Wellborn asked permission to lead his troops against
the Creek Indians; Wellborn to Charles R. Gardner, 16 Aug. 1813, RG 94,
M 566. In other letters he expressed gratitude when ordered to march, and
a hope "to go to the lines" by spring, "if not before"; Wellborn to Gardner,
26 Oct. 1813; Wellborn to Adjutant General, 30 Aug. 1814, ibid. See also
Wellborn to Adjutant General, 22 Sept. 1814, 13 Oct. 1814, ibid.
13. James Wellborn to Daniel Parker, 30 Mar. 1815, RG 94, M 566.
14. James Wellborn to Alexander Smyth, 4 June 1812, undated letter

tuned his superiors in Washington, by-passing General Pinckney in many instances, so that he came to be regarded rather
as a nuisance than as an outstanding officer. He was severely
reprimanded once for not having his troops in Canada instead
of still waiting in Salisbury.[15] No commendations have been
found other than the rather stiff one in which the War Department assured him that his conduct had been always approved. On the other hand, both Major General Lenoir of the
militia and Major Hamilton seemed to find him difficult to
work with. Pinckney almost never mentioned him, whereas he
had high praise for McRee, as well as a few other officers. It
would appear, in the final analysis, to be a case in which the
man, although busy, often feverishly so, and very patriotic,
was not quite big enough for the task.

The final fragments of the Tenth were recruited in the
spring and summer of 1814, and left for Canada in August.
Some two hundred strong, they passed through Salem "on
their march to Washington, and camped beyond the Wach.
They were grateful for the kindness shown to them. Next day
they came once more into the town, and then proceeded on
their way," reported the Moravian records. At Richmond the
two companies were halted and ordered to garrison a fort
below the city, inasmuch as Washington had just been burned
by the British and all of Virginia was anticipating a major
British attack.[16] This seems to have been the last activity of
the Tenth Regiment.

North Carolinians also served in the Third Regiment of
Infantry, one of the old regiments authorized during the war
crisis of 1808. Edward Pasteur of New Bern had been commissioned colonel of this regiment at the time, but resigned in
1810. John Nicks, one of the original captains, remained in
service but was later transferred to the Seventh Regiment
that saw action in Mississippi Territory at Velere's Plantation
below New Orleans in December 1814. Henry Atkinson, cap-

[June 1812?], 27 June 1812, 27 July 1812, RG 94, M 566; Thomas Cushing
to Wellborn, 6 Jan. 1814, RG 94, M 565.

15. Thomas Cushing to James Wellborn, 7 Oct. 1813, RG 94, M 565.

16. James Wellborn to Adjutant General, 30 Aug. 1814, RG 94, M 566;
Adelaide Fries, ed., *Records of the Moravians in North Carolina* (Raleigh,
1947), 7:3,228 (hereafter cited as *Moravian Records*); Wellborn to Adjutant
General, 22 Sept. 1814, RG 94, M 566.

tain in 1808, became a professional soldier and after serving a year as inspector general of the United States army saw active service in three other regiments. He was commissioned a brigadier general in 1820. Archimedes Donoho rose from ensign to regimental adjutant and saw action against the Creek Indians at Holy Ground, Alabama, and against the British at Pensacola, Florida.[17]

Although the Eighteenth Infantry was chiefly recruited in South Carolina, a number of residents of eastern North Carolina enlisted in it. Captain John Vail of New Bern recruited a company which was assigned to the Eighteenth. Captain John Gray Blount raised a company which rendezvoused at Tarboro and from thence marched to Columbia, South Carolina. It was this company at Tarboro that had suffered so badly from lack of supplies and indifference. Some of the men still showed how ill they had been as they marched through Raleigh in the fall, wearing coats made of blankets. As the company left Raleigh, Blount marched them through the suburbs instead of down the main street because they had celebrated pay day too much the preceding night. Blount was too restless to remain in the South, however; he was attached to the staff of Major General Wade Hampton, and then was transferred to the Third Rifle Regiment as a major. His brother, William A. Blount, also served in the Eighteenth Regiment, doing garrison duty on the coast of South Carolina. Lieutenant Colonel Benajah White did not have a distinguished record. Wellborn had remarked that he was valueless as a recruiting officer; during the Creek War he was with General Pinckney and committed some offense for which he was convicted at a court-martial and dismissed from the service. The Eighteenth Regiment saw no combat.[18]

After the Tenth Regiment was ordered northward, the

17. Heitman, *Historical Register*, 1:773; Thomas Pinckney to Secretary of War, 27 Oct. 1812, RG 107, M 221; Heitman, *Historical Register*, 1:174, 378, 2:392-93. Ensigns William Lord Robeson of Fayetteville and John Allen Watson of Wilmington were ordered to Fort Stoddert, Mississippi Territory, to join the 3d Regiment in 1812 (Thomas Cushing to each, 31 Oct. 1812, RG 94, M 565).

18. Thomas Cushing to John Vail, 14 Oct. 1812, RG 94, M 565; *Raleigh Register*, 12 Feb. 1813; Raleigh *Star*, 12 Feb. 1813; Thomas Pinckney to Secretary of War, 11 Apr. 1814, RG 94, M 566; Heitman, *Historical Register*, 1:979, 226, 1,027.

Forty-third Regiment was authorized and assigned to the southern district. Although most of these men were recruited from Georgia, the colonel of the regiment, Nicholas Long, who was in command of the North Carolina coastal defense, made Raleigh the recruiting headquarters. It was from this regiment that D. L. Clinch was transferred to the Tenth in the spring of 1814. Some one hundred men from the western counties of Buncombe and Haywood enlisted in this regiment. The only record found of the United States Senate's refusing approval for a commissioned officer from North Carolina was for Holomon Battle of the Forty-third to be a 3d lieutenant. No grounds were given. The Forty-third was not in combat.[19]

Next to the Tenth Regiment of Infantry, the Rifle Regiment, later the Rifle Corps, had the largest number of North Carolinians. This regiment was created in 1808; in 1809 a company of seventy men marched through Raleigh en route to Washington, North Carolina, clad in handsome uniforms of green coats faced and turned up with brown and yellow, green pantaloons, fringed white vests, leather caps high in front with U.S.R.R. in large yellow characters, completed by tall nodding black plumes. No wonder it was a popular branch of the service! In 1814 it was expanded into a total of four regiments with the original one becoming the First Rifle Regiment; in 1815 the four were consolidated into one; and in 1821 the rifle regiment was disbanded. The best-known North Carolinian in the Rifle Corps was Benjamin Forsyth, who was commissioned a captain in 1808, promoted to major in 1813, breveted lieutenant colonel in 1813, and killed in action 28 June 1814. He became a legendary figure about whom many tales were told. One of these concerned a British prisoner whom he wanted to impress. After arranging for certain marksmen to stroll by his tent at the proper moments, Forsyth engaged the British officer in a conversation about skill in shooting. Signaling to a man who "happened" to walk by, Forsyth asked him to give a demonstration, which he did, sticking a table knife in a tree about fifty paces away and splitting his rifle ball on it. In a few moments, another man passed by, who upon being asked to demonstrate his skill

19. *Raleigh Register*, 11 Mar. 1814, 22 Apr. 1814; Heitman, *Historical Register*, 1:199.

shot the ace of clubs out of a card, both displays astonishing the British officer. The intrepidity of his men also led to popular tales. An anecdote described a rifleman serving as a sentry on the shore of Lake Ontario near Ogdensburg who saw a British schooner sailing along. Taking careful aim, he shot "the best dressed man on board." The men on the schooner replied with muskets, but the rifleman hid behind a tree. When the fire slacked, he peeped out and shot "another tall fellow." The schooner thereupon clawed off shore to a greater distance. When the guard from Ogdensburg came up to investigate the shooting, the sentry replied that he had just had an engagement with a British schooner, but she had "unluckily for him succeeded in getting off with only a small loss in killed and wounded." A typical toast offered at a dinner in Raleigh honored the rifle major thus: "Major Forsyth and his gallant band of North Carolinians; May their Eagles, as heretofore, always summon them to victory and to glory."[20]

Forsyth's commanding officers did not always view his excursions with approval, however, nor was his character entirely flawless, folk hero though he was. Both Major General Henry Dearborn and Brigadier General George Izard had occasion to reprimand him for indiscreet behavior. Dearborn told Secretary of War John Armstrong that Forsyth's "known zeal for a small partisan warfare has induced me to give him repeated caution against such measures, on his part, as would probably produce such retaliating strokes as he would be unable to resist; but I fear my advice has not been as fully attended to as could have been wished." To soften this somewhat, Dearborn added, "He is an excellent officer, and, under suitable circumstances, would be of important service." His zeal indeed got him into trouble, for his raid on Elizabethtown brought the British in full cry after him in Ogdensburg, from which he was driven. Izard gave instructions to his officers to seize *"within our territory"* a notorious British spy named Perkins, and bring him to the American camp. Forsyth, however, raided British territory for Perkins; and although he captured him, the British retaliated by seizing an American

20. Heitman, *Historical Register*, 1:141; Raleigh *Star*, 25 May 1809; Marshall Delancey Haywood, *Builders of the Old North State*, ed. Sarah McCulloh Lemmon (Raleigh, 1968), p. 124; *National Intelligencer*, 14 Oct. 1813; *Raleigh Register*, 29 Oct. 1813.

whom they held for exchange. Izard instituted an inquiry, the outcome of which has not been found. Forsyth also reportedly captured a British officer who was traveling under a flag of truce, an unheard-of military indiscretion. According to the British complaint to General Dearborn, Forsyth "abused us in a most scurrilous manner, made us prisoners, and marched us into their pickets . . . where we remained for two or three hours on horseback." Forsyth demanded the surrender of their dispatches in "a most abrupt and *ungentlemanlike* manner" meanwhile calling the British major a "rascal and scoundrel." The British officer retaliated by calling Forsyth a "person, I cannot call him an officer" and demanded that Dearborn punish him. Before anything was done, if indeed it would have been, Forsyth was killed in action. Forsyth and his riflemen were also blamed for plundering the captured Canadian town of York, "under the pretence of protecting the town." Such criticism of the Americans was not, however, a unanimous complaint by the citizens of York, some of whom felt that they had been very helpful and courteous to noncombatants.[21] It was, however, Forsyth's very vigor, dash, and love of action that caused his death. By making a stand when he was supposed to wait in ambush, he not only caused the failure of the project but also stopped a bullet. Izard reported, "The Indiscretion of poor Forsyth prevented the entire success of the Project—he has paid for it with his life." He called him "gallant but excentric [*sic*] & irregular." Legend accrued around his death. When he was shot through the collarbone, "He immediately expressed a conviction that he must die, and exclaimed 'boys rush on!' " He was called brave, intrepid, gallant, and was reportedly well loved by his men. Following a funeral with military honors, his fellow officers were directed to wear crepe on their left arms for thirty days.[22]

21. Henry Dearborn to John Armstrong, 25 Feb. 1813, *American State Papers: Military*, 1:440; George Izard to Secretary of War, 29 June 1814, RG 107, M 221; W. H. Merritt, "Journal of Events Principally on the Detroit and Niagara Frontiers," in William Wood, ed., *Select British Documents of the Canadian War of 1812*, 3 vols. in 4 (Toronto, 1928), 3:586-87 (hereafter cited as *British Documents of the War of 1812*); *Documentary History of the Niagara Campaign*, 7:177; Edith G. Firth, ed., *The Town of York, 1793-1815: A Collection of Documents of Early Toronto* (Toronto, 1962), pp. 294-96.

22. George Izard to Secretary of War, 29 June 1814, RG 107, M 221; *Niles' Weekly Register*, 16 July 1814, 9 July 1814; *Raleigh Register*, 15 July

Forsyth's riflemen were the advance troops, the shock troops, the raiders. They scoured the forests for Indian enemies; they protected the flanks of marching troops; they raided small British forts and camps, carrying off booty; they landed on the shores and banks in advance of the infantry to gain the necessary foothold for successful landings. Forsyth was indeed a partisan fighter and apparently his temperament made him a successful one; it also explains the types of error he made and why he lost his life. The riflemen were in continuous combat on the Canadian front throughout the war. Illustrations of the rifle corps assignments are legion. When forty Indians led by a British officer seized one of Forsyth's pickets on 10 February 1813, about twenty volunteers went after them, crossed the river, and captured one British lieutenant, two men, and fifteen guns. On 17 August 1813, Major Forsyth and two companies of riflemen accompanied friendly Indians and volunteers from Buffalo on an expedition in which they found and defeated a number of Indian enemies. The Raleigh *Register* of 3 September 1813 reported the number as three hundred Indians and British ambushed, with seventy-five Indians killed and thirteen captured, including a chief. In the attack on the Narrows, on 7 November 1813, Forsyth was posted in the rear of the Elite, advancing on the enemy guns, drawing their fire, and then carrying them off. As General James Wilkinson moved down the St. Lawrence River on his abortive expedition, Forsyth and three other officers were sent ashore with small detachments to beat off the enemy. In February 1814, Forsyth attacked and dispersed a British raiding party headed for a commanding situation about twenty miles from French Mills. This type of winter warfare brought commendation from Secretary of War Armstrong who wrote to Dearborn that "the fortunate issue of Major Forsyth's last expedition shows that small enterprises, at least, may be successfully executed at the present season."[23]

1814; Raleigh *Minerva*, 15 July 1814, said that the news was brought "By the Steam Boat Car of Neptune" to Albany; ibid., 22 July 1814; Benson J. Lossing, *The Pictorial Field Book of the War of 1812* (New York, 1869), p. 857.

23. Henry Dearborn to John Armstrong, 16 Feb. 1813, RG 107, M 221; *National Advocate*, 28 Aug. 1813, quoted in *Documentary History of the Niagara Campaign*, 7:37; *Raleigh Register*, 3 Sept. 1813; Extract from Journal of Major-General James Wilkinson, 7 Nov. 1813, quoted in *Doc-*

When three more rifle regiments were added to the original one, William S. Hamilton was named lieutenant colonel of the Third Regiment and ordered to North Carolina for recruiting. Hamilton was a career officer who had served as assistant inspector general for some six months in 1813, resigning to serve as a major in the Tenth Regiment while it was at Green Leaf Point, and eventually being assigned to the rifle corps. During the summer of 1814 he competed with Wellborn for recruits, meanwhile protesting to the adjutant general because one Lieutenant Colonel Croghan had been listed as outranking Hamilton. By October he had some five hundred men ready to move; in November the march to Virginia from Charlotte began. After a long and exhausting journey the battalion reached Bottom's Bridge, some fifteen miles from Richmond, where the men rested and recuperated briefly. Although Hamilton attempted to convince the adjutant general that it would be wiser to remain there than to undertake a further march to Fredericksburg, he was unsuccessful and the regiment went into winter quarters at the latter town. When spring came, the battalion leaving behind some forty ill soldiers marched northward to Carlisle, Pennsylvania, although the war had been concluded, where in May some noncommissioned officers attempted to excite a mutiny. These men had not received their pay for twelve months, nor had their bounties been paid. Although Hamilton kept the situation under control, he urged the War Department to remedy the grievances immediately. The Rifle Corps was eventually abolished without the Third ever having seen action.[24]

The cavalry were called light dragoons during the War of 1812. A regiment was created in 1808, expanded to two regiments in 1812, and consolidated with the artillery in 1815.

umentary History of the Niagara Campaign, 8:214; Ingersoll, *Historical Sketch of the Second War*, 1:304; Raleigh *Minerva*, 18 Feb. 1814; John Armstrong to Henry Dearborn, 24 Feb. 1813, *American State Papers: Military*, 1:440.

24. Heitman, *Historical Register*, 1:494; William S. Hamilton to John Armstrong, 17 Mar. 1813; Hamilton to Wade Hampton, 28 Aug. 1813; Hamilton to Armstrong, 6 Mar. 1813, RG 94, M 566; Thomas Cushing to Hamilton, 14 Jan. 1814, RG 94, M 565; Hamilton to John B. Walbach, 24 Feb. 1814; Hamilton to Armstrong, 24 June 1814; Hamilton to J. R. Bell, 14 Oct. 1814; Hamilton to Adjutant General, 27 Nov. 1814; Hamilton to Daniel Parker, 6 Dec. 1814, 19 Dec. 1814, RG 94, M 566; *Raleigh Register*, 13 Jan. 1815; Hamilton to Parker, 28 May 1815, 22 May 1815, RG 94, M 566.

Archibald F. Macneill of North Carolina was named lieutenant colonel of the Second Regiment of Dragoons, and was for a time stationed in Salisbury recruiting. Not only did he have to secure men, but also horses. An interesting report states that a middleman who rounded up horses for the troop received 5 percent commission, and twenty-five cents per day for feeding each horse until a quartermaster was acquired and the troops fully organized. Horses averaged about $100 each in price. Saddles, bridles, and valises were also part of a cavalryman's equipment. Macneill's command stayed in the South during the war, at the disposal of Pinckney, who held them in readiness to rush to the scene of action in case of an invasion. Pinckney called them his "disposable troops." Another North Carolinian, Archibald H. Sneed, served as paymaster for the Second Regiment. Although the First Regiment saw action in Upper Canada, it appears that only one North Carolinian was an officer with that troop, Thomas F. Hunt, who was transferred to Hamilton's Third Rifle Regiment when it was formed. Hunt later served in the War with Mexico.[25]

The Second Regiment of Artillery was recruited in North Carolina. Major Daniel M. Forney was the chief recruiting officer, and Robert R. Ruffin was regimental paymaster. About 140 men were recruited and rendezvoused at Salisbury, from which in April 1813 they marched to Charleston where they were posted at various forts along the southern coast. Recruiting for the artillery ceased in 1814 and all officers were transferred to the corps artillery. Some of them were no doubt sent to the Canadian front at this time. Daniel Turner, who graduated from West Point in 1814, was commissioned in the artillery and given duty in erecting defenses for New York City. Lieutenant Edwin Sharpe was the only artillery officer found who remained in the army following the war, not even Turner doing so.[26]

There were perhaps fewer engineers than any other category of troops in the war, not because they were not needed

25. Heitman, *Historical Register*, 1:79, 679, 906, 557; Archibald F. Macneill to Thomas Pinckney, copy, 23 Dec. 1812; Pinckney to Macneill, 21 Dec. 1813, RG 107, M 221.

26. Thomas Cushing to Daniel M. Forney, 25 Sept. 1812, RG 94, M 565; Heitman, *Historical Register*, 1:850, 974, 877; *Raleigh Register*, 16 Apr. 1813, noted the passage through Raleigh of some 140 as "fine looking soldiers as we have ever seen" belonging to Major Forney's artillery regiment.

but because engineering was a new occupation. One of the most outstanding of all the engineers was William McRee, a native of Wilmington, North Carolina, and a graduate of West Point in the class of 1805. Son of an officer in the Continental Line, he was early introduced to the military life. After serving in the southern district under Pinckney, he was transferred to Burlington, Vermont, to serve with Major General Hampton as chief of artillery. A year later he was ordered to New York to the Niagara frontier where he served in the same post under Major General Jacob Brown. Winfield Scott said of him: "In my opinion and perhaps in that of the whole Army he combined more genius and military science with high courage than any other officer who participated in the War of 1812." When the war ended, McRee had attained the rank of breveted colonel. He was sent to Europe on duty to examine military schools, fortifications, and the like, and to collect books for the West Point library. However, perhaps because there was not much future in remaining a colonel of engineers in the peacetime army, McRee resigned in 1819 and moved west.[27]

Seven North Carolina physicians served as surgeons or surgeon's mates in the regular army. Most served very short terms of duty, although one was killed in action and another died while in service.[28]

Pension abstracts reveal personal glimpses of the service of some of the soldiers. James Floyd enlisted as a private in 1812, and served in the dragoons until 1814. At Foxe's Old Fields in Rowan County he was thrown from a horse and his right leg injured so badly that he was never able to perform

27. Heitman, *Historical Register*, 1:682; George W. Cullum, *Biographical Register of the Officers and Graduates of the U.S. Military Academy at West Point, N.Y.* (New York, 1868), pp. 93-94; Thomas Cushing to William McRee, 23 July 1813, 21 Mar. 1814, RG 94, M 565; George W. McIver, "North Carolinians at West Point before the Civil War," *North Carolina Historical Review* 7 (1930):28; Charles Winslow Elliott, *Winfield Scott: The Soldier and the Man* (New York, 1937), p. 201. In 1816, McRee was spoken of to serve as one of two American engineers to consult with General Bernard of France on the subject of national defense; James Monroe to Andrew Jackson, 14 Dec. 1816 (*Monroe Writings*, 5:348-49).

28. The seven were: Egbert H. Bell, Horace Dade (killed 21 Nov. 1814), Reuben Everitt (died 29 Jan. 1814), Isaac Forster, James W. Hunt, Lucco Mitchell (resigned 1822), James Norcom (resigned 1 Jan. 1813), William H. Williams (resigned 9 Sept. 1812). Heitman, *Historical Register*, 1:207, 250, 410, 429, 556, 717, 750, 1,043.

his duties fully thereafter. As late as 1860 he still had a running ulcer in his leg. John Pierce served in the rifle corps and was wounded at Sackett's Harbor in 1813, from which wound he lost his right leg. Elijah Close enlisted at Germantown, North Carolina, in 1812 for five years. He marched to Canada where he engaged in four battles, including that of Plattsburg. At the end of the war he was transferred to Carlisle, Pennsylvania, where he had a fall and was injured; thereafter he received an honorable discharge.[29] Many other entries reveal similar events in the lives of the common soldiers.

Except for the original rifle regiment and one battalion of the Tenth Regiment, none of the regular troops recruited in North Carolina saw action against the British, although a few individuals were in some of the engagements on both the Canadian and the southern frontiers.

Few North Carolinians were in the United States Navy. Of those who were, the most noted was Johnston Blakeley, whose famous ship the *Wasp* engaged in a spectacular raid along the coast of Europe. Blakeley was a career naval officer, having joined in 1800 as a midshipman. He served in the Mediterranean, first under Captain John Rodgers and then under Captain Stephen Decatur. Promoted to lieutenant in 1807, he was given a command in 1811 but was stationed in New Orleans, much to his disgust. At his request, his guardian, Ed. Jones, asked Congressman Gaston to consult Senator Turner and attempt to secure a better appointment on active duty for Blakeley. Finally in 1814 he was placed in command of the newly built *Wasp*. Blakeley was described by a lady who recalled having seen him when she was a child as "very handsome, and the exceeding whiteness of his teeth, and the brightness of his eyes, I shall never forget. My mother has often described him to us as rather small, but well made, with very black hair and eyes; grave and gentlemanly in his deportment, but at the same time cheerful and easy when at

29. U.S., Congress, House, *H. Report* 149, 36th Cong., 1st sess., 1859-60 and U.S., Congress, House, *H. Report* 338, 34th Cong., 1st sess., 1855-56, collected in U.S., Congress, *Congressional Reports Relating to North Carolinians in the War of 1812,* bound in one volume, NCC; Annie Walker Burns, comp., Abstract of Pensions of North Carolina Soldiers of the Revolution, War of 1812 and Indian Wars, 10 vols., typescript in NCC.

home." The *Wasp* disappeared at sea with all aboard. A poem honored him thus:

> No more shall Blakeley's thunders roar
> Upon the stormy deep;
> Far distant from Columbia's shore
> His tombless ruins sleep;
> But long Columbia's song shall tell
> How Blakeley fought, how Blakeley fell.[30]

Thomas N. Gautier was the only other well-known naval officer from North Carolina, although of humbler rank. Commissioned a sailing master, which was in rank above that of midshipman but below lieutenant, he was placed in charge of constructing gunboats at Wilmington, and following the decommissioning of these boats in the spring of 1813, he was given other service until he was promoted to lieutenant and sent back to Wilmington in 1814 in command of a flotilla. He had a good sense of humor as displayed in friendly letters to his commanding officers with whom he had obviously served a long time. He commented of one man that he had no more business in a particular assignment than Gautier had of being Pope of Rome. When an order went out abolishing pipes, drums, and calls on board during wartime, he asked if the men were to be called to quarters by some sort of torpedo. He was an old hand, having as he said "worn a sword for 30 years and am not to be taught at this period what is allowed for, or what the Service requires." He refused to allow "all the trash on hand in Public Stores" to be furnished his vessels by private commissaries. He was proud of the naval service and demanded strict discipline of his officers. He was also proud of the young North Carolina officers who served with him. To the secretary of the navy he wrote, "I am happy in having so many Carolinians with me I trust that in case of emergency they will be found useful to their country," and he named Linch, Belt, Clinch, and Brown. "They appear young

30. Kemp Plummer Battle, "A North Carolina Naval Hero and His Daughter," *North Carolina Booklet* 1 (January 1901): 1-15; Ed. Jones to William Gaston, 11 June 1813, William Gaston Papers, SHC (hereafter cited as Gaston Papers, SHC); William Johnson, "Biographical Sketch of Capt. Johnston Blakel[e]y," *North-Carolina University Magazine* 3 (February 1854): 2, 16.

men of education, character & of moral habits," he continued. His crews also he praised for their good behavior.[31] When the gunboats were launched and put into service he recruited seamen for them. To man the four boats he needed an additional forty seamen, sixty landsmen including some "smart boys," four boatswains, three carpenters, three stewards, and three gunners. It was almost impossible to get seamen at Wilmington because merchantmen's and privateers' wages were higher than those paid by the United States Navy and because in addition any seaman owing money was not allowed by the local magistrates to enlist even though Gautier paid the debts. He was enraged by the unpatriotic and selfish attitude of the Wilmington merchants. A navy clerk, James Taylor, accused the "small merchants" of Wilmington of making such great profits from the timber sold for boat building that they erected brick houses and drank the "best of Wines" much to Taylor's disgust. Nevertheless, by going to Edenton, New Bern, Washington, and Plymouth, Gautier was able to man his gunboats.[32]

One other reference has been found to a naval officer: George F. Kennon served on the United States frigate *Constellation*, but whether he was from North Carolina or Virginia is not clear.[33]

Disciplining new army and navy personnel was a problem, sometimes amusing and sometimes arduous. Drinking was a constant problem. In 1812 Wellborn reported Lieutenant John Macqueen as unfit for an officer "from constant habits of intoxication, and is now confined in gaol for debt in Chatham County." Macqueen was struck off the rolls. Sergeant Nathaniel Mitchell who was commissioned an ensign was "as bad an appointment as could have been made," for he had to be placed under arrest, and it "would be doing him justice to strike him off the rolls of the army." Three young lieutenants were declared unworthy of their commissions because "these men I am afraid will not conduct themselves with that soberness & prudence which their duties require, some from habitual

31. Gautier Letterbook, 18 Jan. 1812; 12 Apr. 1809; 10 May 1809.
32. Gautier Letterbook, Jan. 1812 *passim*, 18 Dec. 1809; James Taylor to William Blackledge, 10 July 1813, Blount Papers.
33. George F. Kennon to Solomon Mordecai, 27 Sept. 1813, Mordecai Papers, Box 1, SHC.

intoxication, others on account of misapplication of public money, but I entertain hope that they may yet be reclaimed."[34] Two young officers behaved in such a "drunken & disgraceful" manner one Sunday on the streets of Georgetown that they were picked up and punished by a court-martial. Midshipman William Mayo was drunk on the streets of Wilmington in uniform. "Ladies noticed you with pity," wrote his commanding officer, "Gentlemen with contempt." Since this was not his first such offense, he was warned that one more would mean arrest and a report to the secretary of the navy. A man named Armour was arrested by Gautier for drinking in his cabin on shipboard with the gunner and the steward. Many Americans who had recently been civilians found military discipline hard to understand and to enforce. The same Armour was reprimanded for spending the night on shore without leaving an officer in charge of his boat; and for engaging in "idle conversation with the men" and permitting himself to be spoken to without respect.[35] When denied a pass, some young officers simply took leave without one, and rendered themselves liable to a court-martial for being absent without leave. Examples of flogging enlisted men without cause, of duelling which was against the law, and of "unofficer-like behavior" were also mentioned.[36] Most amusing was an incident at Green Leaf Point in which some soldiers released "two fair virgins from the confinement of a work house, where the moral magistrate (urging the Law, & *giving love no toleration*) had forced them to do *penance*—by picking *oakum*." The commanding officer persuaded the authorities to let the military rather than the civil courts handle the case. Some, like Lieutenant John Jelks, accepted the opportunity to resign from the service rather than undergo arrest and court-martial.[37]

34. James Wellborn to Thomas Cushing, 13 Aug. 1812; Wellborn to W. R. Bootes, 20 Jan. 1813; Wellborn to Charles R. Gardner, 27 Sept. 1813; Wellborn to Alexander Smyth, 27 June 1812, RG 94, M 566.

35. William S. Hamilton to John B. Walbach, 27 Jan. 1814, RG 94, M 566; Gautier Letterbook, 11 Apr. 1812; 10 Mar. 1812; 16 February 1812.

36. Lt. George R. Bridges of Chatham and Ensign Samuel H. Bryant of Prince Edward County, Virginia, duelled in Washington on 25 Apr. 1814. Bryant was killed (Raleigh *Minerva*, 6 May 1814).

37. William S. Hamilton to John B. Walbach, 22 Jan. 1814; Hamilton to J. R. Bell, 14 Oct. 1814, RG 94, M 566. Jelks had "tarnished the cloth by unofficer-like behavior."

4 NORTH CAROLINA MOBILIZES

The chief defense of the nation had always been the militia. In 1792 Congress passed the organic act creating a citizen militia to be composed of all free, white, able-bodied male citizens between the ages of eighteen and forty-five, properly enrolled and self-equipped. Three years later the president was authorized to call out as many troops as needed for repelling invasion or supporting insurrection, and in 1798 30,000 stand of arms were deposited at suitable places to be available when needed. Each state adjutant general was required in 1803 to report yearly to the president on the number of men in his state. When war clouds darkened in 1808, the federal government was authorized to spend $200,000 annually for arms and equipment for the militia. When war became imminent in 1812, a bill was passed creating the detached militia up to 100,000 in number that could be called into federal service by the president. Two other militia acts, one in April 1814 and the other in January 1815, testified to the need for men over and above those in the regular army. Each state was requested to supply a portion of the total number needed, but it was possible for a state to refuse, which in point of fact was done by Massachusetts, Connecticut, and Rhode Island.[1]

1. Kreidberg and Henry, *Military Mobilization*, pp. 30, 46; Seybert, *Statistical Annals*, pp. 607-11.

In 1812 North Carolina had enrolled 120 artillerymen plus officers, 1,150 dragoons plus officers, and 48,123 riflemen. Out of this number the president called for 7,000 troops organized with one-twentieth as artillery, one-twentieth as cavalry (or dragoons), and the remainder as infantry. Riflemen would be accepted if they numbered not over one-tenth of the total. These men were to be organized and equipped, "in readiness to march at a moment's warning," but not to be kept embodied until further notice.[2] Governor Hawkins immediately directed his adjutant general, Calvin Jones, to raise the state's quota, urging "the utmost activity, zeal, and despatch." Each regiment was to consist of one lieutenant colonel, two majors, one adjutant, one surgeon, ten captains, one paymaster, one quartermaster, two surgeon's assistants, one sergeant major, one quartermaster sergeant, two senior musicians, forty sergeants, forty corporals, twenty musicians, and six hundred privates. Seniority of rank was to be considered in selecting the officers unless it would be injurious to the army. Jones acted without delay, issuing general orders on 27 April 1812. "The Militia of North Carolina," he declaimed, "do not on the present occasion require to be reminded of what they owe to honor and to duty, their Country calls; and their patriotism is confided in." When the 1814 militia call came, Adjutant General Robert Williams issued similar orders, again urging that preference for active duty be given to officers in senior rank unless it should "render the army almost inefficient." He stressed to one major general that he should use his "talents and influence to procure as many volunteers as possible so as to prevent the necessity of a draft." The final call for 2,850 militiamen came in February 1815 after the North Carolina legislature had adjourned, so that the governor was unable to raise this new requisition.[3] Since news of the end of the war came within a few days, however, it mattered not.

Most North Carolinians had faith in the militia as a defense in spite of several bad experiences during the Revolutionary

2. *American State Papers: Military*, 1:332; Hawkins Letterbook 18, 15 Apr. 1812, pp. 119-20.

3. Hawkins Letterbook 18, 27 Apr. 1812, pp. 127-33; 29 Apr. 1812, pp. 138-41. Adjutant General Robert Williams to Major General Calvin Jones, General Orders, 20 July 1814, Calvin Jones Papers; William Miller to James Monroe, N.C., Executive, Letterbooks of Governor William Miller, 21, 7 Feb. 1815, p. 79, NC Archives (hereafter cited as Miller Letterbook).

War. "To the federal government belongs the fortifying our harbors, equipping a navy, and raising a regular military-force," said Governor Benjamin Smith to the North Carolina legislature in 1811, "but it is in our power to do much by improving that natural and powerful safeguard, the militia, one of the strongest pillars of national liberty and security . . . with proper discipline, the militia may be trained to achieve the most brilliant victories." Senator Franklin wrote to Major General Lenoir that should either the British or French invade the nation, the citizenry "woud rise like a Lyon from the forest and quickly do the necessary work upon any invader." Corn Dowd told Governor Hawkins that "I am and always have been opposed to a standing army, and in favour of a well armed and well regulated militia and when I see any thing going on that will injure the militia I feal myself bound to use my feble Efforts against it." Lenoir himself, as a veteran of the Revolutionary War, used militia duty to inculcate not only military discipline and training but to develop patriotism as well. The day before each militia review, he attended a muster of the officers, and the day following, he attended the courts-martial to instruct the officers and explain the principles of discipline. He also spoke at each review, addressing the men on the nature, amiableness, and excellence of the American government, and insisting that a well-regulated militia was very important for such support. In peacetime, he opposed a large standing army. When the militia refused to cross into Canada at the battle of Queenston in 1813, even the anti-administration paper, the *Minerva,* did not blame the militia system; the militia had always defended its country when called upon. Perhaps it had not held at the battle of Guilford Court House, but it had fought at Lexington and Bunker Hill. The task of the militia was not to fight pitched battles, said the *Minerva,* but to harrass the enemy, nor was it intended to invade other territories.[4] The North Carolina militia performed well during the Creek War in 1814. Although militia-men did not engage the Indians, they carried out all that was required of them; they were peaceable and orderly in conduct,

4. Niles' *Weekly Register,* 14 Dec. 1811, supplement; Jesse Franklin to William Lenoir, 15 Feb. 1812, Lenoir Papers; Corn [?] Dowd to William Hawkins, 30 July 1812, Hawkins Papers; William Lenoir to Hawkins, 9 Oct. 1812, Hawkins Letterbook 18, pp. 350-55; Raleigh *Minerva,* 12 Feb. 1813.

accurate and soldier-like in discipline, obedient and respectful to their superiors. Many of his officers, reported Brigadier General Joseph Graham, commander of the Carolina Brigade, would do credit to higher grades. Lieutenant Colonel R. A. Winson also praised the North Carolina militia in the Creek War, saying that it was always ready to perform its duty, and was not surpassed by any militia yet called into federal service in its orderly conduct and military duty.[5] Indeed, after having spent some time in service and having experienced some training, many officers and some men were eager to continue under arms: Major (later colonel) Nathan Tisdale, Captain Frederick Brooks, Brigadier General Graham, and Colonel (later major general) Jesse A. Pearson are examples. As Graham expressed it, he had learned present usage and "intercourse between the different departments," had most of his outfit ready for a campaign, and could go with much less inconvenience than formerly. The Craven County company under Tisdale rapidly learned its trade after only three months of service in 1812, and its officers were young, ambitious, and desirous of learning. The Beaufort County militia wished to remain in service; Captain Brooks reported that his men "will volunteer their servises to go enny whar they may be wanted as soon as their time is out at Beaufort," because "the greater part of us are young men that hath no farms to attend to, nor but little other business." Major Tisdale aspired to "the honor of being continued in the Command" if troops were again needed on the coast, or at the scene of battle. The Bladen County militia at Fort Johnston showed "exemplary conduct" and additionally was "handsomely uniformed and possess[ed] no small share of patriotism."[6]

As obviously dependent as was the national defense system on the militia, one would have expected that serious preparations would be undertaken for war during the winter of 1811-12. However, no laws were passed in either of these years by the North Carolina legislature to provide funds for

5. Joseph Graham to William Hawkins, 16 July 1814; R. A. Winson to Hawkins, 1 Aug. 1814, Hawkins Papers.

6. Joseph Graham to William Hawkins, 8 Sept. 1814, Hawkins Papers; Nathan Tisdale to Hawkins, 8 Oct. 1812, Hawkins Letterbook 18, p. 344; Frederick Brooks to John Gray Blount, 14 Oct. 1812, Blount Papers; John A. Lillington to Hawkins, 8 Dec. 1812, Hawkins Papers.

necessary equipment or provision for furnishing supplies to the militia. In December 1812 the House of Commons passed a bill providing $20,000 to buy arms for the militia but the bill was defeated in the state senate. Governor Hawkins endeavored with all his might to get the state to take measures for defense, but because of his lack of constitutional powers, he was unsuccessful. The legislature was jealous of the powers of the governor; constant debate went on over voting him money to spend for military purposes without specific acts of the assembly. Although the legislature eventually approved giving to the governor such power, the resolution was worded in such a way that it represented a warning to all governors that they must not assume financial prerogatives. Finally in 1813 the legislature authorized the state treasurer to borrow up to $25,000 for arms and munitions, if needed, and to borrow up to $50,000 for food and other supplies for the militia, if needed. In 1814 Archibald D. Murphey drew up a bill to give Governor William Miller the authority to spend $120,000 for arms and supplies, but the bill as enacted provided only $50,000 for the militia and $55,000 for arms and supplies. Attached to the provision for tents and camp equipage was a requirement that the supplies so purchased were not to be allowed to go outside the state. All of the above money was to be borrowed at not more than 6 percent interest, and upon the conclusion of peace all expenditures were to stop immediately.[7] Emergency expenditures arose when the British landed on the North Carolina coast in July 1813. Action had to be taken immediately and finances provided later. Bills and claims connected with this event were presented to the state, and the militia and citizens furnishing supplies were paid; the state then presented the bill to the federal government. Such items were included as $426 for gunpowder, flints, and wagon hire to Norfolk and return; $3 to hire a horse to carry the alarm to Hillsborough; $1,500 for transportation of troops and supplies; and personal bills such as one from Major

7. *Raleigh Register,* 25 Dec. 1812; Raleigh *Minerva,* 2 Oct. 1812; Raleigh *Star,* 4 Dec. 1812; N.C., General Assembly, *Laws of North Carolina, 1809-16* (Raleigh, 1816), *1813,* p. 5; Archibald D. Murphey to Thomas Ruffin, 1 Dec. 1814, *The Papers of Archibald D. Murphey,* ed. William Henry Hoyt, 2 vols. (Raleigh, 1914), 1:77 (hereafter cited as *Murphey Papers*); *Laws of North Carolina, 1814,* chap. 4, p. 4; chap. 3, p. 4.

John A. Cameron including forage for two horses, wood for
his fireplace, and allowance for one servant's rations. The
total expenditures of the state as reflected in its annual budget
showed the impact of the war. In 1812 North Carolina spent
$57,000; in 1813, $80,000; in 1814, $115,000; in 1815, $123,000;
and even in 1816, $63,000 was appropriated to repay war
loans. Some of this expenditure was repaid promptly by the
general government, but in 1833 there was still due $30,-
930.21½ plus interest, according to the state's calculations.
Governor Miller reported to the legislature that the militia
called out in July and August 1813 had not been paid because
there was no United States army officer to inspect the troops
before they returned home. The Raleigh *Minerva* remarked
in high dudgeon that even the Georgia militia had been paid,
but not that of North Carolina, and that such injustice should
be attended to. Several account books were filled with claims
rejected by the federal government for which the state continued to seek repayment. The report submitted in 1833 was
not acted upon; finally after the matter had dragged on for
a century, in 1916 the Committee on Claims of the United
States Congress recommended that North Carolina be reimbursed for her expenditures during the War of 1812. The
money, however, was never appropriated.[8]

At the outbreak of the war, Major General Thomas Brown
was appointed by Governor Hawkins to command the seven
thousand detached militia when it was organized for duty.[9]
Although officers of field rank were elected by joint ballot of
both houses of the legislature, having once been elected the
governor chose from among them in giving assignments.
Thomas Brown, Graham, and later on Calvin Jones were the
only general officers who saw active duty although none of it

8. *Raleigh Register*, 27 May 1814; Governor's Warrant Book (Hawkins),
1813, NC Archives; John A. Cameron to William Hawkins, 19 Feb. 1814,
Hawkins Papers; Archibald Debow Murphey, *Statistical Tables of the Popula-
tion, Agriculture, Commerce, and Finances, of North Carolina* (Raleigh, 1816),
p. 15; *Select Committee on Claims*, p. 2; Miller Letterbook 21, 20 Dec.
1814, pp. 3-5; Raleigh *Minerva*, 25 Mar. 1814; Account Books, 1813-21,
War of 1812, N.C. Military Collection, Box 8, NC Archives; U.S., Congress,
House, Committee on Claims, *H. Report 96*, 64th Cong., 1st sess., 1915-16.
A search through *U.S. Statutes* and an inquiry of the North Carolina State
Treasurer revealed no evidence of payment.

9. Hawkins Letterbook 18, 9 July 1812, p. 224. A complete roster of
commanding officers may be found in Hawkins Letterbook 19, pp. 118-19.

was combat. The others held musters, wrote letters, and sometimes resigned, being replaced at the next session of the legislature.

Many men both old and young, experienced and inexperienced, desired to be officers in the militia, or if already officers, to be chosen for the detached militia that would see actual service. The cavalry, or dragoons, rushed to offer their services, as for example the Wake County troop under Captain Thomas Henderson, Augustus Moore of Hertford County, Lieutenant Colonel James Owen of Fayetteville, and Lieutenant Colonel Edmund Jones of Wilkes County. In accepting the offer of the Wake County cavalry troop, Governor Hawkins expressed his thanks, saying that "this early and voluntary tender made by your Troop of their services, furnished a conspicuous and an honorable proof of their patriotism [and] it also affords a striking example of that enthusiasm & unanimity which the practical enjoyment of a Free Government alone can inspire." The governor of Virginia, in thanking North Carolinians for their offer of help, stated that "we see in the part you are acting, that spirit which bound us together as a band of brothers, during the revolution, and carried us in triumph thro' that glorious conflict; and which, can it be kept alive, will give, under providence, immortality to our confederated republic, the last hope of man."[10] Brigadier generals wrote to the governor offering their services and recommending certain officers under their commands. John H. Hawkins asked to be sent to Norfolk in command of North Carolina troops there. Also writing to the governor were majors, colonels, and an artificer who wished to be a captain in command of cannon, baggage wagons, and blacksmith work. Old men, veterans of the Revolutionary War, organized themselves in Rowan County, Caswell County, and Mecklenburg County, offering their services within their home counties. As one of them wrote, "our bosoms swell with indignation" over impressment and Indian raids. The Mecklenburg men called themselves the "silverlocks" and enrolled six full companies.[11]

10. Hawkins Letterbook 18, 2 May 1812, p. 143; 1 July 1812, p. 220; 21 July 1812, pp. 245-46; 22 July 1812, p. 247; 3 May 1812, pp. 144-45; J. S. Barbour to Calvin Jones, 15 July 1813, Calvin Jones Papers.

11. Hawkins Letterbook 18, 30 June 1812, p. 212; 3 June 1812, p. 174; 14 May 1812, p. 161; 2 June 1812, p. 179; 20 May 1812, p. 180; Isaac T.

When the second request for detached militia was made in 1814, another flurry of offers and requests for appointments flooded the governor's office, including those from Brigadier General Graham and Colonel Jesse A. Pearson, both veterans of the Creek campaign.

About half as many resignations were tendered as were offers to serve. Most of these gave no reason; two have been identified as accepting commissions in the regular army—Thomas Taylor and James Wellborn. One was honest enough to say that he lacked experience in military tactics and thought he would be useless.[12] On the whole, however, it appears that many of the militiamen were either young enough, eager enough, patriotic enough, or ambitious enough to relish the opportunity of participating in the war—or at least in the militia.

Unity, however, was lacking within the militia. It was difficult to tell where the lines of organization ran and who was making decisions. The governor gave orders to the adjutant general, the same orders to the major general, and then by-passed both to give orders to a major. The sudden death of Brigadier General William Arrington of Nash County left his troops incompletely organized. The same lack of efficiency and discipline or organization was true for the commissary and the militia pay, although there was more reason for the problems incurred in the two latter. When Major General Brown reached Fort Johnston, he found both a state and a federal supply contractor there, each uncertain of his duties, and both finding overlapping responsibilities with commissaries and quartermasters.[13] Major General Lenoir pointed out that in 1799 and 1808 when the militia was called up, "the negligence of Officers . . . makes me doubt" that orders would be carried out as promptly in 1812 as they should be. Lenoir resigned within a few months because he felt he had lost the confidence of the governor, because a colonel was appointed over his two recommendations of better qualified men, and because in ad-

---

Cushing to William Hawkins, 11 July 1812, Hawkins Papers; Niles' *Weekly Register*, 15 Aug. 1812, 26 Dec. 1812.

12. Hawkins Letterbook 18, 13 May 1812, p. 157; 6 Nov. 1812, p. 359; 18 May 1812, p. 162, and others.

13. Calvin Jones to ———, 12 Nov. 1812, Calvin Jones Papers; Hawkins Letterbook 18, 17 July 1812, pp. 238-39; 1 Aug. 1812, pp. 260-61.

dition Major General Brown was twice given the command of the active militia when Lenoir believed it only fair to pass the command on to another general—namely, himself. A militiaman from Bertie County accused Brigadier General Jeremiah Slade of dismissing all the officers who reported to him from Bertie and naming others in their stead, an unwarranted extension of his authority; privates were promoted over gentlemen who had equipped themselves, volunteered, and already served as militia officers. Colonels were especially jealous of their seniority and watchful lest others be advanced ahead of them.[14] In such complaints as these it is easy to see class lines, because of which the gentry felt that their social standing gave certain prerogatives regardless of the military capabilities of some men of lesser standing. Another factor influencing antagonisms and rivalries among militia officers was the heritage of the American Revolution. One Nathan Horton, who had been a Tory in the Revolution, came in for much criticism, lest he "might not only make a sacrifice of my Life but a sacrifice of my Country," as Thomas McGimsey wrote the governor. Horton, however, received his commission. One Moses Kerr who "crope" into the office of captain although he was "an alien enemy" was also exposed to the governor.[15] Conversely, men descended from patriots who had fought at Kings Mountain or Guilford Court House were regarded by many as well qualified for commissions.[16] The feelings of the privates were much more considered in the choice of officers then than today; whether authorized or not, the general practice for the lesser ranks was that of election. Calvin Jones

14. William Lenoir to William Hawkins, 22 May 1812, Hawkins Letterbook 18, pp. 199-200; Lenoir to Hawkins, 9 Oct. 1812, ibid., pp. 350-54; Jona. T. Jac[torn], to Hawkins, 10 Oct. 1814, Hawkins Papers; Col. John Martin to Hawkins, 4 July 1812, Hawkins Letterbook 18, p. 218. Lieutenant-Colonel Edmund Jones of Wilkes County complained of "some improprieties as to seniority of some of the back country officers" (Jones to Hawkins, 22 July 1812, ibid., p. 248).

15. Thomas McGimsey to William Hawkins, 9 Nov. 1812, Hawkins Letterbook 18, p. 348c. Four officers to Hawkins, 30 Oct. 1812, ibid., p. 348, pleaded with the governor not to let Horton lead "this Honorable Regiment into the Fields of battle"; two men to Hawkins, 24 Nov. 1812, Hawkins Letterbook 19, pp. 11-12.

16. William Lenoir recommended for a colonelcy one man whose father was killed at Kings Mountain and another who also was descended from Patriots. Lenoir to William Hawkins, 9 Oct. 1812, Hawkins Letterbook 18, p. 353.

recommended to the legislature that it might be as well to legalize the election of captains and lieutenants because this was actually practiced. When the Hillsborough volunteers did not care for the officers proposed for them by their colonel, they elected their own. The adjutant of the regiment acquiesced and requested commissions from the governor for those elected. Even physicians for the troops were sometimes elected, as in 1814 when an election was held at Fort Hampton between Dr. James Manning and Dr. J. J. Verell.[17]

Militiamen to fill the ranks of the detached militia were first given a chance to volunteer, and then if necessary were drafted. There was thus a limit, wrote A. Plunkett to a friend, "even to freedom in the freest country on earth." In June 1812 musters were held at nearly all the muster grounds, at which time volunteers were called for. In Granville County, all had to be drafted; in Orange, about half; in Franklin, Warren, and Person, all were volunteers; in Wake and Edgecomb, so many volunteered that a draft was held to choose among them. When Jonathan S. Tayloe became eighteen, he volunteered at Windsor to keep someone else from being drafted, since he was anxious to fight because "some weak-kneed patriots predicted that the King of England would have the Prince Regent in the President's House in ninety days." In Wilkesboro, "a general spirit of Patriotism appeared to pervade [*sio*] the whole company," but in Wilmington when a muster was called not more than half the men appeared "and them without order or discipline." Solomon Mordecai regarded the men who turned out for a muster at Warrenton as a "ragamuffin Crew."[18] Exempted from militia service and hence from the draft in North Carolina were Quakers, "Menonists," Dunkards, and Moravians, until December 1814. Although both Moravians and Quakers expelled members who partic-

17. N.C., General Assembly, House of Commons, *Journals of the House of Commons of the State of North Carolina, 1812*, p. 14 (hereafter cited as *N.C. House Journal*); Willie Shaw to William Hawkins, 25 Aug. 1812; Dr. J. J. Verell to Hawkins, 17 Mar. 1814, Hawkins Papers.

18. A. Plunkett to Samuel Mordecai, 2 Aug. 1812, Mordecai Papers; William Hawkins to Calvin Jones, 5 May 1812, Hawkins Letterbook 18, p. 148; *Raleigh Register*, 26 June 1812; U.S., Congress, Senate, *Petition from Jonathan S. Tayloe*, Misc. Doc. 76, 42d Cong., 3d sess., 1872-73; Edw. Jones to Hawkins, 6 June 1812; John A. Lillington to Hawkins, 26 May 1812, Hawkins Papers; Solomon Mordecai to Samuel Mordecai, 2 Sept. 1814, Mordecai Papers.

ipated in musters, military parades, or even watched them, the Moravians made provision for paying substitutes while the Quakers did not. Each Moravian man of draft age was to pay eight dollars into a draft fund, so that if any one of them were to be called up after December 1814, the money would be available to hire a substitute. Others also hired substitutes. Ebenezer Pettigrew thought Republicans should be glad to serve for patriotism's sake since they seemed to want the war, rather than expecting to be paid. Young men of little or no property eventually tended to wait for the draft, and then make themselves available as substitutes for someone of more wealth.[19] Lack of manpower, however, was not one of the problems of the war; an adequate number of militiamen was always available.

Not only was arming and supplying the militia a greater problem than it was for the regular army, but trying to equip two separate armies doubled the nation's headaches. In 1812, on paper at least, North Carolina had enough small arms and artillery to care for her militia, but much of it was outdated and some was even in the possession of private individuals. There were enough muskets and rifles for each of the seven thousand men to have one, but only one-third could have cartridge boxes, only half could have one cartridge to fire, the musket bearers could each fire seven times only, and while all could have powder pouches and horns, there were no flints, no wagons to haul supplies, and only 284 knapsacks.

19. *N.C. Senate Journal, 1812,* p. 45; *Laws of North Carolina, 1814,* chap. 1, p. 3. Heinrich Wernly and Samuel Krause of Bethabara were reinstated by the Moravians when they testified that their names were "enrolled by the captain at a muster of militia without their permission and would be withdrawn" (*Moravian Records,* 7:3,236). Certain young people were disapproved because they "have repeatedly occupied themselves with marching, soldier fashion, with drum and fife, near the town and in the evening, which must be considered disorder and must be suppressed so far as possible" (*Moravian Records,* 7:3,237). For particulars of the draft fund, see *Moravian Records,* 7:3,548-49. Quakers Rick Elliott and Thomas Duke Lawrence of Rich Square were visited by their brethren and admonished "for frequenting Musterfields and other places for Diversion. . . ." After a year of vain efforts to reform the two men, both were expelled (Monthly Meeting Minutes, Men, 1760-1943, Quaker Church of Rich Square, Northampton County, 17 July 1813-16 Apr. 1814, microfilm, NC Archives); Ebenezer Pettigrew to William Shepard, 6 Sept. 1814, Pettigrew Papers, SHC, *Raleigh Register,* 12 Aug. 1814. See also Sarah McCulloh Lemmon, "Dissent in North Carolina during the War of 1812," *North Carolina Historical Review* 49 (1972): 107.

No tents at all were available. Yet the North Carolina militia had more federal arms than any other state except Vermont. Although according to federal records North Carolina had no artillery, this was not correct; for there were two brass field pieces locked up in a building owned by former Governor Smith, and at Edenton some twenty-seven pieces of artillery under the private care of Dr. John Beasley but belonging to the state. The Edenton cannon were rather ancient, six having come from Ocracoke where they were used in 1775, and others dating from the administration of President John Adams. The two brass field pieces from Governor Smith were finally obtained in December 1812, while the other artillery pieces were gradually distributed along the seaboard at fortifications erected there.[20] The small arms were chiefly in the federal arsenal at Fayetteville where they had been placed during Adams's administration when the provisional army was called up. Although all militiamen were required to report for duty bearing their own arms, this was hardly reasonable to expect nor workable in practice considering the fact that many guns were homemade in that period. Governor Hawkins therefore spent a considerable amount of time trying to get federal arms for the militia, as authorized by the Act of 1808; it was *"indispensably necessary"* he wrote the secretary of war that effective arms be supplied. The most readily and immediately available arms were those at Fayetteville, which after much correspondence the governor obtained from the secretary of war and from which he distributed 130 muskets to John Cameron for his Fayetteville troop.[21] Another two thousand stand of arms were sent to Fort Johnston, near Wilmington, from which the militia guarding Fort Johnston and Fort Hampton were armed and the remainder stored at the Fayetteville arsenal.[22] The legislative session of December 1812 specified that 128 stand of arms were to go to the New Hanover

20. *American State Papers: Military*, 1:334, 329, 333; Hawkins Letterbook 19, 8 Dec. 1812, p. 16; Letterbook 18, 18 Sept. 1812, p. 323; Miller Letterbook 21, 14 Jan. 1815, p. 41; 31 Jan. 1815, pp. 68-69; 6 Feb. 1815, pp. 81-82.

21. John A. Cameron to William Hawkins, 22 May 1812, Hawkins Papers; Hawkins Letterbook 18, 3 June 1812, p. 170; 1 Feb. 1812, p. 78; 26 Feb. 1812, p. 80; 26 Apr. 1812, p. 128; 6 May 1812, p. 154; 15 May 1812, p. 155; 12 June 1812, p. 201.

22. Hawkins Letterbook 18, 8 June 1812, p. 202; 9 July 1812, p. 223.

County militia, 96 to Onslow and Currituck, 64 each to other
eastern counties, and 82 to Wake County. Eventually Haywood and Buncombe counties were also given 64 stand each.
Governor Hawkins then distributed the arms to the aforesaid
counties, calling for bids for their transportation; one such bid
for delivering the guns from Fayetteville to the two western
counties was $128.[23] However, the governor did not have the
power to purchase powder and lead for these weapons; but
when the necessity arose, not only the governor but junior
officers used their money and credit to supply the necessary
ammunition, with only the hope of reimbursement. After the
defeat of Napoleon in Europe, when the southern coast anticipated a major British offensive, Hawkins asked for additional
arms for the coastal forts, securing thereby one thousand
stand more that were sent to the commandant at Fort Johnston.
Legally, all these arms were the property of the United States,
yet many men took them home when their militia duty was
over. In 1819 the adjutant general of North Carolina issued a
plea for their return in order that they might be cleaned, re-
paired, and kept in a place ready for emergency use.[24]

Clothing and shelter were not for the most part a problem
for the militiamen, for their term of service was brief. There
were, however, some exceptions. The troops called out during
the summer of 1812 to man the forts until the regular army
could take over found themselves still in service as September
wore on. The nights began to get cold and their commanding
officers feared that "to many it may prove fatal" unless clothes
and blankets were soon secured. Log houses "covered well
with clapboards" were erected for shelter. These men were
eventually relieved by the regulars. A more difficult situation
arose in 1814 and 1815, when the militia again went on duty
along the coast, some to Norfolk and others to Fort Hampton
and Beacon Island. The men had marched with their summer
clothing and, as in the case of Wellborn's Tenth Regiment,

23. *Laws of North Carolina, 1812,* chap. 12, pp. 11-12; Raleigh *Minerva,*
19 Mar. 1813; William Hawkins to Robert Cochran, 18 July 1812; Receipts
for arms, 31 July 1812, 31 Aug. 1812; Hodge Rabun to Hawkins, 23 Mar.
1813, Hawkins Papers.
24. Hawkins Letterbook 19, 1 July 1813, p. 270; Thomas Pinckney to
Secretary of War, 31 Aug. 1814, RG 107, M 221; Francis K [R?]. Huger to
Nicholas Long, 2 Nov. 1814, Hawkins Papers; Robert Williams, *An Order*
(n.p., 1819), a printed form to be filled in as arms were returned (NCC).

were not supplied with winter clothing before cold weather came. Appeals were made in the press for gifts to help these soldiers secure clothing and blankets. The situation at Norfolk was "almost incredible" reported Colonel Duncan McDonald to Governor Miller; some 160 men had already died in his regiment. The men on Beacon Island had no wood for fires, and indeed no fireplaces; their only clothing was summer homespun. Of the 451 men stationed there, only 180 were in good health and able to report for duty. Every soldier at Wilmington was in need of clothing; 70 men were ill on the day Colonel Maurice Moore reported their needs.[25] The legislature appropriated $10,000 for the relief of the militia, which act Governor Miller immediately implemented. Writing each commander, he asked for lists of supplies needed; the response was pitiful. Items such at 300 blankets, 400 pairs of shoes, 360 pairs of socks, 321 pairs of pantaloons per regiment, may be found in these lists. The money was divided amongst the four regiments then in service, and purchasing agents scoured the surrounding areas to find supplies at reasonable prices. Norfolk, New Bern, and Tarboro were searched; a privateer in the harbor of Wilmington loaded with prize cargo made available some blankets; unable to get clothing, Colonel Moore bought cloth at Fayetteville, rowed four days by boat down the river to Wilmington, and then had it made up into coats and pants.[26] This was the greatest period of need experienced by the North Carolina militia. Ironically, while troops suffered for proper clothing, officers were concerned with the impression their uniforms might make. Colonel Polk was anxious that Brigadier General Graham should have proper buttons, sword, and epaulettes in order to impress the South Carolina militia and the United States regulars during the Creek campaign. Cadwallader Jones appreciated his appointment as aide-de-camp to Calvin Jones, but inquired if it would be proper for him to wear his late United States army uniform. Governor Hawkins himself designed the official uniform for field officers

25. Hawkins Letterbook 18, 19 Sept. 1812, pp. 329-30; 1 Aug. 1812, pp. 260-61; Hawkins Letterbook 20, 22 Oct. 1814, p. 426; *Raleigh Register*, 4 Nov. 1814; Miller Letterbook 21, 16 Jan. 1815, pp. 42-43; 24 Jan. 1815, pp. 52-54; 22 Jan. 1815, pp. 50-52.

26. Miller Letterbook 21, 20 Jan. 1815, p. 49; 24 Jan. 1815, pp. 63-65; 26 Jan. 1815, pp. 66-68; 30 Jan. 1815, pp. 72-73; 23 Feb. 1815, pp. 117-18.

of the North Carolina militia: dark blue coats with buff linings and yellow buttons; white vests; blue pantaloons for winter and white for summer; Suwarrow boots; black cockades with golden eagles; red sashes; and yellow hilted swords.[27] Apparently gold was not expected.

Food and daily supplies for the militia were let to private concerns by the awarding of contracts. Jarvis & Brown of New Bern furnished food at fifteen cents per ration, each consisting of three-quarters pound of pork or 1.25 pounds of beef, eighteen ounces of bread or flour, and one gill of whisky, brandy, or rum. Soap, candles, vinegar, and salt were also arranged for. Who was to pay for these rations, however, was unclear. Hawkins feared that there would be a period of time during which federal supplies would not yet be available and credit would have to be used. He instructed Major General Brown, therefore, to secure a commissary and assure the suppliers that "there cannot be the least shadow of doubt" that the United States would eventually pay. He also wrote to the secretary of war reporting that there were no provisions for the troops at Fort Johnston and Fort Hampton: while eventually he knew that the federal government would furnish the supplies, he had made temporary provisions to prevent "inconveniences" to the men. This procedure was approved.[28] Perhaps because there was a state government on hand to fill in the gap when the federal government acted tardily, one does not find the complaints against the commissary or the contractors furnishing the militia that one finds against those furnishing the regular army.

The state did not find it necessary to appoint surgeons or surgeon's mates except at times when the troops were on active duty. The United States engineers had not provided a hospital or surgeon's quarters at Fort Johnston when it was constructed during 1810-11; Dr. George Clitherall who was resident surgeon there for fifteen years had to rent a private house in which to live. Major General Brown secured the

27. William Polk to Joseph Graham, 8 Mar. 1814, Joseph Graham Papers, 1780-1836, NC Archives; Cadwallader Jones to Calvin Jones, 2 Aug. 1813, Calvin Jones Papers; Hawkins Letterbook 19, 12 Mar. 1813, pp. 109-12.

28. Jarvis & Brown to Col. [Simon] Bruton, 22 July 1813, Hawkins Papers; Hawkins Letterbook 18, 17 July 1812, pp. 238-39; 26 July 1812, p. 249; 31 July 1812, p. 252.

services of a navy surgeon for the initial troops at Fort Johnston. By 1814, however, the legislature realized the need for better medical care and created the position of brigade inspector, surgeon, and surgeon's mate for each brigade of militia, these men to be commissioned by the governor just as any other officer. Many physicians were interested in attending such large groups of men, especially if located in their home towns. Dr. John Poythress of Beaufort asked for a commission, only to have a rival candidate, Dr. James Manney, urged upon the governor. Poythress was represented by his enemies as a fraud, who had first come to North Carolina as a Methodist preacher, but "shortly became too *visibly* apostate to be permitted to continue that vocation" after which, "between the paroxisms of intoxication" he read medicine and hung out his shingle. Most of the enlisted men supported Poythress while most of the officers petitioned for Manney.[29] Conditions of service, unfortunately, were such that illness was much too common. A report that twenty men out of five hundred had died in three months was considered a good record. Illnesses at Deep Water Point in late fall of 1813, at Beacon Island and at Norfolk during the winter of 1814-15, were the most serious. Because the men at Beacon Island had been working in mud and water for two or three months building fortifications, by December two hundred of the six hundred there were ill. Measles invaded the camp of the First Regiment at Norfolk, relapses from measles causing twenty deaths. By February 1815 a total of two hundred men had died in that regiment alone. The men of the Fifth Regiment also at Norfolk experienced so much illness that the adjutant general ordered military police to remove all filth, put sand in the streets between huts, and construct proper sinks and necessaries. The cleaning and airing of huts was strongly enforced. Thin tents and an irregular supply of food contributed to the bad conditions, so that James Campbell after a gruesome account lamented to a friend, "Oh! what a fine thing it is to be a soldier!" When the First Regiment was dis-

29. Petition of Dr. George C. Clitherall, U.S., Congress, House, *H. Doc. 363*, 23rd Cong., 1st sess., 1833-34; Hawkins Letterbook 18, 1 Aug. 1812, pp. 260-61; *Laws of North Carolina, 1814*, chap. 1, p. 3; T. A. Patterson to William Hawkins, 4 Oct. 1812; Petitions to Hawkins, 6 Oct. 1812, 8 Oct. 1812, Hawkins Papers.

charged from service on 4 February, three hundred men were ill, of whom one hundred "can never be fit for service again."[30]

The militia, like the regulars, found the federal government exceedingly tardy with its pay. The first troops did not even know who their paymaster was. After two months without pay, Major John A. Lillington's men required assurance from Governor Hawkins that "they will certainly receive their pay." By this time it had been ascertained that the district paymaster at Petersburg, Virginia, was responsible; but several companies were discharged from service after three months without ever having received any pay. Major Tisdale rightly pointed out the excellent propaganda this would make for the antiwar party.[31] Throughout all correspondence between militia officers and the governors runs the refrain of lack of pay, so that the men having no money in pocket were unable to alleviate their shortages of clothing, food, and blankets.

Under such conditions of supply shortages, pay arrears, and poor health conditions, it is not surprising that there were a number of desertions from the militia. In fact, since some of these were drafted men, while all of the regulars were volunteers, one might expect the incidence of desertion to be higher in the militia. Again, the few days of muster that was all the training most militiamen had experienced was hardly enough to prepare them for uncomfortable field service of some duration. Major Lillington was surprised that he had not had more desertations than actually occurred. Another reason for desertion was misunderstanding of the terms of service. At Wilmington in 1815 the militia discovered that because it had been federalized, it could not go home at the end of its three-month enlistment term; "there were various indications of a meeting & a general desertion." After two desertions, the major in

30. *Raleigh Register,* 5 Nov. 1813; Miller Letterbook 21, 26 Dec. 1814, pp. 29-31; 13 Feb. 1815, pp. 102-5; 1 Feb. 1815, pp. 69-71; Adjutant General's Order, 15 Jan. 1815, and Colonel Atkinson's General Orders, 9 Jan. 1815, N.C. Militia Papers, 5th Regiment, SHC; James Campbell to Thomas Ruffin, 16 Jan. 1815, Thomas Ruffin Papers, SHC; *Raleigh Register,* 10 Feb. 1815; Raleigh *Minerva,* 10 Feb. 1815.

31. Hawkins Letterbook 18, 12 Aug. 1812, p. 262; 10 Sept. 1812, pp. 280-81; 8 Oct. 1812, p. 344; 11 Nov. 1812, p. 360; Raleigh *Minerva,* 28 Jan. 1814. Pay scales were low: a captain received $40 per month; 1st lieutenant, $30; 2d lieutenant, $25; 3d lieutenant, $23; ensign, $20; enlisted man, $11 (accounts of Captain James Graham, N.C. Militia Papers, 5th Regiment).

command arrested two privates and anticipated no further trouble. Seven soldiers deserted in 1813 when they learned that their company had been placed under a different captain than their own; they had volunteered to serve under him and no one else. Again, personal problems must have caused many of the desertions, as in the case of a man who deserted because his family was in distress. When he found that he "was not to be harrassed over the world" but merely stationed at Norfolk, he gave himself up. The greatest number of desertions reported came from the Seventh Regiment of militia that marched to Alabama to serve in the Creek War. Newspapers reported that eighteen men deserted as they neared the Ocmulgee River at the borders of Indian country; twelve men were tried for desertion at the camp headquarters during the active campaign; thirty names from the same regiment were listed in August with a $10 reward offered for each if brought to Fort Johnston. A final court-martial to try deserters from the Seventh Regiment was held in Salisbury in January 1815, although the campaign had been over since July.[32] Punishment was prescribed by the legislature, but additional ideas were sometimes thought of during courts-martial. The legislature had no provisions for the punishment of deserters until December 1813. At that session a law was passed punishing deserters by the loss of all pay, a fine from $20 to $50, imprisonment of one to six months, and service in the regular army of double the militia term. Sentences actually administered included a $50 fine and two months' imprisonment; hard labor on the fortifications for three days at half rations with hands tied to the handles of the wheelbarrows; and hard labor in general. In one instance it was too difficult to keep the prisoner at hard labor because the regiment had run out of construction work, and since it would be a nuisance to keep the man under guard, he was set free and his name erased from the muster rolls provided he left the area. Governor Miller pardoned one deserter for whom a petition was sub-

32. Kreidberg and Henry, *Military Mobilization*, p. 53; Hawkins Letterbook 18, 19 Sept. 1812, p. 329; Miller Letterbook 21, 13 Jan. 1815, pp. 39-41; Petition, 29 Sept. 1813; William W. Bryan to William Hawkins, 9 Nov. 1814, Hawkins Papers; *Raleigh Register*, 29 Apr. 1814; Orderly Book, 29 Apr. 1814, p. 44, Graham Papers; Raleigh *Minerva*, 5 Aug. 1814; Miller Letterbook 21, 22 Jan. 1815, pp. 56-58.

mitted; he also remanded some convictions because the court-martial was not properly constituted. Another time, Brigadier General Graham remanded part of a sentence because the punishment was cruel. A mutiny almost occurred when, at the crossing of the Ocmulgee River en route to Indian territory, nine-tenths of the Rowan County company refused to obey the first command to cross.[33] Since the militia was not in actual combat at any time, since the troops had little or no training in military discipline and obedience to orders, and since they were usually near home and could casually come and go, the number of desertions is probably about what might be expected.

The first call for seven thousand troops from North Carolina produced more men on the rolls than were needed; only a small number were called into active service. Five companies were sent to Fort Johnston near Smithville, and four to Fort Hampton near Beaufort, to remain until regular army troops could be recruited and replace them. Most of these men were back home again by December 1812. In July and August 1813 militia from nearly every coastal county and as far inland as Wake County and Orange County were called up to repel a British invasion. Although they served only a few days, some troops remained on duty until winter to supplement regular forces. In January 1814 a regiment from North Carolina was called up from the western counties to march to Alabama to join Andrew Jackson in the defeat of the Creek Indians. These troops served six months and were discharged. In August 1814 President Madison called for another levy of seven thousand detached militia. While many of the same men were enrolled, this was a different levy. In at least one instance, men who had already been designated as available for the past two years were exempted from this call by their commanding officer. From these new men, two regiments were called into service at Norfolk, and one each at New Bern and Wilmington. An additional order was issued for a regiment to rendezvous at Wadesboro in order to march to the defense of the southern frontier, including Thomas Lenoir,

33. *Laws of North Carolina, 1813,* chap. 1, p. 3; Miller Letterbook 21, 20 Jan. 1815, p. 62; Orderly Book, 30 Apr. 1814, p. 49; 29 June 1814, no page number, Graham Papers; Miller Letterbook 21, 22 Jan. 1815, pp. 56-58; *Raleigh Register,* 29 Apr. 1814.

the son of Major General Lenoir; but upon receipt of the news of the peace treaty the men were sent home.[34] While the North Carolina militiamen were not called upon to serve as often, as long, or as arduously as those of New York, Pennsylvania, Tennessee, or Kentucky, nevertheless they answered every call and it was not their fault that they won no glorious victories.

34. Summarized from N.C., Adjutant General, *Muster Rolls of the Soldiers of the War of 1812: Detached from the Militia of North Carolina* (Raleigh, 1851); Francis L. Davey to Calvin Jones, 20 Aug. 1814, Calvin Jones Family Papers, microfilm; Thomas Lenoir to William B. Lenoir, 9 Mar. 1815, Lenoir Papers; Miller Letterbook 21, 1 Feb. 1815, pp. 73-74.

5 *THE WAR ON LAND*

The major fronts during the War of 1812 were in Upper and Lower Canada, in the Old Northwest against British and Indians, in Alabama against the Indians, and along the lower Mississippi River in defense of New Orleans. The North Carolina troops in the regular army were engaged at Niagara and along the St. Lawrence River, and the North Carolina militia was called into active service for the Creek Indian War in Alabama. The Rifle Corps and one battalion of the Tenth Regiment of Infantry were employed against Canada, the chief engagements centering around Ogdensburg, New York; Fort George, Fort Erie, and York in Upper Canada; and Chateaugay in Lower Canada.

The first major event on the Canadian frontier was Major General Hull's inglorious surrender at Detroit, for which he was court-martialed and suspended from the service. Colonel Wellborn asked permission for his regiment, then being recruited in North Carolina, to march at once to Canada so that "we may contribute our mite in taking vengeance on our enemies." Governor Hawkins issued an appeal for volunteers calling on each man's desire for "glory and renown" as well as his "bravery and patriotism," but only a slight increase in enlistments occurred as a result.[1] A concentration of troops

1. James Wellborn to Thomas Cushing, 13 Aug. 1812, RG 94, M 566; *Raleigh Register*, 25 Sept. 1812.

began at Plattsburg, New York, with an advanced post at
Sackett's Harbor, in preparation for a spring attack on Upper
Canada. Early in August, Captain [later brevet colonel] Benjamin Forsyth arrived at Sackett's Harbor with a company of
riflemen, the first regulars to appear on that part of the frontier. The rifle corps was popular with young American men—
it enjoyed prestige, the best in arms and ammunition, and it
saw plenty of action often in small, personal combat. Before
long, Forsyth had 185 men in his company which he was
anxious to augment to a regiment with himself as colonel. In
spite of the severe winter, Forsyth informed the newspapers
that the troops enjoyed "high health in that country, not one
having died since their arrival there." By the winter of 1813-
14, Forsyth was in command of 263 men.[2]

Within a month after his arrival at Sackett's Harbor, Forsyth made one of his famous bold dashes into Canada. With
about eighty men, joined later by nineteen New York militia
volunteers, he set out on 18 September 1812 for Gananoque
some forty miles away to capture a reported one hundred
Canadian troops under a Colonel Stone. Embarking down the
river in small boats, with adverse winds slowing their journey,
they did not reach their goal until daybreak of the twenty-first.
Five men became lost and missed the ensuing excitement.
While they were hastily and secretly landing, the enemy inside
the garrison discovered them and gave battle. Unfortunately
for the Canadians, they were firing too high and Forsyth was
able to advance "with a very rapid movement . . . which
caused them to retreat to the woods and leave the garrison in
about fifteen minutes." The Americans took twelve prisoners,
thirty barrels of flour, beef, forty-one muskets, twenty-five
bayonets, one boat and sails, and other spoils of war. With no
means of transportation for heavy objects, they were forced to
abandon the flour and beef, which they burned together with
the storehouse rather than let the Canadians recover them.
One American was killed and one wounded. Private property,
or loot, which had been seized by the soldiers, and which was
estimated by Forsyth at $10,000 in value, was given to them

2. Lossing, *Pictorial Field Book*, p. 370; Benjamin Forsyth to William
Eustis, 24 Oct. 1812, RG 107, M 221; *Raleigh Register*, 22 Jan. 1813; Report
of Adjutant General of General James Wilkinson's army, in *Documentary
History of the Niagara Campaign*, 8:247.

THE WAR IN THE NORTH

Map by James E. Thiem III

by militia Brigadier General Jacob Brown. Perhaps Forsyth was more vicious here than he would normally have been, for Colonel Stone had been a Tory during the Revolution, a "notorious enemy and opposer to the Government of the United States."[3] Brown, commander of the New York militia and ranking officer on the frontier, complimented Forsyth on the attack, speaking of his "gallant conduct on this occation [*sic*] and that of those brave men you had the honor to command."[4] This was no major engagement, but coming hard on the heels of Hull's surrender at Detroit, it lifted American morale and induced great pride in the hearts of North Carolinians.

The cold winter wore on. In February 1813 Forsyth, unable to remain inactive, led a raid across the St. Lawrence River on Brockville (or Elizabethtown) in Upper Canada, across the river from the American garrison at Ogdensburg whose command he had been given. The British, on 4 February, had captured several Americans and placed them in jail; Forsyth determined to rescue them. The Canadian village had some very handsome houses with a church and a courthouse. It was protected by a small troop of cavalry, a volunteer rifle company, and some militiamen, most of whom were absent at their homes much of the time. On the night of 6 February, Forsyth with a party of riflemen, all volunteers, leaving about 10:00 P.M., marched twelve miles up the river to Morristown, rested briefly, crossed the mile-wide river on the ice, and then marched back down the Canadian side. About 3:00 A.M. they surprised the British garrison sound asleep in bed. Liberating the American prisoners, they took 52 prisoners of their own, 134 stand of arms which had been taken from Hull at Detroit, a peculiar pleasure no doubt, and other stores. The raiding party was home again by 8:00 A.M. Forsyth was gleeful over the raid, praising his men and saying that they treated the prisoners "with great hospitality" and paid "due respect to private property." The home town newspapers in North Carolina were bursting with delight and pride over the expedition, one of them calling it "the best *generalship* since the commencement of the war" and planned by a man who was only a captain![5]

3. Benjamin Forsyth to William Eustis, 23 Sept. 1812, RG 107, M 221.
4. Jacob Brown to Benjamin Forsyth, 23 Sept. 1812, RG 107, M 221.
5. Lieutenant-Colonel T. Pearson to Major General de Rottenburg, 7

Two weeks later the British retaliated by striking Forsyth at Ogdensburg. About 7:00 A.M. on the morning of 22 February 480 troops came across the river ice with a heavy snowfall on the ground and attacked the town. Forsyth was not taken by surprise, yet he did not have the defenses necessary to drive off the enemy. Although he repulsed one assault, his cannon were frozen fast so that the fortifications could not be defended. Within an hour, the Americans were driven out of the town. The British emptied the magazine, burned the old and new barracks as well as two schooners and some gunboats, and carried off all the ordnance, commissariat and marine stores and a quantity of camp equipage and clothing, enough for three months. The American losses were twenty-six killed and wounded while the British lost six killed and thirty-four wounded. Forsyth retreated to Black Lake, about nine miles away, and sent a call for help to Major General Dearborn. Give him three hundred men, he begged, and "all shall be retaken & Prescott too or I will lose my life in the attempt." Although reinforcements were ordered to Ogdensburg, it was for greater strategic reasons than Forsyth's immediate need, and they became part of a larger operation. Accounts of this skirmish provide a good example of propaganda and self-defense, for each side enlarged upon the numbers of the enemy forces and of their killed and wounded, the British to make their attack more glorious and the Americans to make their defeat more palatable. The Americans credited the British with having anywhere from 800 to 1,200 men, although the British records state their number at 480; Forsyth claimed to have killed two British for every American killed, or at least 60 men, although the British records give 40. The British claimed that there were 500 Americans in the

Feb. 1813, in *British Documents of the War of 1812*, 2:13-14; Lieutenant-Colonel R. H. Bruyere to Sir George Prevost, ibid., 2:64-65; Benjamin Forsyth to Henry Dearborn, 8 Feb. 1813, RG 107, M 221; *Raleigh Register*, 3 Mar. 1813; *Hornet's Nest*, 4 Mar. 1813. Two accounts state that Forsyth's party traveled in sleighs: Lossing, *Pictorial Field Book*, p. 576, and Niles' *Weekly Register*, 27 Feb. 1813. Forsyth uses the term "marched" in his report. The distance covered was not too great for men on foot, and was reported at a rate of 4 miles per hour; nowhere is any mention made of horses to pull the sleighs. In fact, Forsyth later asked for sleighs to carry his wounded. It seems therefore that the sleighs were a picturesque addition by some news writer.

garrison, whereas the figures show 400.[6] It is obvious that the Americans made the most distorted claims, which might have been expected since they were the losers in the engagement.

Immediately following the attack on Ogdensburg, Forsyth was ordered to Sackett's Harbor in order to take part in plans for the capture of York, scheduled for late spring when the weather would permit a combined amphibious and land operation. York was on a bay where the remains of the old French fort of Toronto stood. The American troops were to be conveyed in vessels to a point just above York, where they were to land and proceed to attack the town. By late April the plans were completed. Forsyth's platoons were to lead the way in the landing, to cover the following infantry as it came ashore. Hopefully there would be no resistance; Forsyth was to make prisoner every person passing, without firing, and send them to Dearborn. After all the troops had been landed, the riflemen were to lead the column with front and flank guards as the army marched toward York.[7]

On 26 April, the little American fleet of fifteen vessels arrived at the bay and stood in toward land, sighted by the British. The next morning the assault began. Major Forsyth led the way with his men in two boats. It was intended to land in an open field, where a few acres of ground had been cleared, but the strength of the wind blew the boats below this opening to a bank with heavy woods on top. The British and Indians, about two hundred in all, were drawn up on the higher ground waiting for them; as the boats neared shore, in spite of supporting fire from the vessels the British approached the brink and fired directly down into the boats.

6. Report of Lieutenant-Colonel G. Macdonell to Lieutenant-Colonel and Deputy Adjutant General J. Harvey, 25 Feb. 1813, in *British Documents of the War of 1812*, 2:24; Major George Macdonnell to Colonel Baynes, 22 Feb. 1813, ibid., 5:74-77; *Hornet's Nest*, 18 Mar. 1813. Benjamin Forsyth to Alexander Macomb, 22 Feb. 1813, RG 107, M 221, Henry Dearborn to John Armstrong, 25 Feb. 1813, RG 107, M 221, reports that Dearborn sent the reinforcements in sleighs. Lossing, *Pictorial Field Book*, pp. 577-81, dramatizes the American defense. *Poulson's American Advertiser*, quoted in *Documentary History of the Niagara Campaign*, 5:77, refers to the "rabble from Canada." Macomb claimed the British force was double that of the Americans, while British losses were three times greater (Macomb to Dearborn, 23 Feb. 1813, in ibid., 5:77-78); Niles' *Weekly Register*, 6 Mar. 1813, reported the British force at 1,200 men.

7. Lossing, *Pictorial Field Book*, 585-86; Charles G. Jones, Brigade Order, 25 Apr. 1813, in *Documentary History of the Niagara Campaign*, 5:162.

For nearly half an hour the struggle to land went on, with other boats and other troops rowing toward shore. General confusion followed in the woods, with Indians whooping and bugles blowing. The gallant Brigadier General Zebulon Pike leaped into a boat, thinking that the riflemen were faltering, to lead the way ashore. But Forsyth's men were in the forefront of the fighting; as they drove back a charge on the brink of the hill, the Indians "shouted and retreated in much disorder." One account reports that the Indians gave "a diabolical yell and fled in all directions" from the mere sound of Forsyth's bugles, so formidable was his reputation supposed to have been.[8] The Americans formed in rank after successfully completing their landing, marched on to York driving the little British force before them, and captured the town. Pike, however, was killed. A young Canadian reported his own very narrow escape from the riflemen as he was "going through a corner of the woods that I might have a better view of the ships firing on the batteries." He heard several shots as he ran through the bushes but they all missed "and I came off safe." During the occupation of York, Forsyth was reputed to have found a white man's scalp suspended over the speaker's chair in the house of parliament. This scalp created a great furor and was accepted as proof that the British were encouraging Indian warfare on the frontier. The gruesome object, together with the mace and the British standard, were sent to Secretary of War Armstrong, who refused to receive the scalp. The riflemen were accused by some Canadians of pillaging in the town, "professedly in retaliation of British outrages at Ogdensburg." One Canadian, however, praised the troops for their good conduct. "They used the people with

8. Colonel Cromwell Pearce's Account of the Battle, in Firth, *Town of York*, pp. 303-6; *United States Gazette*, 24 May 1813, in *Documentary History of the Niagara Campaign*, 5:214; *Philadelphia Aurora*, May 1813, ibid., 5:180; Niles' *Weekly Register*, 5 June 1813; Major General Sir Roger Hale Sheaffe to Sir George Prevost, 5 May 1813, in *British Documents of the War of 1812*, 2:90. On p. 96, the District General Orders claimed that 2,500 Americans had landed, and that "It was not disgraceful for 200 to retreat from such a force." Dearborn's report stated that the British force consisted of 700 regulars and militia, and 100 Indians; he said the Americans constituted "a far less number" (*American State Papers: Military*, 1:443). Ingersoll, *Historical Sketch of the Second War*, 1:270, called Forsyth "a bold and dashing soldier, always forward for action, who on this occasion sustained it with great spirit for a long time."

great civility," he said. "They did not allow their men to plunder any property that could be prevented. In the night they put a sentry over every store." As to their fighting qualities, Dearborn reported to Armstrong that "our troops behaved with great firmness and deserve much applause, especially those who were first engaged, under circumstances that would have tried the firmness of veterans."[9]

Preparatory to an attack on Fort George in Upper Canada immediately after the capture of York, Colonel Winfield Scott and Major Forsyth were to lead a landing party at Newark, just above Fort George. On the morning of 25 May some four hundred infantry, Forsyth's riflemen, the two flank companies of the Fifteenth Regiment of Infantry, and one small piece of artillery crossed the river to attack. Many Americans stood on their shore to watch, while a small American flotilla protected the troops with a cannonade. The British were ready for them, firing so rapidly that the water near the Canadian shore "appeared in foam" from the bullets. Dearborn said that the landing was "warmly and obstinately disputed," which was a mild way to express it. After a sharp fight the landing was made good, and the first brigade followed the shock troops across. The British general, John Vincent, described the two-mile long line of ninety to one hundred barges and scows loaded with fifty or sixty men each, rowing across the river while the American riflemen advanced through the "Brush-wood." The battle lasted three or four hours with "very severe loss" for the British. Scott's and Forsyth's commands sustained the brunt of the action. Following the capture of the fort two days later, the enemy was pursued by Brigadier General Morgan Lewis with some of the riflemen included among his troops. The enemy did not make a stand as expected at the Beaver Dams, but broke up and marched on, thus escaping. "Distinguished marks of respect" were received by the riflemen and the volunteers from the towns of Baltimore and Albany, and from Brigadier General John

9. Isaac Wilson to Jonathan Wilson, 5 Dec. 1813, in Firth, *Town of York,* pp. 292-93; Ingersoll, *Historical Sketches of the Second War,* 1:273; *New York Statesman,* 29 May 1813, in *Documentary History of the Niagara Campaign* 5:171-72; Henry Dearborn to John Armstrong, 28 Apr. 1813, *American State Papers: Military,* 1:443.

Parker Boyd. Forsyth lost two men killed and ten wounded in the actions at Newark and Fort George.[10]

Meantime General Wilkinson and General Hampton had been sent north to take command of a two-pronged attack on Montreal, with Wilkinson to go down the St. Lawrence River from Lake Ontario and Hampton to march north along the Lake Champlain route. As Hampton left the southern district and passed north through North Carolina to assume his command, he selected Captain John Gray Blount as one of his aides. Blount wrote a few letters home in which he described the struggles of the troops as they crossed the wilderness in northern New York. Hampton concentrated his troops at Burlington, Vermont, from thence proceeding down the Chateaugay River toward Montreal, hacking out a road and fighting off Indian attacks as he went. Blount damned the road from Plattsburg north as one "of the worst description and all our supplies are brought from there." "This is a woodland country," he wrote to his brother, "& requires to be on the alert to keep off the copper skins who are lurking about our camp." In October with severe weather beginning, the men were sleeping with only one blanket or none nor had they any tents. Day after day they cut trees to make a road. One Canadian remarked that "they must have been good woodsmen to clear a road as they did, but the Americans were mostly all first rate axemen." The first battalion of the Tenth Regiment from North Carolina joined Hampton as he moved along the Chateaugay Road, bringing his troops up to about four thousand strong.[11] Finally Hampton reached an open area some seven miles across, on the other side of which the enemy, mostly French Canadians, had entrenched themselves under Lieutenant Col-

10. *Buffalo Gazette*, 8 June 1813, in *Documentary History of the Niagara Campaign*, 6:28-29; Winfield Scott, 25 May 1813, ibid., 6:107; Elliott, *Winfield Scott*, p. 93; Henry Dearborn to John Armstrong, 27 May 1813, *American State Papers: Military*, 1:444; Brigadier General John Vincent to Sir George Prevost, 28 May 1813, in *British Documents of the War of 1812*, 2:104-6; Morgan Lewis to Dearborn, 27 May 1813, *American State Papers: Military*, 1:445; Dearborn to Armstrong, 29 May 1813, ibid.; Niles' *Weekly Register*, 19 June 1813; Returns of Killed and Wounded in the Action of the 27th May 1813, RG 107, M 221.

11. *Hornet's Nest*, 15 Apr. 1813; John Gray Blount, Jr., to Thomas H. Blount, 7 Oct. 1813, Blount Papers; Montreal *Gazette*, 11 May 1895, in *British Documents of the War of 1812*, 2:425-26; Wade Hampton to John Armstrong, 12 Oct. 1813, RG 107, M 221.

onel Charles de Salaberry to make a stand. Hampton's carefully made plans for the attack went awry when Colonel Robert Purdy's troops became lost in the swamps and woods and fired on each other; but he decided to attack anyhow about two o'clock in the afternoon of 25 October. The Canadians, posting buglers in the woods, sounded the charge and Hampton, believing that he was vastly outnumbered, pulled back all the way to his position of 21 October. The French Canadians under de Salaberry were elated at their success, an eyewitness proudly saying, "The enemy, to use a favorite phrase, did indeed 'pollute our soil,' but he was repulsed by Canadians not the one twentieth part of his force, led on by a Canadian commander." Hampton's forces went into winter quarters and the action was over until the following spring should arrive.[12]

The western prong of the march on Montreal left Sackett's Harbor on 16 October and moved down the St. Lawrence in a flotilla of small assorted vessels. Winter snow, rain, and sleet set in. Along the shore marched twelve hundred elite troops under Colonel Alexander Macomb including Forsyth and his riflemen to protect the flotilla from the British who were trailing them from Kingston. By 11 November the army had reached Chrysler's Island where the British attacked. After a severe battle lasting most of the day in the sleet and snow, with the coming of darkness the battle ended in a draw. In view of the fact that the Americans outnumbered the British, it was really a defeat for them. Wilkinson called off the further march on Montreal, crossed over to the American side, and went into winter quarters at French Mills. Although Forsyth was wounded in the battle, it appears not to have been serious.[13]

Following a grim winter at French Mills, Wilkinson, suspecting that he would probably be relieved of his command, decided to launch an early spring attack that might retrieve his reputation. On 29 March he marched from Plattsburg, to which some of his troops had been moved, twenty-two miles

12. Lieutenant Colonel Charles de Salaberry to Major General L. de Watteville, 26 Oct. 1813, in *British Documents of the War of 1812*, 2:386, 391; de Watteville to Sir George Prevost, 27 Oct. 1813, ibid., 385; Michael O'Sullivan, "An Eye-Witness Account," ibid., 2:405-12.

13. Lossing, *Pictorial Field Book*, pp. 652-54.

to LaColle Mill, with his advance commanded by Colonel Isaac Clark and Colonel (by brevet) Forsyth. Setting up a battery in the woods, the American advance began to fire on the mill from the rear, while the other troops launched a frontal attack. This mill located at the end of a bridge was a heavy stone structure with walls eighteen inches thick and windows barricaded with heavy timbers. In front of it was open ground, muddy from the melting snow, with the narrow road blocked by cut trees. It was defended by only two hundred men. American assaults on the mill failed to breach the walls; on the other hand, British attempts to capture the battery in the woods behind them also failed. Wilkinson withdrew and returned to Plattsburg, and within a week was relieved from command. Newspapers were bitter about Wilkinson's failure. Niles' *Weekly Register* praised Clark and Forsyth, but of Wilkinson said, "Our force under the command of gen Wilkinson was between 3 and 4,000 men; *and they did not take a mill!* It appears also that they *missed the road* that should have led them to their object!"[14] Two months later, in nearly the same spot, Forsyth met his death. About the middle of June Forsyth staged a raid on Odell Town, which having had advance warning sent out some two hundred infantry after him. Forsyth withdrew about a half mile and posted part of his men in a house, with the residue around it, and gave battle. After a brisk fire, the enemy retreated and left the colonel "master of the ground." Two riflemen were killed and three wounded, but according to deserters who came across the lines, the British had three killed and five wounded.[15] A few days later, Forsyth tried again to raid Odell Town. A small body of troops under a Major Morgan feinted at the village on 28 June and retreated, intending to draw the British after them into an ambush of Forsyth's riflemen. When they reached Forsyth's stand, with two hundred British in pursuit of them, the plan broke down. Forsyth "inconsiderately advanced upon them [the British] instead of retreating and drawing them after him as he was ordered." The British took alarm and escaped, but the Americans lost "the services of that valuable officer. He was killed while

14. *British Documents of the War of 1812*, vol. 3, pt. 1, p. 15; Lossing, *Pictorial Field Book*, pp. 790-91; Niles' *Weekly Register*, 23 Apr. 1814.
15. Letter from Plattsburg in Raleigh *Minerva*, 15 July 1814.

advancing on the enemy who were driven off by the Riflemen and one Company of the 12th Infy only."[16]

When Major General Brown succeeded Wilkinson in command of the troops along the St. Lawrence frontier, Robert Ruffin of North Carolina reported that the prospects for the summer campaign were good. By mid-June Brown was ready to march, aided by Winfield Scott, Eleazar W. Ripley, and Peter B. Porter. Major William McRee was his chief engineer. On 4 July 1814 Scott fought the battle of Chippewa Creek against the British commander Major General Phineas Riall and defeated him. The British thereupon concentrated at Fort George and sent out frequent sorties to annoy the American army. Brown had to decide whether to attack Fort George or Riall's army first. Scott voted for Fort George; McRee, Porter, Ripley, and several other officers voted for Riall's army. The decision was made for them by Riall, who pushed down to occupy a hill at Lundy's Lane near Niagara Falls just a few miles north of the Americans. Discovering him, Scott led his troops forward and engaged him. British reinforcements were rushed to the spot and, when Brown heard the guns, American forces dashed "with all speed" to the scene of action. As Brown arrived, he consulted with his engineers, McRee and Lieutenant Colonel Eleazar D. Wood, who reconnoitered the British position. McRee reported that the British had taken a new position and occupied a height with artillery that was the key to their whole position and had to be taken. Brown directed McRee to take the Second Brigade on the Queenston Road and order Colonel James Miller to take the height. By moonlight Miller stormed the height and the enemy was routed. Although McRee attempted to remove the British guns from their positions, he found that without drag ropes or horses the task was impossible; his men thereupon engaged themslves in carrying the wounded off the field. Brown praised Wood and McRee highly. They were "greatly distinguished on this day, and their high military talents exerted with great effect; they were much under my eye, and near my person, and to their assistance a great deal is fairly to be ascribed; I

16. Brigadier General Smith to George Izard, 28 June 1814, RG 107, M 221.

most earnestly recommend them, as worthy of the highest trust and confidence."[17]

Although the Americans were improving daily in their discipline and military skills, the British were transferring across the Atlantic by the early summer of 1814 their veterans of the Peninsular Campaign, whether with designs against the northwest, the seacoast, or the Gulf coast the Americans did not know. Brown therefore ordered as rapid a fortification of Fort Erie as possible in preparation for an anticipated British attack following the battle of Lundy's Lane. The fort covered an area of fifteen acres, facing a cleared area where there was a good field of fire. Its fifteen-hundred-yard front was well protected by parapets, ditches, and abatis with two batteries in operation and emplacements for two more. McRee and Wood, the engineers in charge, had supervised and planned the work, although it was not yet finished. The commanding general reported to the secretary of war that "our position is growing stronger every day by the exertions of Majors McRea[sic] and Wood and the officers and men generally." On the evening of 14 August McRee and Wood examined every part of the entrenchments carefully, for an assault was in the wind. About 2:00 A.M. the attack came, with some twenty-two hundred British and Canadians against three thousand Americans inside the fort. McRee personally managed one of the six-pounder guns during the attack. The initial assault failed, but the British hung on with grim determination until a great explosion blew up the fort, wrecking the bastion and killing many of the assaulting party. The Americans promptly retook the bastion. Brigadier General Edmund Pendleton Gaines, commanding the fort during Brown's illness, praised McRee: "To Major McRea [sic], chief engineer, the greatest credit is due for the excellent arrangement and skilful execution of his plans for fortifying and defending the right, and for his correct and seasonable suggestions in regaining the bastion." A month later, on 17 Sep-

17. William Ruffin to Sterling Ruffin, 20 May 1814, Ruffin Papers; Narrative of General T. S. Jessup, in *Documentary History of the Niagara Campaign*, 2:477-80; Major General Jacob Brown's Diary, ibid., 2:467-71; Colonel James Miller to ———, 28 July 1814, ibid., 1:105; Evidence of Captain MacDonald, 15 Mar. 1815, ibid., 2:348; *British Documents of the War of 1812*, vol. 3, pt. 1, p. 162.

tember, with General Brown again well enough to be in command, the garrison of Fort Erie launched an all-out assault to break the British siege. Although their immediate object was not met, within a few days the British evacuated and fell back, leaving Fort Erie again free. McRee and Wood were highly praised by Brown for their actions during the battle. "Licut Colo McRee and Lt Colo Wood of the corps of Engineers having rendered to this Army services the most important," he wrote to the secretary of war in his official report, "I must seize the opportunity of again mentioning them particularly. On every trying occasion I have reaped much benefit from their sound & excellent advice. No two officers of their grade could have contributed more to the safety and honor of this Army." Wood died in the battle, but "McRee lives to enjoy the approbation of every virtuous & generous mind, and to receive the reward due to his services & high military talent."[18] A few skirmishes later, the Americans blew up Fort Eric and retired to the American side of the river. On Lake Champlain, Macdonough defeated the British who thereupon retreated into Canada. The fighting died down, winter came, and by the following spring when the weather would have permitted the resumption of warfare, the war was over.

On the southern frontier, with the exception of the Georgians who greatly desired Florida,[19] most Americans expected any fighting to be with the Indians. Beginning in 1811, uneasiness was sweeping the western country because of the activities of the Prophet and his warrior brother Tecumseh, combined with friction caused by settlements of white persons on Cherokee lands. Haywood County, in extreme western North Carolina, felt exposed, and its citizens recognized that "if there is a British War there will be an Indian War also, and our frontier extends from Georgia to Tennessee a distance of at least sixty miles and only this [one] regiment for its defense." Militia Brigadier General Thomas Love of

18. Brigadier General Edmund Pendleton Gaines to Secretary of War, 23 Aug. 1814, 29 Aug. 1814, in *Documentary History of the Niagara Campaign*, 1:153-55, 159; Battle of Fort Erie, ibid., vol. 3, pt. 1, pp. 188, 195; General Jacob Brown to Secretary of War, 29 Sept. 1814, RG 107, M 221; Lossing, *Pictorial Field Book*, pp. 832-35.

19. John E. Talmadge, "Georgia's Federalist Press and the War of 1812," *Journal of Southern History* 19 (1953): 488-500.

Waynesville heard reports that a trader had been arrested in Tennessee for selling powder and lead to the Indians; six persons had been murdered on Sandy River; the Tennessee militia had been called out. While it is true that there is little evidence to show that western North Carolinians accused the British of creating this trouble, nevertheless some of the leaders in that section requested aid in case war should come. "I fear from the present aspect of things," wrote Love to Governor Hawkins, " that if a War with England should take place, (and I believe there is but little doubt to be entertained on that head) that we shall have a general Indian war." Hawkins asked the secretary of war for the right to call into service the North Carolina militia for protection against the Indians when and if necessary; but in Washington it did not appear that there was an Indian menace in the southwest. Indian agents had uniformly reported on the "friendly disposition" of the nearby Indians, largely Cherokee, and Secretary of War William Eustis declined to approve the use of troops by the governor.[20] But the activities of the prophets began to reach into Creek country in Alabama by 1813. Benjamin Hawkins, Indian agent, sent a mission to the Creeks asking for a denial that they intended to create trouble. Salem Moravians, heeding a report from two of their missionaries on the Flint River that war talk and "spreading animosity" were making their situation precarious, sent a baggage wagon to meet them at Milledgeville, Georgia, to bring them home. Colonel Hawkins requested troops, writing to Wellborn asking for all the recruits he could spare; Wellborn received orders in August to march with his troops to Fort Hawkins, which orders he ignored because he had received prior orders to march toward the north.[21] The flame and the fury erupted on 30 August at Fort Mims, Alabama, where some 550 men, women, and children were massacred by Indians in a three hour orgy. Tennessee militia under Andrew Jackson and Georgia militia under John Floyd rose in arms, General

20. *National Intelligencer,* 16 Nov. 1811; Hawkins Letterbook 18, 16 Apr. 1812, p. 147; Thomas Love to William Hawkins, 15 June 1812, ibid., pp. 229-30; Hawkins to Secretary of War, 26 July 1812, ibid., p. 249; Secretary of War to Hawkins, 31 July 1812, ibid., pp. 252.

21. *Raleigh Register,* 30 July 1813; *Moravian Records,* 7:3,206; James Wellborn to Charles R. Gardner, 9 Aug. 1813, RG 94, M 566; *Raleigh Register,* 20 Aug. 1813.

Pinckney was directed to take over the campaign until victory was achieved, and the war was on.

The Cherokee Indians had hesitated a long time over joining with the prophets. For them, it was essentially a struggle between the old ways and the new, between an older generation and a younger. Indians were implored by the conservatives to "put off the white man's dress, throw away the mills and looms, kill the cats, put on paint and buckskins, and be Indians again." The new generation, on the other hand, praised the generosity of the United States, saying, "You forgot the past, established our boundaries, provided for our improvement, and took us under your protection. We have prospered and increased, with the knowledge and practice of agriculture and other useful arts. Our cattle fill the forests, while wild animals disappear. Our daughters clothe us from spinning wheels and looms. Our youth have acquired knowledge of letters and figures. All we want is tranquility." In a council at Hiwassee the Cherokees approved an address wishing America well in her war against England. As tension mounted among the Creeks, their traditional enemies, however, the Cherokees became nervous. When the Creeks killed a Cherokee woman near Etowah, Georgia, the tribe abandoned its tranquility and prepared for war. Some eight hundred of them, from Georgia, North Carolina, and Tennessee, joined Jackson and took part in the campaign.[22]

Although Jackson's little army engaged the Creeks and defeated them in several engagements, the militia began to long for home when their enlistment terms were up. The Tennessee militia went home in December 1813, except for 130 men; the Georgia militia's terms would expire in February. Pinckney called, therefore, for Carolina troops in December to replace those of Georgia, while Tennessee sent eight hundred fresh troops to join Jackson. North Carolina and South Carolina each supplied one regiment, both of which were commanded by Brigadier General Joseph Graham of North Carolina. Pinckney had no time to consult the secretary of

22. John P. Brown, *Old Frontiers* (Kingsport, Tenn., 1938), pp. 460-61; Ingersoll, *Historical Sketch of the Second War*, 1:322; Circular from Thomas Pinckney, Hawkins Letterbook 20, 27 Dec. 1813, pp. 49-51; Henry T. Malone, "Cherokee-White Relations on the Southern Frontier in the Early Nineteenth Century," *North Carolina Historical Review* 14 (1937): 9.

war; he cut the red tape and action resulted. In order to
expedite the movement of these troops of detached militia,
supplies were sent directly to Fort Hawkins to be awaiting
them there. Shoes and blankets were furnished by deducting
the cost from the soldiers' pay. Difficulties in securing forage
led to the cancellation of the orders for two troops of dragoons.
Since the quartermaster in Charleston was out of funds, Pinckney sent $2,000 personally to Salisbury, North Carolina, to
get the militia under way. Fifteen hundred shirts, twelve hundred fatigue frocks, and twelve hundred pairs of trousers
were promptly supplied.[23] One must remember that this was
1814; much had been learned since the hectic first months of
the war, with Pinckney certainly profiting by his experiences.
These troops were requested, assembled at their rendezvous,
marched, and arrived in the Creek Nation in less time than
Wellborn had spent trying to get winter clothing for his men
eighteen months earlier.

Both Brigadier General Graham and Colonel Jesse A. Pearson, commanding the North Carolina regiment, wrote volumi-
nous letters to the governor describing their march and experiences. From the first days at camp in Salisbury until the
discharge of the men after their tour of duty it is thus possible
to reconstruct their every important activity. On the day the
first troops arrived at Salisbury for their rendezvous freezing
rain fell. Only half enough huts and no tents were ready,
but food was plentiful and the men managed to be in good
spirits. When the troops were organized and transportation had
been provided, the march through Georgia to the Creek Nation began. Broken in two parts for marching, the regiment
was led by Lieutenant Colonel Atkinson commanding one
battalion followed by Pearson commanding the second. General Graham marched with Pearson. By 18 March the regiment
reached South Carolina, with a few desertions along the way
and with one crisis when the riflemen from Lincoln County
refused to continue. This trouble having been averted, an-

23. *Raleigh Register,* 21 Jan. 1814; Thomas Pinckney to Secretary of War,
27 Jan. 1814, RG 107, M 221; Joseph Graham to William Hawkins, 27 Feb.
1814, Hawkins Letterbook 20, pp. 109-10; Pinckney to Secretary of War,
10 Feb. 1814, 18 Oct. 1814, 11 Feb. 1814, 10 Mar. 1814, RG 107, M 221;
W. Bourke to ———, 4 Apr. 1814, ibid; John K. Mahon, "The Carolina
Brigade Sent against the Creek Indians in 1814," *North Carolina Historical
Review* 28 (1951): 421-22.

other arose in the form of measles, so that near Milledgeville, Georgia, the men stopped to care for the sick and to wash their clothes. Major Turrentine broke his leg and had to ride in one of the wagons.[24] In spite of these relatively small problems, the North Carolina troops continued steadily on toward Fort Hawkins (now Macon, Georgia), to meet the South Carolina regiment.

While these troops were on their way, Jackson and his men defeated the Creeks at the battle of Horseshoe Bend. The Thirty-ninth Regiment of United States Infantry, 150 Cherokees under Colonel Morgan of Knoxville, and 80 friendly Creeks, General Coffee with a brigade of mounted riflemen, and several hundred Tennessee militiamen, the latter group including some North Carolina volunteers, defeated the Creek stronghold defended by some 800 warriors. The Cherokees swam the river to destroy the Creek canoes and cut off their escape. Junaluska was one of the young men participating. Years later, when Jackson ordered the Cherokees to be removed to Oklahoma, Junaluska is reported to have said, "If I had known that Jackson would drive us from our homes, I would have killed him that day at the Horseshoe." At the end of the day some 560 Creeks had been killed and many wounded, the few remaining scattering into the wilderness. Jackson's losses were 49 dead, of whom 18 were Cherokees and five were friendly Creeks; and 154 wounded. "GREAT VICTORY" shouted the headlines in the *Raleigh Register*.[25]

The North Carolina regiment of militia reached Fort Hawkins by 1 April, with transportation ready to cross the Ocmulgee River to proceed to Fort Hull. The troops were praised even by officers of the regular army, bragged Pearson. Perhaps the praise was spoken too quickly, for when the time came to cross the river, thereby leaving "civilization" and heading into the thick of Indian country, four men from the

24. Raleigh *Minerva*, 18 Feb. 1814; *Raleigh Register*, 18 Feb. 1814; Jesse Pearson to William Hawkins, 18 Mar. 1814, Hawkins Letterbook 20, pp. 145-46; Pearson to Hawkins, 23 Mar. 1814, ibid., pp. 148-49; Raleigh *Minerva*, 15 Apr. 1814.

25. Joseph Graham Letterbook, Graham Papers; many drawings are included. The Cherokees were under the command of Colonel Morgan of Knoxville. Lossing, *Pictorial Field Book*, p. 779; Glenn Tucker, *Poltroons and Patriots*, 2 vols. (New York, 1954), 2:453; Andrew Jackson to Secretary of War, 2 Apr. 1814, RG 107, M 221; *Raleigh Register*, 15 Apr. 1814.

Rowan County militia refused to cross. Since Rowan County was a hotbed of Federalism and opposition to the war, Republican supporters magnified the incident until Pearson, himself from Rowan, submitted affidavits from the company commanders that only one man, "and he a substitute" refused, plus three others who deserted.[26] Upon reaching Fort Hull the news was received of the victory at Horseshoe Bend. The brigade pressed on immediately to Fort Decatur in a nerve-racking march, with double sentinels posted at night, frequent alarms and battle line formation being called in the darkness; but no fighting occurred. Pinckney caught up with the troops at Fort Decatur and continued with them until they effected a junction with Jackson at the meeting of the Coosa and Tallapoosa rivers. The fighting was over and the Indians in retreat with their towns burned by army scouts. The North Carolinians were "chagrinned," said Graham, "thinking it will be an inglorious campaign, not having an opportunity to discharge a single musket at an enemy." Pearson enjoyed having guests from Jackson's army who ate North Carolina "bacon & Bread" and said that many from that state were in Jackson's army.[27]

Pinckney soon left to return to the nearly defenseless seacoast, Jackson went to Tennessee to rest briefly, and the Carolina Brigade together with the Thirty-ninth Regiment manned the forts and proceeded with a pacification program. The two groups worked in harmony with each other, the Thirty-ninth having inspired confidence in the militia by their "gentlemanly & dignified conduct." The militia developed a sense of order and discipline and made progress in their knowledge of military affairs. Graham expressed the hope that eventually the charges of desertion and mutinous conduct would be forgotten by the public. Two major tasks were undertaken by the brigade: construction of four forts in Indian country, and a mopping-up operation down the Alabama

---

26. Jesse Pearson to William Hawkins, 1 Apr. 1814, Hawkins Letterbook 20, p. 151; Raleigh *Minerva*, 8 July 1814; *Raleigh Register*, 29 Apr. 1814, 8 July 1814.

27. Jesse Pearson to William Hawkins, 12 Apr. 1814, Hawkins Letterbook 20, pp. 172-73; *Raleigh Register*, 20 May 1814; Thomas Pinckney to Secretary of War, 18 Apr. 1814, RG 107, M 221; Joseph Graham to Hawkins, 26 Apr. 1814, Hawkins Letterbook 20, p. 181; Pearson to Hawkins, 18 Apr. 1814, ibid., p. 179.

River. Fort Bainbridge complete with a drawbridge was built
in March 1814, the best fort in the Creek Nation except for
Fort Jackson. Although it had a capacity of 300 men, only 108
were stationed there. During April fortifications were erected
at Fort Decatur. Located on a high bluff one hundred feet
above the Tallapoosa River, it was matched by a smaller fort
named Burrows on the opposite bank to protect the ferry
across the river. While these two forts could accommodate a
battalion, only 67 were stationed at Burrows and 217 at Decatur, the latter equipped with two pieces of artillery. Fort
Jackson on the Coosa River was erected in May and June by
the brigade and the Thirty-ninth Regiment. Its parapet was
proof against artillery, although one would hardly expect the
Indians to have artillery. At that time, however, there was
great fear that the British would land in Florida and cut behind
the settled portions taking the United States from the rear;
hence all precautions were taken in erecting these frontier
forts. Fort Jackson had a drawbridge like Bainbridge and was
surrounded by the encampment of the troops. Camp Jackson
had a hospital, kitchen areas, sutter's area, and quarters, with
the Thirty-ninth Regiment on the south of the road, the South
Carolina regiment to its northeast, and the North Carolina
regiment across the road to the northwest. The entire encampment was surrounded by sentinels.[28]

Pearson's men finally had the opportunity to engage in
an expedition that promised more excitement than did building forts. Pearson was ordered by General Graham to take
three hundred infantry, seven thousand rations, small boats
to carry the heavy equipment, and to advance down the
river to mop up any remaining bands of unfriendly Indians.
Upon his return he was to be met with wagons on the "federal
road" which would bring him back to Camp Jackson from the
east side of the Alabama River. Pearson chose his infantry
equally from South and North Carolina; he took the North
Carolina riflemen, the South Carolina dragoons, and seventy
Indians. Each village he discovered was surrounded, asked
to surrender, and the warriors taken prisoner. Without blood-
shed, Pearson's expedition returned with 540 captives, having

28. Joseph Graham to Thomas Pinckney, 21 May 1814, RG 107, M 221;
Graham Orderly Books, *passim,* drawings included, Graham Papers.

broken up "the only remaining assemblage of hostile Creek Indians," according to Pinckney who was highly gratified with the entire expedition.[29]

There was ordinarily too little to do, however, with only garrison duty every day, so that some of the men fell into mischief. Much disorder and many courts-martial resulted, all for petty offenses. For drinking or swearing, the punishment meted out was that a man had the left side of his face dry-shaved, and then he had to beat the ground with a maul for three days. A soldier who swindled forfeited half his pay for two months, lost his liquor ration for the remainder of his service, and was drummed up and down the lines three times to the tune of the "Rogue's March." Accusations of subalterns against each other for chicken stealing and cheating were not unheard of. It was fairly easy to sentence the men to hard labor as long as the fortifications were being built, but after their completion it was a nuisance to discover a means of punishment. When Pearson, however, sentenced a man to have his hands tied to a wheelbarrow as he worked on the fortifications, Graham rescinded that part of the sentence as too cruel.[30]

Although the enlistment term of the Carolina militia was due to expire on 16 July, no replacements had arrived to man the fortifications. When an appeal was made for volunteers to remain until relieved, 350 men did so. One Captain Hood from Mecklenburg, however, after having promised to remain at Fort Decatur, on the day of expiration of enlistments simply walked away, taking all his men with him. Part of Captain Frider's company from Rowan and of Captain Gingle's from Lincoln also followed him.[31] The remainder, however, stayed and were shortly relieved by the Georgia militia. The troops

29. Joseph Graham to Jesse Pearson, 18 May 1814, Graham Letterbook, Graham Papers; Pearson to Graham, 1 June 1814, copy, RG 107, M 221; Pearson to Graham, 13 June 1814, ibid; Pearson to Graham, 15 June 1814; Hawkins Letterbook 20, pp. 214-25; Graham to Thomas Pinckney, 14 June 1814, RG 107, M 221; Pinckney to Secretary of War, 25 June 1814, ibid; *Edenton* (N.C.) *Gazette,* 11 July 1814; *Raleigh Register,* 15 July 1814.

30. Mahon, "Carolina Brigade," p. 424; Official Charges against Major David Kerr, 18 June 1814, Graham Papers; Graham Orderly Book, 30 Apr. 1814, p. 49, ibid.

31. Joseph Graham to William Hawkins, 16 July 1814, Hawkins Papers; R. A. Winson to Hawkins, 1 Aug. 1814, ibid.

were disbanded from Fort Hawkins, after being mustered, inspected, and relieved of their arms and accoutrements. With permission, any who wished to return home on their own were allowed to do so, but the others marched with transportation and provisions supplied. All reported at Salisbury for their final discharge. Graham and Pearson, before leaving Georgia, enjoyed a meeting at Fort Mitchell with Indian chiefs, some of whom had never before seen Americans. Attending this meeting with Colonel Benjamin Hawkins, the Indian agent, the Americans attempted to impress the Indians with their military might. By camping in single file they supposedly induced the Indians to believe that they had twice as many men. Drills and maneuvers were staged to illustrate the power of the army. Graham was convinced that garrisons alone would adequately serve the purpose of peace-keeping from that time on.[32]

General Pinckney praised Graham and the Carolina Brigade. The general, he said, had "conducted his Brigade with judgment and propriety, and that he and the officers and men under his command have displayed much zeal, patriotism and attention to discipline; and have executed with fidelity the orders they received." Graham was proud of the fact that 350 men volunteered to stay on beyond their enlistment term, regarding it as previously unheard of in the annals of militia service. The Indian campaign was over, even though the Carolinians did not participate in the great victory. Peace, however, was brought to that land. Maria Crump wrote from Huntsville, Alabama, to a relative that "all is at peace now, you need never be afriad [sic] to bring your family to this country on account of the Indians they are complexly [sic] whip-d."[33]

Before returning to North Carolina, Graham inquired if his men should march to Florida where a British landing was reported. Since the enlistments would have expired before the men could have reached there, the answer to his query was

32. Joseph Graham to William Hawkins, 16 July 1814, Hawkins Papers; A. W. Cannon, Orderly Book, 17 July 1814, no page number, Graham Papers.

33. Thomas Pinckney to Secretary of War, 30 July 1814, RG 107, M 221; Joseph Graham to William Hawkins, 24 Aug. 1814, Hawkins Papers; Maria Crump to Joseph Michaux, 12 June 1814, Michaux-Randolph Papers, NC Archives.

negative. Jackson, however, marched on Pensacola with a thousand regulars, including some few North Carolinians, charged the town on 7 November 1814 and the Spanish surrendered. The British blew up the fort and left.[34] It was apparent that the British were preparing to mount a large-scale attack somewhere along the Gulf coast. Pinckney asked Governor Miller of North Carolina to call up another regiment of militia for service in the Mississippi Territory. This regiment was requested by the governor to rendezvous at Wadesboro on 23 February 1815; but even as the men were wending their way to Wadesboro, the news came of Jackson's victory at New Orleans, followed shortly by the news of the signing of the peace treaty. The regiment destined for New Orleans halted in its tracks and then returned home.[35]

During the entire war on land, eighteen men from North Carolina were among the known killed in action. Their families received pensions of some six or eight dollars per month for the remainder of their lives. Others who had service-connected disabilities also were pensioned. As late as 1883 there were still ninety-five North Carolina men receiving such pensions, and the number of widows who were pensioned was too numerous to count.[36]

The military record of North Carolinians on land has a few high spots, such as the Rifle Corps under Forsyth and the excellent work of Major McRee, but this is chiefly the work of individuals rather than of large organized bodies of troops from the state. The Carolina Brigade could have earned a military reputation but for the fact that the Creek War was over before they arrived on the scene. Colonel Wellborn and the Tenth Regiment never fought as a unit, since one battalion served without Wellborn under Wade Hampton and the other never saw combat service. Because most of the fighting was in the far north, and because there was a strong belief that the militia should fight only in its home state or for its defense in the immediately neighboring territory, the North Carolina

34. Raleigh *Minerva*, 5 Aug. 1814; Lossing, *Pictorial Field Book*, p. 1,023.
35. *Raleigh Register*, 27 Jan. 1815; Miller Letterbook 21, 1 Feb. 1815, pp. 73-74; Thomas Lenoir to William B. Lenoir, 9 Mar. 1815, Lenoir Papers.
36. U.S., War Department, *North Carolina Pension Roll* (Washington, D.C., 1835), pp. 20-23; U.S., Congress, Senate, *List of Pensioners on the Roll, 1 January 1883*, Exec. Doc. 84, 47th Cong., 2d sess., 1883, 5:161-80.

militia was never engaged on the Canadian front. One may conclude, therefore, that they acted when called upon, that when they were engaged in action North Carolina units performed well, that, in short, North Carolina contributions to the land warfare during the War of 1812 were unspectacular but, under the circumstances, all that could have been expected.

6 *THE DEFENSE OF THE COAST*

The seacoast of North Carolina from Cape Lookout to Roanoke Island is protected by the Outer Banks from attack by a large enemy fleet. Conversely, of course, the banks have hindered trade and commerce and the development of large seaports. During the colonial period and the Revolutionary War the banks held off enemy fleets and provided a screen behind which small coasting vessels traveled with food and fiber. The most popular route through the banks from the ocean was at Ocracoke [then spelled Ocracock or Occacock] where ships of nine-foot draft could cross the bar at high tide. At this inlet was the village of Portsmouth, a trading post known as Shell Castle owned by the John Gray Blount business interests, a customs office, and a revenue cutter that had been requested in 1808 by Secretary of the Treasury Gallatin because the customs boat there frequently had to put to sea and needed a commissioned captain and mates. Cargoes from vessels too large to cross the bar were transferred to smaller boats and then shipped to Edenton, Washington, and New Bern, the chief ports on the great sounds. South of Ocracoke at Cape Lookout the coastline turns sharply west, and at this point Beaufort had developed into a seaport free of the barricading banks. However, only vessels of five-foot draft could anchor there. At Bogue Point on a small island forming the

Virginia

North Carolina

Norfolk

Gates Court House

Currituck Inlet

Chowan River

Edenton

Albemarle Sound

Washington

Neuse River

Pamlico River

Pamlico Sound

New Bern

Beacon Island

Ocracoke Inlet

Portsmouth

Ft. Hampton

Beaufort

Cape Fear River

JET III

Wilmington

ATLANTIC OCEAN

Smithville

Ft. Johnston

0 miles 35

north

COASTAL NORTH CAROLINA

Map by James E. Thiem III

harbor of Beaufort was a fort, then called Fort Hampton but later moved to Fort Macon. The best seaport on the North Carolina coast was that of Wilmington, reached by sailing up the Cape Fear River. Where the Cape Fear emptied into the Atlantic on the west bank was the town of Smithville, nestling up to Fort Johnston, still in use by the United States Army as late as 1903. Hampton and Johnston were considered the only fortifications needed for the Carolina coast because of the protection afforded by the banks.[1]

When the seven thousand militiamen from North Carolina were called up in 1812, Hawkins was instructed to place them under the command of Major General Pinckney to be used for the defense of the coastal fortifications. Pinckney, after ascertaining the "equipage & military stores in general" of the militia, instructed Hawkins in July to send four infantry or artillery companies to Smithville near Fort Johnston and the same number to Fort Hampton, so that the manning of the forts would discourage attack. Companies were called up by Major General Brown from Bladen, Brunswick, New Hanover, and Duplin counties for Fort Johnston; power of attorney was requested by him to secure two thousand stand of arms; blank commissions were obtained for some of the new officers; arrangements for feeding the troops were made. Brown thought that some cavalry might also be stationed there "to guard against a rebellion of the blacks, so probable, and so much to be dreaded in this section of the State."[2] The Independent Volunteers from Bladen County and the Wilmington Volunteers staged a review for General Brown in Wilmington. The general arrived on the revenue cutter's barge, thanked the men for their courtesy, after which "refreshment was instantly provided." All drank to the health and success of the general and the country. On the following day, Brown and the Bladen company went to Smithville to man the fort. The Duplin company and others arrived within the next few days. Pinck-

1. U.S., Congress, House, *A Report of the Engineer Department in Relation to a Survey of the Waters of Virginia and North Carolina,* H. Doc. 125, 19th Cong., 1st sess., 1825-26, pp. 7, 9; Albert Gallatin to House of Representatives, 2 Dec. 1808, *American State Papers: Finance,* 2:306; Heitman, *Historical Register,* 2:479, 481, 506, 513.

2. Hawkins Letterbook 18, 21 May 1812, p. 169; 6 June 1812, p. 197; 4 July 1812, p. 221; 14 July 1812, pp. 235-36.

ney sent Major Joseph Swift of the Engineers to assist in laying out the camp, with particular attention to the healthfulness of the location; directions were issued to protect the persons and property of the citizens living nearby. Fort Hampton was garrisoned by troops from Lenoir, Beaufort, Craven, and Onslow counties, under the command of Major Nathan Tisdale of Craven County. The troops assembled at New Bern the last day of July and marched to Beaufort. Arriving there, they camped in a church and the courthouse until the barracks were constructed. Twice a day Tisdale drilled the troops. Muskets arrived at the end of August, but no powder, ball, or cartridge boxes. Each company took its turn at garrison duty along with the few regulars who were permanently stationed there.[3]

When no British attack materialized, Pinckney ordered two companies from Fort Hampton and one from Fort Johnston sent home. Governor Hawkins was distressed over what he regarded as bad news. General Hull had just surrendered at Detroit and Hawkins anticipated that all regulars in the South would be ordered at once to Canada, leaving the coast stripped of protection if the militia was discharged. As Pinckney, however, received no orders to send his regulars northward, he continued to reduce the militia on active service and his orders concerning the three North Carolina companies were carried out. One company from Fort Johnston and two from Fort Hampton were therefore sent home. The remaining companies continued to garrison the forts until the end of the year when 235 regulars and eleven officers of the newly recruited Tenth Regiment were marched from Salisbury to the coast to replace them. Pinckney then thanked the militia for its service, saying that President Madison was "highly gratified with the patriotic disposition displayed"; Tisdale turned over Fort Hampton to the regulars on 20 January 1813, thanked the governor for his promotion to colonel in the militia and asked for a commission in the regulars as a major if Hawkins could recommend him; the militia was ordered by Hawkins

3. Raleigh *Star,* 14 Aug. 1812; William E. Morris to John A. Lillington, 1 Aug. 1812, Hawkins Papers; Hawkins Letterbook 18, 10 July 1812, p. 227; 9 July 1812, p. 226; Nathan Tisdale to Calvin Jones, 8 Sept. 1812, ibid., p. 306. Tisdale's letter is extremely descriptive.

to stand ready for an emergency if it should occur beyond the reach of the troops at the two forts.[4]

The defense of Wilmington was undertaken by the gunboats stationed there under Gautier, and by local volunteer companies. While to some extent its defense was dependent on Fort Johnston, nevertheless other measures were also involved. Robert Cochran, collector of the port of Wilmington, explained to the governor: "I do not know that much danger is to be apprehended in this quarter from the Enemy; nature has fixed barriers to impede any formidable Naval force, we ought nevertheless to be well prepared for a case of emergency." He feared that an enemy force could land at night a few miles from the town which, under cover of darkness, could create "much mischief" and return to its fleet before morning. Four companies of volunteers were ready for such an eventuality, if the governor could arm them. Also active in the defense of Wilmington were Captain David Callender and Colonel Maurice Moore. Moore, concerned and knowledgeable, recommended "flying artillery" as the best means of defense. Sea fencibles were suggested by Pinckney; and indeed the pilots of Wilmington offered to organize a company of sea fencibles for service in case of attack. Joshua Potts, on the other hand, was of the calculated opinion that Fort Johnston should be abandoned for two new forts, one on Oak Island and one at Federal Point; his analysis was essentially correct although not put into effect during the War of 1812. Brigadier General William Watts Jones did not believe Wilmington to be in much danger from the British; for although the town in actuality was weakly defended, her appearance was so strong that the British would probably not attack. However, the citizens easily panicked, and Jones ordered militia reviews occasionally to keep them pacified.[5] One such review took

4. Hawkins Letterbook 18, 27 Aug. 1812, p. 267; 10 Sept. 1812, p. 281; 12 Sept. 1812, p. 288; 19 Sept. 1812, p. 321; 26 Sept. 1812, p. 326; 26 Sept. 1812, p. 324; Thomas Pinckney to Secretary of War, 5 Oct. 1812, RG 107, M 221; James Wellborn to Thomas Cushing, 13 Nov. 1812, RG 94, M 566; Hawkins Letterbook 18, 4 Nov. 1812, p. 358; 4 Nov. 1812, p. 355; Hawkins Letterbook 19, 20 Jan. 1813, pp. 75-76; Hawkins Letterbook 18, 4 Nov. 1812, p. 355.

5. Hawkins Letterbook 18, 18 July 1812, pp. 242-43; 13 July 1812, p. 237; Maurice Moore to William Hawkins, 12 Nov. 1814, Hawkins Papers; Joshua Potts to Hawkins, 28 Aug. 1813, ibid.; Hawkins Letterbook 19, 16 July 1813, pp. 207-8.

place after the Ocracoke landing, on 29 July 1813, when Major General Brown and Adjutant General Robert Williams were among those present. Calvin Jones made a speech, fourteen infantry companies, two cavalry units, and two rifle companies passed in review, and then marched to the Episcopal Church where the Reverend Adam Empie held a service; after this, the companies were dismissed and returned home.[6] This was of course an unusually large number of men, occasioned by the pressing danger, but it was a great morale builder for the Wilmingtonians. A final call for the militia to defend Wilmington came in the late fall of 1814, when a British attack was feared either on the Atlantic coast or in the Gulf of Mexico; after these troops remained briefly on duty, they were discharged following the certainty that the attack would be on New Orleans and not on the Atlantic seaboard.[7] Wilmington defenses also included Gautier's flotilla of gunboats. These little boats carried out such duties as surveying the bar, laying buoys, enforcing the American embargo passed by Congress in April 1812, and challenging all boats cruising in Wilmington waters. Just before the declaration of war, for instance, Gunboat Number 168 stopped the ship *Fernando* of New York and took its papers, whereupon the British brig *Sappho*, which was in the vicinity, came up and demanded the papers. After shots were exchanged, the ships parted, with no damage to the gunboat and the loss of some rigging by the brig. These boats were not designed for ocean service, but for river duty. Although Gautier agreed with his commanding officer that he should help to enforce the war-time embargo by looking in on Swansboro and some northern ports, he pointed out that he had only one man whom he could trust over the bar with his vessel. The boats seem to have been somewhat dangerous to serve in, for two of them blew up at different times, in one case killing eight men including two "free men of color" and in the other, killing nine. Yet there was faith by the people in the ability of the gunboats if necessary to attack the British; Congressman Blackledge believed that North Carolinians knew more about sailing gunboats than the best British sailor on a man-of-war.[8]

6. Raleigh *Minerva*, 6 Aug. 1813.
7. *American* (Fayetteville, N.C.), 13 Oct. 1814.
8. Gautier Letterbook, 15 Feb. 1812, 11 Apr. 1812, 4 May 1811, 16 Nov.

Ocracoke was guarded by the revenue cutter under collector of the port Thomas S. Singleton, who exerted himself to inquire of John Gray Blount if he could purchase some twelve pound carronades on board one of Blount's vessels, as well as two hundred shot for them. James Taylor of Wilmington also inquired of Blount if he could assist in fitting out two vessels for the defense of Ocracoke, equipped with thirty-two-pounders. John Stanly of New Bern, concerned for gold specie in the bank at New Bern, asked Congressman Gaston to solicit the support of other North Carolina representatives in Washington to secure the stationing of a vessel armed with ten or twelve guns within the Swash to protect Pamlico Sound and incidentally the New Bern bank. Whether as a result of these importunities or not, for a short time two gunboats were at Ocracoke, but not when they were needed. Further north, at Currituck Inlet, Brigadier General Jeremiah Brite kept a six-pounder gun ready and the militia on call in case of an attempted landing.[9]

Such were the defenses of coastal North Carolina, vulnerable to a strong attack, able to put up a decent defense only at the two garrisoned forts, yet as in the days of the Revolution dependent in time of trouble on a rising of the militia to give the British a good fight and possibly even drive them off.

Part of the British strategy was to harry the coast from Norfolk to the southward, and to destroy any American vessels found. Sir John Borlase Warren, Vice Admiral of the Blue, planned to harrass and alarm, capture and destroy trade and shipping, carry hostile efforts into American harbors, and if possible destroy ships of war. Warren recognized the great vulnerability of Delaware, Maryland, and Virginia by reason of their waterways and the easy access by an enemy to food supplies. The states farther to the south he saw as somewhat less vulnerable. Warren requested from the British Admiralty six fast-rowing boats, which would be "peculiarly well cal-

---

1812; Raleigh *Minerva*, 12 June 1812; *Raleigh Register*, 9 Sept. 1814; Niles' *Weekly Register*, 6 Oct. 1814; *National Intelligencer*, 21 Mar. 1812.

9. Thomas S. Singleton to John Gray Blount, 8 Apr. 1813, Blount Papers; James Taylor to John Gray Blount, 10 July 1813, ibid.; John Stanly to William Gaston, 31 May 1813, Gaston Papers; Hawkins Letterbook 19, 22 June 1813, pp. 276-77.

culated for Reconnoitering and intercepting any of the Whale Boats employed upon the desultory Expeditions of the Americans." He also ordered a number of mortars and Congreve rockets. Finally, he purchased one large and two small schooners "of the Baltimore built and most approved models" to communicate from his base in Bermuda with Cockburn at Norfolk, and also to be used "against the Enemy with their own Class of Vessels in Shoal Waters and Rivers." Rear Admiral Sir George Cockburn was accordingly sent to blockade the Chesapeake and Delaware regions, with thirteen vessels, enough to "enforce a most strict blockade." The fleet under Cockburn appeared off Norfolk on 4 February 1813 to begin its task.[10]

Cockburn quickly earned a detestable name for himself from the Americans. "Market shallops, oyster smacks, pleasure boats . . . became the prey . . . of commanders and admirals," charged Ingersoll; "notorious Cockburn" carried fire and destruction against "defenseless plantations and fishing towns" complained George Coggeshall. He was a "notorious free-booter," a leader of "modern Goths" who in Chesapeake Bay engaged in "the gallant destruction of Havre-de-Grace, Hampton, and many other small defenceless villages . . . illustrious acts and deeds" that contradicted the "vaunted boast of superior civilization" by the English. "The enemy," said Ingersoll, "taught us not only to detest, but to despise him."[11] On the other hand, the British government greatly appreciated Cockburn and his zealous activity in contrast with the inertia of certain other naval officers. The Lords of the Admiralty upon two occasions thanked him for "the zeal and gallantry displayed by himself and the Officers and Men employed under his orders on these several occasions." This was the com-

10. Sir John Borlase Warren to British Admiralty, 24 Sept. 1813, Letters Received by the British Admiralty from Admirals on the North American Station, Admiralty 1/502-507 (1811-14), Adm 1/504, Public Record Office, London (hereafter cited as Adm 1/——); Warren to Admiralty, 20 Feb. 1813, 28 May 1813, Adm 1/503; 7 Aug. 1812, Adm 1/502; 22 Feb. 1813, Adm 1/503; Raleigh *Minerva*, 12 Feb. 1813.

11. Ingersoll, *Historical Sketch of the Second War*, 1:198, 196, 201-4; George Coggeshall, *History of the American Privateers, and Letters-of-Marque, during Our War with England in the Years 1812, '13 and '14*, 2d ed. (New York, 1856), pp. 75-76, 396-97.

mander, in his flagship the *Sceptre,* who directed the activities off the Carolina coast in 1813-14.[12]

In spite of the declaration of a blockade, small vessels still used protected inland water routes from Norfolk to Charleston with great success, thus avoiding seizure by the British. By using the Dismal Swamp Canal, only three miles of portage were needed between Albemarle Sound and the Cape Fear River; only two miles between the Cape Fear and the Little River; a canal could be constructed, or portage used, of six or seven miles in length to the Waccamaw River, thus completing an entirely secure commercial route. Alternatively, a vessel reaching Pamlico Sound from Norfolk could proceed by inland navigation to Beaufort, from thence sailing outside to Charleston, a riskier route but much easier for transporting cargoes. Although the Thirteenth Congress debated the completion of the first route, no action was taken at the time.[13] However, enough vessels escaped the British so that Admiral Cockburn began to turn more of his attention to the southern coast. He therefore extended the official blockade to cover the "outlets from the Albemarle and Pamlico sounds, connected by inland navigation with the port of Norfolk, the ports of Beaufort and Ocracoke, North Carolina, Cape Fear river, and Georgetown, S.C.," delivering his proclamation by a schooner at Ocracoke and a gun brig at Beaufort. The Ocracoke blockading fleet consisted of a brig, a schooner, and another smaller schooner. Although two frigates and two sloops became the permanent blockading fleet, they were insufficient to secure all the ports, even though the naval historian Mahan considered it as a fairly successful blockade.[14]

The blockading vessels not only harried small coasting

12. Admiralty to Alexander Cochrane, 6 Oct. 1814, Letters from the Office of the British Admiralty, Admiralty 2/932-933 (1808-15), Adm 2/933, p. 235, Public Record Office, London, photostats in Library of Congress (hereafter cited as Adm 2/——); Admiralty to Cochrane, 12 May 1815, Adm 2/933, pt. 2, p. 80; Admiralty to John B. Warren, 3 Mar. 1813, Adm 2/932, p. 235.

13. Thomas Pinckney to Secretary of War, 24 Oct. 1812, 28 Jan. 1813, RG 107, M 221; *Annals of Congress,* 13th Cong., 2d sess., 1813-14, pp. 813, 822, 844, 1,696, 1,767, 1,881.

14. Raleigh *Minerva,* 15 Oct. 1813; Hawkins Letterbook 19, 15 Sept. 1813, pp. 418-19; *Raleigh Register,* 24 Sept. 1813; Alfred Thayer Mahan, *Sea Power in Its Relation to the War of 1812,* 2 vols. (London, 1905), 2:204-6.

boats and seized those departing from the ports if they could, but also landed from time to time in search of food and refreshment. Since Currituck County lay close to Norfolk, it received a number of unwanted visitors. Three British frigates ran a sloop ashore, cutting a hole in the mainsail but not otherwise damaging it; however, they captured two schooners. When, upon landing at Indian Town upon another occasion, the British "demanded provision, and the inhabitants refused to supply them," in retaliation the British burned two windmills. The local militia major, Caleb Etheridge, called out two companies of troops and asked the governor for arms and food. In the fall of 1813 the militia at New Inlet captured seventeen prisoners, eleven of whom were black. They were the crews of two boats from the British privateer *Mars*, which was chasing two small vessels loaded with shingles. One of the two boats upset on the bar and its crew was seized by the Americans. When bad weather forced a small schooner into port at Indian Town, Colonel Brickhouse Bell seized it and discovered it to be an American schooner that the British had previously captured only a few days before. In the fall of 1814, the British came in at Currituck Inlet with nine barges and three hundred men. They captured three coasting boats and burned three others; chased oyster boats and canoes and fired on them; killed a dozen or more cattle; spent the night on Church's and Knott's islands and destroyed Thomas Walker's furniture; and left the following morning.[15]

Beaufort had more alarms than raiding parties. On one occasion a British sloop of war appeared off Cape Lookout, signaled for pilots whom they then detained, decoyed another pilot off Beaufort bar together with his son and two Negroes, and then returned to Cape Lookout where the men landed and carried off all the stock. The militia under a Lieutenant Bauer and seventy-five sea fencibles from Fort Hampton turned out and almost captured seventeen of the men. A newspaper politically opposed to the war remarked that the British had wanted only a swim and some wood, not plunder![16]

15. *Edenton Gazette*, 3 Jan. 1813; Hawkins Letterbook 19, 17 June 1813, p. 260; Josiah Flower to Joseph H. Bryant, 28 June 1813, Hawkins Papers; *National Intelligencer*, 6 Nov. 1813; Raleigh *Minerva*, 15 July 1814; *Raleigh Register*, 4 Nov. 1814.

16. Raleigh *Minerva*, 22 July 1814; *Raleigh Register*, 29 July 1814.

Wilmington had an alarm in June 1814. Two ships and a brig stood off the main bar of the Cape Fear for several days, apparently after the salt works. They captured three pilots, but released them within a few days. The next month the sloop *Peacock* approached Federal Point and was spotted by the militia. Gathering to repel a possible attack, the militia hid behind sand dunes and awaited the landing. When one American was spotted by the British, the boats hastily backed away to safety while the disappointed militia fired from the shore with no effect. South of Wilmington the *Lacedemonian* sent a barge ashore after cattle. The men, unfortunately for themselves, left their muskets in the boat with only two guards. The local militia captured the entire party. Three schooners for Charleston were chased into New Topsail Inlet by an armed brig, which ran them aground and burned two. The British then shot some cattle and departed before the militia under a Colonel Nixon could arrive. Another small fleet of six coasting vessels en route from Elizabeth City to Charleston laden with flour, tobacco and cordage, was captured by four barges from a British frigate, probably the *Lacedemonian,* just before the ratification of the peace treaty ending the war.[17]

There was more difficulty at Ocracoke than at any other location on the Carolina coast. In May 1813 a British schooner falsely flying American colors lured four pilots on board on pretense of wishing to cross the bar. Since the water was too shallow, the British filled the pilot's boat with their men and began to row in, hoping to burn the revenue cutter. On the way they met another pilot boat coming out to investigate, which turned around and hastened to give the alarm. The British thereupon let the four pilots go free and departed, remarking that they "would soon return better prepared to execute their design." Two days later they returned and seized a sloop. The alarm spread by this event caused Colonel Tisdale to call out the New Bern town militia companies in case the British should cross the bar at Ocracoke, enter the sound, and attack New Bern. The rumor spread to Washington that the British had gotten across the bar, and one citizen com-

17. *Raleigh Register,* 3 June 1814; Raleigh *Star,* 10 June 1814; Hawkins Letterbook 20. 20 July 1814, pp. 270–71; Myer Myers to Samuel Mordecai, – Nov. 1814, Mordecai Papers; *Raleigh Register,* 2 Sept. 1814, 17 Feb. 1815.

plained that the "cannon lays rusting on the wharf without carriages" thus leaving Washington also open to a possible attack. The ruse for seizing pilots was used again in September when three pilots were captured by a schooner. Two were forced to jump overboard and swim to shore; the other was later released. Once, however, the Americans were able to capture a British tender which became separated from its convoy and ran aground on Ocracoke Bar.[18]

It was at Ocracoke that the only large-scale coastal attack of the war came. Admiral Warren decided on an assault because he had heard that several enemy vessels were at that time at Ocracoke. He hoped to glean information as to the extent of the commerce coming out of Ocracoke, and to put an end to its use as a substitute for Norfolk. Cockburn therefore took the *Sceptre, Romulus, Fox, Nemesis, Conflict,* and two tenders and sailed for Ocracoke.[19] Arriving after dark on July 12 Cockburn and his commander of the marines decided to take immediate advantage of their position even though the weather was not the best and they could not discern the defenses. The plan of attack was for the advanced division of "the best pulling Boats" including rocket boats with armed seamen and some marines from the *Sceptre* to go in and attack enemy shipping and attract the fire of armed vessels, if any were present. The flat and heavier boats, loaded with as many of the 102d Regiment and artillery as they could carry, were to follow, and the men were ordered to occupy land positions as rapidly as possible. The final division consisting of small vessels and tenders was to take ashore the remainder of the troops.[20] Unfortunately for Cockburn, the Ocracokers saw the British and notified collector of the port Singleton at Portsmouth before daybreak. Singleton placed his trunk with money and custom house bonds on board the revenue cutter under Captain David Wallace at daybreak,

18. John Gray Blount to William Hawkins, 25 May 1813, Hawkins Letter-book 19, p. 227; Nathan Tisdale to Hawkins, 1 June 1813, ibid., pp. 236-37; Thomas Trotter to Ebenezer Pettigrew, 1 June 1813, Pettigrew Papers, NC Archives; James Bradley to John Gray Blount, 26 Sept. 1813, Blount Papers; *Raleigh Register,* 25 Nov. 1814; Niles' *Weekly Register,* 3 Dec. 1814.

19. Sir John B. Warren to Admiralty, 22 July 1813, Adm 1/504.

20. Sir George Cockburn to Sir John B. Warren, 12 July 1813, Adm 1/504.

and Wallace got under way as soon as he could see the stakes in the channel, heading for New Bern.[21]

The British began rowing in at 2:00 A.M., but due to the long distance from the bar to the harbor, and due also to the heavy swell running, it was well after daylight before the advanced forces arrived. As they rounded Shoal Point, heavy fire opened upon them from the armed brig *Anaconda* and the schooner *Atlas*. Opening a "very precise" rocket fire, the British headed straight for the two vessels and boarded both of them, finding only a few men on board each. Neutral ships at anchor were not disturbed, but a number of small American boats that had come to load cargo on the larger vessels took off in flight up the sound, pursued by the British until they kept grounding on the shoals and found the American boats drawing farther and farther away. One of these vessels was the revenue cutter, which crowded on every inch of canvas and cut away her long boat in order to increase her speed. The British finally gave up the chase and returned to Portsmouth and Ocracoke. By this time all the other barges had landed with their troops and the inhabitants had surrendered. Cockburn ordered "that no mischief shall be done to the unoffending inhabitants, and that whatever is taken from them shall be strictly paid and accounted for." He requested that cattle be driven in for purchase and "for the Refreshment of our Troops & Ships."[22] The degree to which this order was obeyed is open to question. The Americans claimed that the troops destroyed furniture of all kinds, ripped open feather beds, carried off clothing, and tore up the law books in the customs office. Some two hundred head of cattle, four hundred sheep, and sixteen hundred fowl were carried off. Singleton felt that the $1,600 that was paid represented only half the value of the cattle alone. He further reported that old Richard Casey was shot in the chest, although not fatally, for being slow to return to shore when he and his family tried to escape in their boat. Cockburn was alleged to have said, "point out the man who did it and he shall be corrected," but, said Singleton, how could you recognize one

21. *Raleigh Register*, 30 July 1813.
22. Sir George Cockburn to Sir John B. Warren, 12 July 1813, Adm 1/504.

man among so many British soldiers?[23] Upon inquiry, Cockburn discovered that neither Washington nor New Bern
harbored vessels of any size "nor other object worthy our
attention." Learning that all other exits through the Outer
Banks were filled up and impassable for any vessel drawing
more than eight feet of water, he decided that there was no
additional purpose to be gained by staying. As soon as the
cattle were on board and the ships manned, therefore, he
released Singleton whom he had kept in custody for two
days, manned the privateer *Anaconda* that he had captured,
and returned to Norfolk. Admiral Warren praised the attack
on Ocracoke, saying that Cockburn "has performed this Service with his accustomed Zeal & Alacrity."[24]

The revenue cutter meanwhile sailed swiftly to New Bern
under the skilful hands of Captain Wallace. About five in
the evening of the fateful day of landing, she neared the town,
firing her guns in alarm. Colonel Tisdale, hearing the news,
called out the New Bern militia and sent one express to Major
General William Croom who commanded in Lenoir and Jones
counties and another to Raleigh to inform the governor. John
Stanly decried the efforts of the New Bern militia to prepare
for an attack, calling it "madness" to attempt to defend the
town against a thousand British regulars. Croom, when he
received Tisdale's message, without waiting to receive orders
from the adjutant general left for New Bern, arriving there
with his troops three days after Wallace's alarm. By that
time four hundred local troops had gathered, a force indeed
formidable, reported Croom, if only they had guns! The townsmen of New Bern furnished the food and paid other expenses
"in this moment of peril."[25] It was not only from nearby
counties that troops rallied to the call, but from Raleigh within twenty-four hours after receipt of the news, a company of
volunteers was on the road to the coast accompanied by the
state adjutant general himself. Two days later the governor

23. Hawkins Letterbook 19, 24 July 1813, pp. 338-41; same letter reprinted in *Raleigh Register*, 30 July 1813.

24. Sir George Cockburn to Sir John B. Warren, 12 July 1813, Adm 1/504;
Admiralty to Warren, 28 Dec. 1812 [1813], Adm 2/933, p. 80; Warren to
Admiralty, 22 July 1813, Adm 1/504.

25. Hawkins Letterbook 19, 14 July 1813, p. 293; 16 July 1813, p.
299; John Stanly to William Gaston, 19 July 1813, Gaston Papers, SHC;
Hawkins Letterbook 19, 16 July 1813, pp. 297-98.

and a troop of cavalry marched, followed the next day by the Wake County militia. A company of militia marched off to New Bern from Chowan County "in high spirits and eager to meet the brutal foe. God grant that they may do honour to themselves and country," said the *Hornet's Nest*. Major S. Turrentine ordered a muster at Hillsborough to be ready for orders, and a company from Warrenton prepared to march. The Hyde County regiment of three hundred men plus a company of volunteers were under arms for four days, fed by generous donations of beef and meal from the citizens and supplied with ammunition by Lieutenant Colonel William Watson himself. Some of the Hyde County men, however, were slow in mustering because "they kept themselves hid so that," said Captain Beverly New, "I was one weake giting them or others in thare place."[26] The countryside was scoured for powder and lead; five hundred pounds of lead were located in Raleigh; General Thomas Davis at Fayetteville sent the supply in the arsenal to New Bern. The governor dispatched a special emissary to Norfolk who obtained one thousand pounds of lead from the commanding officer there, but could not get any powder. Without money, he found no credit until the commanding general guaranteed his good name, whereupon on sixty-day credit he purchased two thousand gun flints, one thousand pounds of loose powder, and four reams of cartridge paper. It took eight days for wagons and teams coming and going to bring the supplies from Norfolk to New Bern. New Bern was an armed camp, with cannon mounted, plenty of powder and ball ready, and the men eager to fight, when the news came that the enemy had departed. Perhaps the greatest appreciation expressed by the citizens of the town was to the governor for coming in person to their assistance. The Committee of Safety paid "homage to the motive which urged your Excellency in such haste to our town, to share in our toils, to mix in our dangers, and to give a more certain combination, force and effect to our means of resistance; but above all, to express the warm and lively sentiments of exultation and confidence which the appearance

26. *Raleigh Register,* 23 July 1813; *Hornet's Nest,* 22 July 1813; Hawkins Letterbook 19, 19 July 1813, p. 317; William Watson to John Gray Blount, 11 Aug. 1813, Blount Papers; Beverly New to William Hawkins, 27 Aug. 1813, Hawkins Papers.

of your Excellency amongst us, at such a time as this, has inspired in all our hearts."[27]

A shudder of fear and anticipation ran along the entire seaboard. At Edenton, Lieutenant Colonel Duncan McDonald sent to Norfolk for powder and lead, and unlimbered the cannon. He personally bought food for the men on duty and distributed it every morning. For "a young officer without any actual experience" he did very well indeed. Some citizens evacuated their families from the exposed situation of the port to more remote plantations, as did James C. Johnston, who told his aunt Mrs. Hannah Iredell that "we shall be extremely uneasy not to have you with us—we have plenty of room to accomodate you without the least inconvenience to ourselves." At Elizabeth City, Colonel Thomas Banks ordered an immediate "parade" for which 507 men turned out, armed with 150 shotguns. Banks stationed 130 men to defend the town and 20 sailors to man the artillery. The owner of a privateer offered all its small arms and ammunition as well as eight cannon, while many "respectable citizens" of Currituck volunteered service and arms "without even being invited." The Fayetteville Independent Light Infantry Company rushed to Wilmington to aid in its defenses. As Ann Nessfield wrote to Mrs. John Steele, "we have been in a state of warfare, every decent man was calld [sic] to Wilmington they b[e]ing in companies of Horse or foot, scarcely enough left for a guard." This company served as Governor Hawkins's personal bodyguard when he visited Wilmington to inspect its defenses. Not all the Wilmingtonians were eager to fight, however; Maurice Moore castigated them for preparing "not for fight, but for flight, safe creeks and swamps are diligently inquired after." Some militia were still under arms there several weeks later.[28] When the news of the landing reached Beaufort, the

27. Hawkins Letterbook 19, 17 July 1813, p. 303; 20 July 1813, pp. 326-27. Total cost of munitions was $791.00, plus $6.00 per day for wagon and team, and $20.00 personal expenses for the emissary, Joseph H. Bryan; The Committee of Safety likewise thanked the Wake County troops for "submitting to a long, fatiguing, and rapid march," calling it "worthy and elevated conduct . . . ," (23 July 1813, ibid., p. 335); *Raleigh Register,* 6 Aug. 1813.

28. Hawkins Letterbook 19, 15 July 1813, pp. 308-9; James C. Johnston to Mrs. Hannah Iredell, 18 July 1813, Charles E. Johnson Collection, NC Archives; Hawkins Letterbook 19, 19 July 1813, pp. 318-19; Ann Nessfield to Mrs. John Steele, 23 Sept. 1813, *Steele Papers,* 2:713-15; James C. MacRae,

alarm guns were fired for the people to assemble. Hurriedly they took up their arms, made cartridges, set lookouts and guards. The country people were summoned to come into town for greater safety. The privateer *Roley* lent them arms, and the cannon were loaded. Part of the militia was stationed at the straits to annoy the enemy should he sail in, with orders to retreat to Beaufort as the ships passed through. Within the next two weeks, an earthen fort with ten guns was constructed in the center of town and forts also erected east of the town and on Shackleford Banks, all built and manned by 310 militiamen. By the end of the month, the enemy would have received a warm welcome had he arrived.[29] The town of Washington also called out its militia, about 300 men, who erected at the lower end of the town a breastwork which mounted four long eighteen-pounders, and sent a reconnoitering party down the river by boat. Governor Hawkins toured the coast looking for sites for forts, inspiring patriotism, and preparing material for a report to the federal government criticizing it for lack of protection. Most of the troops thereupon returned to their homes.[30]

A few persons regarded the entire affair as something of a tempest in a teapot. The Federalist *Minerva* did not think that the loss of featherbeds and lawbooks at Portsmouth was much to complain about. The number of British who landed was regarded by some as an exaggeration. Even one of North Carolina's United States senators told the governor to remember that if the whole American navy had been at Ocracoke, it would have been insufficient to attack the British. To much of the nation, however, it was a shocking event. The *National Intelligencer* editorialized that "NORTH-CAROLINA We had supposed, would have been safe from the enemy's ravages. But she, too, has enjoyed the honor of a visit from the Cockburns and the Beckwiths, and their myrmidons." Describing then the rapidity with which the militia responded, the

"The Fayetteville Independent Light Infantry Company," *North Carolina Booklet* 7 (1908): 252; Hawkins Letterbook 19, 17 July 1813, pp. 311-12; 7 Aug. 1813, p. 366.

29. Report by Adjutant Matthew Morris, 12 July–30 July 1813, Hawkins Papers.

30. Thomas Latham to William Hawkins, 17 July 1813, Hawkins Papers; *Raleigh Register*, 30 July 1813, 20 Aug. 1813.

Intelligencer praised the people and government of the state, saying that they "will at least have the proud satisfaction of knowing, and their neighbors will see, that they have shewn a disposition to perform their duty as citizens and men by fronting the first appearance of danger." There was a general impression of zeal and ardor in defense, of the forgetting of party spirit in rallying to repulse the British.[31] A sad effect of the invasion was the death of Mrs. William Gaston, wife of the congressman from New Bern, who reportedly died of sheer fright because of the invasion.[32] The federal government, however, was not willing to pay for all this patriotism that had saved it from much expense in sending its own troops long distances; Governor Miller in 1815 was still attempting to secure funds to reimburse individuals and the state government for calling out and supplying the militia in July 1813.[33] At least the state did not wait for all the red tape to be cut; like Pinckney when the Creek Indian War broke out, she acted first and then counted the cost.

Following the summer's excitement, six companies of militia remained on duty on the coast until December when Pinckney sent Colonel Nicholas Long to take command. Long made a thorough study of coastal defenses from Elizabeth City to Fort Johnston, recommending a fortification at Ocracoke on Beacon Island which, he believed, would thus protect practically all of the commerce of the state. The details of his report indicate clearly the inadequate and unprotected condition of the coast. Ordnance available, he discovered, included twenty-seven iron and two brass cannon at Edenton, under the care of Dr. John Beasley, but the iron ones were not mounted and had no ammunition. At Washington there were six guns also not mounted and without ammunition. Fort Hampton had six mounted guns, two small guns on trucks, and two iron ones on trucks, all ready for service. However,

31. Raleigh *Minerva,* 6 Aug. 1813; Niles' *Weekly Register,* 24 July 1813; *National Intelligencer,* 22 July 1813; Hawkins Letterbook 19, 23 July 1813, pp. 342-44; *National Intelligencer,* 30 July 1813; Hawkins Letterbook 19, 30 July 1813, pp. 359-61; Raleigh *Star,* 23 July 1813.

32. Ingersoll, *Historical Sketches of the Second War,* 1:126-27; Raleigh *Star,* 23 July 1813; Joseph Herman Schauinger, *William Gaston, Carolinian* (Milwaukee, 1949), p. 70.

33. William Miller to Tobias Lear, 14 Feb. 1815, Miller Letterbook 21, pp. 86-87.

the larger guns were awkwardly mounted and required too many men to service them. The garrison consisted of one company of militia. The fort was capable only of "annoying vessels going up the river, is accessible by land, & non defensible if assailed on that quarter." It had 17 barrels of powder, a few cartridges, 180 round shot, but no cannister and no flints for muskets. In fact, there were no flints to be had anywhere in the state. While vessels of more than six or eight feet in draught had to pass under the guns of the fort, barges could slip by out of range. The muskets were so rusted that he had sent them to New Bern for repairs. At Fort Johnston, a company of artillerymen was in good shape as far as readiness and discipline were concerned. As a fortification, however, Johnston was "a mere apology" and was even less defensible than Fort Hampton. The battery was placed so near the water that at high tide it was damaged, while only thirty feet behind it was a bluff of oyster shells that would scatter like shrapnel if hit by enemy shot. The artillery at Johnston consisted of eight long guns and a blockhouse with seven other guns. The blockhouse was so flimsy that it could be laid prostrate by a few enemy shots. The homes in the village of Smithville were built so close to the battery that they would be destroyed in any attack. Ships could cross the bar and anchor safely out of reach of the guns, while lighter vessels could come in through New Inlet and reach Wilmington completely bypassing the fort. A battery on New Inlet was obligatory. To place the coast in a respectable defense position would cost, Colonel Long thought, $70,000 at Fort Johnston, $50,000 at Fort Hampton, and $30,000 at Beacon Island. Lieutenant Gautier in command of the flotilla at the Wilmington station had only six gunboats to defend the entire coast of North Carolina; he needed four more gunboats and six barges distributed with four boats and two barges at Ocracoke, two boats and two barges at Beaufort, and four boats and two barges at Cape Fear.[34] Based on this report, Pinckney requested from the secretary of war twelve companies of infantry and two hundred artillerists for North Carolina, with

34. Thomas Pinckney to Secretary of War, 5 Sept. 1813, 21 Dec. 1813, RG 107, M 221; Report of Colonel Nicholas Long on the state of North Carolina defense, from Elizabeth City to Ft. Johnston, Long to Pinckney, 15 Feb. 1814, RG 107, M 221.

larger numbers for South Carolina and Georgia, still relying on geography to aid in the protection of North Carolina.[35] The Creek Indian War intervened, however, and attention was diverted from the coast. Many militiamen were not replaced by regulars and had to spend the winter at Fort Hampton and Fort Johnston, while the fortification at Beacon Island was not even begun until the late summer of 1814, a year after its recommendation. Upon his return from the Creek War, Pinckney visited the coast and examined the defenses, with an eye to an attack by the British on a large scale following Napoleon's defeat. Because of rumors of great fleets passing in the Atlantic laden with veterans of the Peninsular Campaign, five hundred militiamen were authorized for Wilmington; the governor asked for and received one thousand stand of arms from the federal government; the townsmen of New Bern erected their own defenses at Union Point, the old palace green, Hanging Point, and Pocosin Point. Five hundred men worked frantically in the cold and the mud of late fall on the fort at Beacon Island. The twenty-seven cannon at Edenton were gradually moved to the most exposed parts of the coast, the citizens of Wilmington requesting six cannon from Edenton "*as soon as possible,*" twelve going to New Bern, and most of the remainder to Beacon Island. No citizen was ever reimbursed for his work on the New Bern defenses because the state law provided that only arms and ammunition would be paid for out of the public treasury.[36] Because the enemy did not attack the coast but instead sailed to the Gulf and landed at the mouth of the Mississippi, the defenses were never tested.

35. Thomas Pinckney to Secretary of War, Feb. 1815, RG 107, M 221.
36. Raleigh *Minerva,* 30 Sept. 1814; Nicholas Long to William Hawkins, 11 Nov. 1814, Hawkins Papers; Resolutions of the New Bern Committee of Safety, 3 Sept. 1814, ibid. The citizens of New Bern spent $4,000 on fortifications and munitions for the Flying Artillery (John Guion to William Miller, 16 Jan. 1815, Miller Letterbook 21, pp. 43-45); Miller to New Bern Committee, 21 Jan. 1815, ibid., pp. 55-56. Concerning the fort at Beacon Island, Thomas H. Blount wrote: "We are progressing in our work & think even at this time, a pretty formidable defense could be made, we have on the Island 300 men. 200 will be here to-morrow—ammunition abundant—so that nothing but courage is wanting, & I flatter myself that will not be wanting—the walls in front are nearly high enough, they will now cover a man to his chin, & we daily add to their height" (Blount to John Gray Blount, 31 Oct. 1814, Blount Papers); William Watts Jones to William Miller, 27 Dec. 1814, Miller Letterbook 21, p. 20.

Although Norfolk was in Virginia, it was a constant source of concern to North Carolina because of its proximity and the fact that much of the state's trade was carried on through the port of Norfolk. When, therefore, after the occupation of Washington the British fleet returned down the Chesapeake, the nation feared an all-out attack on Norfolk and coastal Virginia. Two regiments of the North Carolina militia were consequently ordered to the defense of that city to join the Virginia troops and the regulars already there. Norfolk had been an armed camp since the initiation of the naval blockade in the winter of 1813, although the British strangely never launched an attack on the city. Troops were stationed there from the Tenth Regiment as soon as the blockade was announced; volunteers from North Carolina such as Calvin Jones and Colonel Beverly Daniel, aide to Governor Hawkins, offered their services to the governor of Virginia both before and after the British occupation of Washington and were accepted with "grateful acknowledgments for your affectionate and magnanimous conduct." The city was a veritable beehive of activity in many ways, yet dead in others. Thomas Trotter, following a business trip there, reported that "all business seems stagnated there, even with the Lawyers, some of the most eminent has received Commissions in the Army, there was 6400 troops there, I never saw such preparations for war before, and what the Virginians are to do another Year I cannot tell." The fields in Virginia were only one-third planted because of the absence of men who were in military service. Prices had risen to inflationary levels, "everything in the Stores are dear," he reported. As an example of another kind of hardship, consider Mrs. Jane Collins whose property was used for an army camp so that for three years she could not cultivate the land; the fences were broken down, and a hundred head of cattle turned loose; she took her children for safety to North Carolina and went back to Norfolk to attempt to keep her property together. Her petition in later years for reimbursement by the government was rejected.[37]

The North Carolina militia, when called up in 1814, moved

37. Thomas Cushing to James Wellborn, 27 Mar. 1813, RG 94, M 565; Wellborn to Francis R. Huger, 24 Apr. 1813, RG 94, M 566; Niles' *Weekly Register*, 24 July 1813; *Raleigh Register*, 9 Sept. 1814; Thomas Trotter to Ebenezer Pettigrew, 1 June 1813, Pettigrew Papers, SHC; U.S., Congress,

swiftly. "Our sister State Virginia is threatened at every point assailable by the Enemy," proclaimed Governor Hawkins. "She is literally a military Camp." North Carolina, he added, was expected to be efficient; it was urgent to be prompt! He asked citizens to furnish supplies to troops without waiting for official requisitions in order that haste might be made. Militia rendezvous were ordered for New Bern, for Gates Court House, and for Hillsborough, some men coming from as far away as Stokes and Surry counties, although most were from the central and eastern counties. Calvin Jones, still aspiring to a military career, asked the governor to be appointed the major general in command of the action. Instead, he was requested to organize supplies and transportation, from which position after getting the troops safely to Norfolk he resigned. The men with "willing alacrity" set off for Norfolk, ready "to front their breasts to the enemys steel."[38]

The service of the First and Fifth regiments of the North Carolina militia at Norfolk was entirely a waiting one, for no battle was ever fought. Most of the time was spent in drilling and in trying to guard the health of the troops. Captain James Iredell, Junior, who marched to Norfolk with the Bertie men much against his mother's wishes, served as judge advocate for the court-martial there. His daily routine, as he described it to his younger sister, called for rising between daylight and sunrise. From 9:00 A.M. until 11:00 A.M. he drilled his company; then, until sunset, drill was conducted by regiments. He lived in a hut just large enough for three officers, who hired a cook and attempted to provide for better sustenance than army food. The cook made a pudding now and then; baskets held bread, cold meat, bacon, ham, a quarter of mutton, onions, and sausages; the contents of a jug of brandy and one of cider were poured into a junk bottle used as a

House, *Petition of Mrs. Jane Collins*, H. Report 41, 34th Cong., 3d sess., 1856-57.

38. Hawkins Letterbook 20, 15 Sept. 1814, pp. 341-42; Raleigh *Minerva*, 23 Sept. 1814; *Moravian Records*, 7:3,230, 3,248; Calvin Jones to William Hawkins, 31 July 1814, Calvin Jones Family Papers, microfilm; Jones to Hawkins, 1 Oct. 1814, Hawkins Letterbook 20, pp. 389-90; Adjutant General Robert Williams ordered the cavalry to round up and jail delinquents and deserters (Raleigh *Minerva*, 25 Nov. 1814). Transportation of Richard Atkinson's regiment from Hillsborough to Norfolk cost the state $1752.33 (Miller Letterbook 21, 16 Feb. 1815, p. 92).

decanter. The furnishings were simple: a table, four chairs and a bench, two bedsteads and a cot swung from the joists, with wall decorations of cloaks and swords. As Iredell told his sister, she could perceive that "we are yet in no danger [of] suffering from famine."[39] It does not appear that the enlisted men suffered from lack of food, either, but the terrible winter killed many from cold, damp, and disease. Both regiments were discharged in February without having seen action.

Coastal defense was exceedingly poor. The federal government supplied muskets, ammunition, a few companies of infantry, a very few officers from the regular army, some trained artillerists, and six gunboats. All the rest was supplied by the government of the state of North Carolina and by private citizens and corporate townships. It is not to be wondered at that the state felt the federal government had broken the agreement contained in the preamble to the Constitution to "provide for the common defense."

39. Mrs. Hannah Iredell to James Iredell, Jr., 15 Oct. 1814, Charles E. Johnson Collection; Iredell to sister, 3 Nov. 1814, ibid.; Iredell to Mrs. Hannah Iredell, 9 November 1814, ibid.

7 *THE WAR ON THE SEAS*

The United States Navy, in spite of its importance to the nation in the war as a whole, played only a small role in North Carolina's part in the war, with the exception of the dramatic career of one naval officer, Johnston Blakeley.

The naval forces of the United States were insufficient to prevent the British blockade or to do anything else except raid commerce on the high seas. In 1812 the entire fleet consisted of ten frigates, two not seaworthy even with repairs; three corvettes; three brigs; four schooners; four bomb ketches; and 170 gunboats.[1] Not until the end of the war were any additional vessels authorized. Added to this force were merchant vessels, many of which were well suited to become war vessels. These were commissioned as privateers or letter-of-marque ships. Throughout the British naval correspondence for this period are many remarks praising the structure and sailing ability of these American merchant ships. Indeed, early in the war upon capture of an American ship the British usually straightway commissioned it for their own navy.

Faced only with this weak force, and with two of the eight serviceable frigates in European waters, the British admiralty sent Vice Admiral Sir John Borlase Warren to command in North American waters. Using Bermuda as his base,

1. Seybert, *Statistical Annals*, p. 648.

Warren sat there like a cat watching several mouseholes supervising the coming and going of his ships. When the hurricane season came, he moved north to Halifax, Nova Scotia, and back to Bermuda again for the cold winter months. Bermuda was a hospital and a prison station, as was Halifax.[2] In Bermuda the main licensing offices operated. This licensing system was an effort by the British to allow trade to continue with America and with the colonies of Napoleonic France as long as it supplied their own needs, either in Canada or in Europe. Warren arrived in Halifax from England in September, examined the situation, and on 26 December 1812, proclaimed a blockade of the United States from Maine to Norfolk. Not until the following February did he send Cockburn to Hampton Roads with two ships of the line, four frigates, and several smaller vessels to enforce the blockade. In November 1813 he extended the blockade from Norfolk to the mouth of the Mississippi River. Warren prosecuted the war with less zeal than some of his subordinates, such as Cockburn, and was therefore relieved in 1814 by the appointment of Vice Admiral Sir Alexander Cochrane who commanded a force totaling, by then, thirty-six vessels and nine troop ships. Cochrane did his best to intensify the blockade, upsetting thereby the citizens and military of Canada who had been supplying many of their needs through trade with the New England ports. In spite of the tighter blockade, however, many American vessels continued to slip through. At the height of the blockade, November 1814, a schooner from Currituck sailed on an eleven-day voyage to New York seeing no British cruisers on the entire voyage. How frustrating it must have been for a seventy-four-gun man-of-war to watch idly while American privateers and private armed vessels as well as merchant ships slipped past them because the British were to leeward and a strong breeze was aiding the smaller vessels![3]

2. Vice Admiral Herbert Sawyer to Admiralty, 6 June 1812, Adm 1/502; Sir John B. Warren to Admiralty, 14 Aug. 1813, Adm 1/504; Sawyer to Admiralty, 4 June 1812, 18 July 1812, Adm 1/502.

3. Sir John B. Warren to Admiralty, 5 Oct. 1812, Adm 1/502; Ingersoll, *Historical Sketch of the Second War,* 1:194; Proclamation, 16 Nov. 1813, Adm 1/504; Admiralty to Sir Alexander Cochrane, 25 Jan. 1814, Adm 2/933, pp. 91-94; Admiralty to Cochrane, 14 July 1814, ibid., p. 177; *Edenton Gazette,* 14 Nov. 1814; Coggeshall, *American Privateers,* p. 76, noted that "If the enemy's ships were to leeward, and a strong breeze blowing, our

Many vessels were captured, nevertheless, by the British, some of them off the Carolina coast. On a cruise from Nantucket to Cape Hatteras, Warren destroyed twenty-nine American vessels. The fact that most of such vessels listed in the naval reports were not Carolina-owned ships is indicative of the scarcity of such shipping and the effect of the Outer Banks on shipping in general. Out of 120 ships seized by the British during the first five months of operation, only one, the schooner *Enterprise*, was from North Carolina. During the next six weeks, however, four vessels from Carolina were captured, all laden with corn and engaged in the coastal trade with the New England states. It was a year before any others were captured; then in the period from March to November 1813, seven were seized, two of them during the Ocracoke landing. Many more were driven into port than were seized, partly one must suppose because the smaller ships could navigate the shallow waters of coastal Carolina while the British frigates could not. Occasionally a Carolina vessel sailed to Europe. One ship from Beaufort was en route to Nantes, France, when captured.[4] Exciting events sometimes occurred. The sloop *Betsey* was captured off Currituck by the *Lacedemonian* in November 1813. Putting five men on board her, the British tried to reach Hampton Roads with their prize. Captain Henry H. Kennedy, and one other sailor who had been left on board to work the vessel under the British prize crew, battened their captors below decks and headed for safety. When the British climbed out the cabin window to scramble for the deck, the prize master fell overboard and was rescued by Kennedy, thereupon giving his word not to attempt the recapture of the *Betsey*. Reaching Ocracoke, the Americans got over the bar in a gale, but finding the wind still

privateers and private armed vessels would slip out in spite of them, even at mid-day." Coggeshall was himself a privateer captain during the war, commanding the schooner *David Porter* of New York.

4. Sir John B. Warren to Admiralty, 20 Feb. 1813, Adm 1/503. Lists of vessels captured are dated 26 Feb. 1813, 22 Mar. 1813, 17 Apr. 1813, in Adm 1/503; 23 July 1813, 11 Nov. 1813, in Adm 1/504; 4 Oct. 1813, 25 Dec. 1813, 30 Dec. 1813, in Adm 1/505. Other captured vessels were reported in *National Intelligencer*, 18 Jan. 1813, 17 Nov. 1813; Thomas Trotter to Ebenezer Pettigrew, 25 Dec. 1812, Pettigrew Papers, SHC; Rear Admiral Lord A. Beauclerk to Admiralty, 14 May 1813, operating off the European coast, Adm 1/503.

unfavorable for New Bern, they eventually reached Wilmington and turned in their British prisoners who had once made prisoners of them.[5] Not such a happy ending was the fate of the schooner *Vixen*, laden with rice and turpentine, which was captured by the *Belvidere* en route to Philadelphia from Wilmington. After a seven-hour chase and twenty-six shots, the *Vixen* was taken and its crew plus five passengers made prisoners. The schooner *Lily*, of New Bern, Captain Joseph G. Wicker, was captured a few leagues south of Ocracoke, and the captain and crew put on board a Spanish ship which then landed the men in Wilmington. The antiadministration paper, the *Minerva*, made great capital of the generous and handsome treatment accorded the Americans by their "enemies," the British.[6]

The American navy was not entirely idle, however. The *Enterprize* and the *Rattlesnake* put to sea on 2 January 1814, and arrived safely in Wilmington after seizing several vessels including the Spanish brig *Isabella*. After a six weeks' rest and refitting, the *Rattlesnake* again put to sea in May. The British lost the *Highflyer*, a tender to the *San Domingo*, in a naval action with an unnamed schooner when Warren sent her into the shallow waters off Cape Hatteras to destroy "small Privateers of the Enemy, as well as Coasting Vessels of light draft of Water [which] were lurking in the shallow harbours and Creeks near Ocracok Inlet." Because an American schooner "of very superior force" according to the British seized her, Warren received a reprimand from the Admiralty.[7]

The British licensing system offered an opportunity for lucrative trading with the enemy that was taken advantage of by many New England merchants and a few in other parts of the nation. Congress passed a law in July 1812 prohibiting American vessels from proceeding to or trading with the enemy, and established heavy penalties for accepting British licenses for trade. This "traffic, intercourse, and intelligence,

5. *National Intelligencer*, 9 Dec. 1813; Coggeshall, *American Privateers*, pp. 154-55.
6. *National Intelligencer*, 17 Mar. 1814; *Carolina Federal Republican*, 21 Aug. 1813; Raleigh *Minerva*, 12 Feb. 1813.
7. *National Intelligencer*, 21 Mar. 1814, 23 Feb. 1814; Edward Gordon to Captain John Pickell, 25 May 1813, Adm 1/503; Admiralty to Sir John B. Warren, 9 July 1813, Adm 2/933, pp. 6-8; Warren to Admiralty, 15 Oct. 1813, Adm 1/504.

is carried on with great subtilty and treachery by profligate citizens," said the secretary of the navy, who ordered the United States Navy to exercise the strictest vigilance to stop it, watching particularly for small boats that normally would not attract much attention. Further to attempt to prevent this illicit trade, Congress passed an embargo in December 1813 that, because it was ineffectual, was repealed the next April. While most of the trading with the enemy was carried on from New England, there was some of it from southern ports from whence vessels found it easy to reach Bermuda, Nassau, Jamaica, and Porto Rico. Flour and rice sold well in the British West Indies and such commodities were encouraged by licensing. Grain bound for Spain and Portugal was permitted to pass in order that the British armies in the peninsula could be fed. Timber, too, for the royal navy, was allowed to proceed. When Cochrane relieved Warren, however, the granting of licenses ceased in the interest of tightening the blockade. Yet even Cochrane supplied his officers with American dollars for the purchase of fresh vegetables and meat as they became available.[8]

Efforts to secure food and supplies in the West Indies led to actual solicitation of applicants for British licenses in 1813. One Woccason Banks, Junior, wrote to John Gray Blount offering him the facilities of his firm if he so desired. Licenses were available, he informed Blount, in Cuba "for the purpose of facilitating the commercial objects of our friends, either under the American flag or that of neutrals, all vessels being safe (except French) under such licenses bringing provisions & lumber to Kingston as therein specified." Convoys were provided by Admiral Warren for such as cared to take advantage of them. If Blount were not interested, concluded Banks, would he please tell his friends about their firm?[9] Congress-

8. *Annals of Congress,* 12th Cong., 1st sess., 1811-12, pp. 1,571-72, 1,574, 2,354-56; *National Intelligencer,* 3 Sept. 1813; Ingersoll, *Historical Sketch of the Second War,* 1:504-5; Frances Armytage, *The Free Port System in the British West Indies* (New York, 1953), pp. 132-33; Sir John B. Warren to Admiralty, 18 Oct. 1812, Adm 1/502; Herbert Sawyer to Admiralty, 18 July 1812, ibid.; Admiralty to Warren, 26 May 1813, Adm 2/932, p. 265; Admiralty to Sir Alexander Cochrane, 22 Feb. 1814, Adm 2/933, pp. 119-20; Cochrane to Captain David Milne, 27 Apr. 1814, Adm 1/506.

9. Woccason [?] Banks, Jr. to John Gray Blount, 10 Mar. 1813, Blount Papers.

man William Blackledge was so incensed over the trade with
the enemy, which he believed would "be carried on right or
wrong with or without law," that he suggested legalizing the
purchase of British goods rather than to have such smuggling
going on. All sorts of stratagems, he understood, were being
used to accomplish such importation illegally, thus keeping
large northern cities well supplied in spite of the embargo
while southern planters were hurt. Dark deeds are suggested
by Thomas Trotter's letter to Ebenezer Pettigrew saying,
"I see in the papers of a privateer under British Colours, has
taken a great many Co[a]sting Vessels to the Northard, it is
reported she is commanded and manned by Yankees, and
sends the vessles [*sic*] taken into British ports, but this is
nothing more than I expected from the first." The British in
turn protested against French privateers using United States
harbors to fit themselves out and then to pursue British ships.
Although the American government allowed these privateers
to come and go freely, it attempted to prevent their being
outfitted, but occasional oblique references may be found to
French privateers preparing for sea or to the British searching
for French privateers in American harbors.[10]

The tainted trade eventually touched Currituck, North
Carolina. Vessels carrying corn plied a heavy trade between
Albemarle Sound and the north, much of it in northern ships.
Since much protest was being raised against the blockade,
why then, asked the *Hornet's Nest,* did so many northern
speculators come to Currituck? Perhaps, insinuated the editor,
the British bought the corn from them? In June one William
R. Smith was on a British ship as prisoner of war when the
ship seized a sloop off Ocracoke, finding on her a British
license to trade with Halifax. Smith both saw the license and
heard the sneering remark that the American government allowed "one half to be feeding them while the other half were
fighting." This information was passed on to Governor
Hawkins, who alerted the port collectors in Wilmington,
Edenton, New Bern, Washington, Ocracoke, and Beaufort

10. William Blackledge to John Gray Blount, 25 Nov. 1812, Blount Papers;
Thomas Trotter to Ebenezer Pettigrew, 25 Dec. 1812, Pettigrew Papers,
SHC; A. L. Burt, *The United States, Great Britain and British North America
from the Revolution to the Establishment of Peace after the War of 1812*
(New Haven, 1940), pp. 295-96.

to be on guard. Thomas H. Blount, collector at Washington, sent officers from there to watch for violations in his area; Samuel Tredwell of Edenton reported that no northern vessels had been there for some time, although now and then one arrived at Plymouth.[11] The national government sent a special agent, Robert E. Steed, to investigate. Steed reported at length that there was no doubt the enemy was well supplied with fresh provisions. The people whom he interviewed blamed five men, by name, for this trade, stating that they had purchased British licenses for $20 each. It was "well known," said the inhabitants of Currituck, that ships were cleared to carry "shingles" to Baltimore whereas in actuality cattle were on board and were sold to the British either at sea or at Hampton Roads. Solicitor James Iredell, Jr., was instructed to collect evidence of this, if possible. Brickhouse Bell was assigned to the task. The evidence collected by Bell indicated that only one man was guilty, this one being Jasper Pickel. The charges against the others, Bell believed, were maliciously intended to hurt the reputations of certain leading citizens of the area, citizens who were as patriotic as any to be found but objects of jealousy by some. Clearance papers, said Bell, indicated no ships leaving ostensibly for Baltimore as alleged: indeed, only three ships had cleared during the entire time spoken of, none of which was for Baltimore.[12] No more was heard about the matter.

Although the famous *Wasp* was not built in nor paid for by North Carolina, her captain was a native son, Johnston Blakeley, whose successful cruise and mysterious ending added color to the naval history of the war. As commanding officer of the United States brig *Enterprize*, Blakeley captured the British privateer *Fly* off Cape Porpoise after a chase of eight hours and carried her into Portsmouth, New Hampshire, in

11. *Hornet's Nest*, 28 Jan. 1813; Robert B. Taylor, commanding officer at Norfolk, to William Hawkins and James Monroe, 3 June 1813, Hawkins Papers, had reason to believe that "a very nefarious trade with the enemy is now carrying from the ports of North Carolina." Affidavit by William R. Smith, 3 June 1813, Hawkins Letterbook 19, pp. 232-34; Hawkins to ports collectors, 15 June 1813, ibid.; Thomas H. Blount to Hawkins, 29 June 1813, ibid., p. 278; Samuel Tredwell to Hawkins, 5 July 1813, Hawkins Papers.

12. Robert E. Steed to William Hawkins, copy, 30 Aug. 1813, Hawkins Papers; *Raleigh Register*, 8 Oct. 1813; James Iredell, Jr. to Brickhouse Bell, 16 Oct. 1813, Charles E. Johnson Collection; Bell to Hawkins, 8 Nov. 1813, Hawkins Papers; *Raleigh Register*, 19 Nov. 1813.

late 1813. Early in 1814 he was named to the command of the new *Wasp,* under construction at Newburyport. Blakeley completed the supervision of the vessel, hired the crew, checked out the armament, and on 1 May 1814 sailed from Portsmouth with "a fine breeze at North West." Although the British vessel *Junon* was blockading Portsmouth and Boston, it was unable to watch both ports at the same time and thus let the *Wasp* slip out.[13] Twenty days after sailing, Blakeley spoke the French brig *Oliver* and sent a message home, saying that all was going well with the new vessel. His official orders were to cross the Atlantic, take up a station off the Azores northwest of Corvo and Flores and cruise there for ten or twelve days, capturing what shipping he could. Moving to a post sixty leagues west of Ushant [Ouessant], France, he was to cruise there for a month, heading after that for Cape Clear, Ireland, and spending two or three weeks in that vicinity. Circling out and back near Cape Finisterre in northwest Spain for twenty or twenty-five days, he was to head as far south as Cape St. Vincent at the southwestern tip of Portugal and cruise eight or ten days there. Following this, he was to station himself between Ireland and the Shetlands to try to intercept the British fleet returning from Archangel, Russia. By 10 September, he was to head for France for water and provisions at L'Orient. When autumn came, he could seek warmer climes such as the Madeira Islands, Cayenne, French Guiana, and Demerara [Georgetown], British Guiana, from there coming into the Gulf of Mexico and home to St. Mary's, Georgia, "where you will touch for information and refreshment." Any prizes he might capture were to be destroyed rather than sent in, as the latter would reduce the size of his crew below the effective level. He was strictly forbidden to give or accept a challenge to single combat with any ship of the British navy.[14]

13. Niles' *Weekly Register,* 4 Sept. 1813; Raleigh *Minerva,* 3 Sept. 1813; *National Intelligencer,* 26 Nov. 1813; William Jones to Johnston Blakeley, 16 Nov. 1813, Naval Records Collection of the Office of Naval Records and Library, Record Group 45, Microcopy 149, NA (hereafter cited as RG 45, M 149); Blakeley to Jones, 1 May 1814, RG 45, M 124; C. Upton to Admiral Edward Griffith, 4 Apr. 1814, Adm 1/506.

14. Johnston Blakeley to William Jones, 20 May 1814, RG 45, M 124; Official Orders from Jones to Blakeley, Confidential Letters Sent, 3 Mar. 1814, RG 45.

The *Wasp* was "a beautiful ship," wrote one of her officers, "and the finest sea-boat, I believe, in the world; our officers and crew, young and ambitious—they fight with more cheer fulness than they do any other duty. Captain Blakel[e]y is a brave and discreet officer—as cool and collected in action as at table." The *Wasp's* crew consisted of 173 men, all American citizens. She carried twenty guns, two of which were long twelve-pounders and the remainder thirty-two-pound carronades. During the long cruise to his European station, Blakeley drilled and trained his crew into an effective fighting machine, the results of which were readily seen in his successful engagements with larger British vessels.[15]

On the first portion of its cruise, from 1 May to 6 July, the *Wasp* captured and destroyed six vessels and used a seventh as a cartel for carrying the wounded and prisoners from the other six. The outstanding success was the victory of the *Wasp* over the *Reindeer,* a British warship of twenty-one guns. Near Lands End the two fought an action for twenty-five minutes. Twice the *Reindeer* came close enough for her crew to board the *Wasp*, but they were beaten off. The American gunners cut the *Reindeer* to pieces at the waterline by their effective fire. The captain and twenty-one seamen were killed; the remainder were taken aboard with their baggage and the *Reindeer* burnt. Blakeley praised his crew: "all did their duty and each appeared anxious to excel." Under fire, the "cool and patient conduct of every officer and man" was pointed out, plus the "animation and ardor" when the boarding attempts were repelled. The *Wasp's* foremast, rigging and sails were "a good deal injured" so that she put directly into L'Orient in order to make repairs and to care for her wounded. The Americans were well received in France, supplied with fresh beef and offered "every civility." The British newspapers stated that Blakeley was exceptionally polite to the *Reindeer* crew but they made unpleasant remarks about the "brutality and insolence" of the "Scotchmen and Irishmen" who, they further alleged, composed the crew of the *Wasp*. Congress voted Blakeley a gold medal for his victory, and he has been praised by such later writers as

15. Niles' *Weekly Register*, 19 Nov. 1814; James Ripley Jacobs and Glenn Tucker, *The War of 1812: A Compact History* (New York, 1969), pp. 166-68; Mahan, *Seapower in Its Relation to the War of 1812*, 2:255.

Theodore Roosevelt, James Fenimore Cooper, and Frederick Stanhope Hill.[16]

Fourteen wounded Americans were treated in the French hospital, two of whom, both midshipmen, died. Two who had been badly wounded were sent home from L'Orient, thus escaping the fate of the remainder of the crew. Prize money of $108 each was paid these men; presumably the others would have received their shares upon safe return to the United States. All repairs to the *Wasp* were carried out by her own crew except for the foremast that had to be repaired on shore. Finally, on 27 August, with favorable winds, the *Wasp* sailed on the second leg of her journey.[17]

Almost immediately she fell in with a convoy of ten ships, guarded by a seventy-four-gun frigate. Under the nose of the frigate Blakeley cut out a brig laden with military stores and burned her. Late in the afternoon he saw four more ships and gave battle to a brig that turned out to be the *Avon*, a heavier class of ship than the *Wasp*. Nevertheless, the *Wasp* after a battle of forty-five minutes defeated the *Avon*, but before she could rescue the crew from the water, the three remaining brigs approached and the *Wasp*, after exchanging one round of shot with them, departed into the darkness. The American crew fought so well that the British papers claimed three hundred men were aboard and said the *Avon* was very brave to engage the *Wasp*. Said Niles' *Register*, "THE WASP, after a FROLIC, took a REINDEER then like the bard of AVON, conn'd the notes of Yankee harmony, to JOHNNY BULL. If captain Blakel[e]y should return to France, as it is probable he may, after catching a few more of the enemy, what will the FRENCHMEN think of him and us?"[18]

Sailing on toward the Azores, the *Wasp* captured six

16. Johnston Blakeley to William Jones, 5 July 1814, 8 July 1814, RG 45, M 124; Lossing, *Pictorial Field Book*, p. 979; R. D. W. Connor, "Captain Blakel[e]y in the War of 1812," *North Carolina Review*, 6 Apr. 1913, pp. 12-13; descriptions of the battle drawn from Blakeley's reports may be found in Niles' *Weekly Register*, 29 Oct. 1814, and citations from British newspapers in ibid., 10 Sept. 1814.

17. Johnston Blakeley to William Jones, 10 July 1814, 27 Aug. 1814, 11 Sept. 1814, RG 45, M 124; approval by Blakeley to pay prize money, 1 Sept. 1814, RG 45, M 625; affidavits by mother of wounded sailor, 13 June 1816, ibid.

18. Johnston Blakeley to William Jones, 11 Sept. 1814, RG 45, M 124; a description drawn from Blakeley's report may be found in Niles' *Weekly*

prizes, the last one being the *Atalanta*. Because there was some doubt as to the nationality of the *Atalanta*, Blakeley did not burn her but put a prize crew on board and sent her to Savannah, Georgia, laden with wine, brandy, and silk, under the command of Midshipman David Geisinger. The *Atalanta* reached Savannah safely in mid-November, having among her passengers R. Stewart of Philadelphia who had taken passage on the *Wasp* in France in order to return home, and an incorrigible midshipman, Thomas D. Ponnsville, whom Blakeley had been unable to make "attentive [to] his duty."[19] This was the last word ever received from the *Wasp*.

As the days and weeks passed without word from the ship, rumors began to fly concerning her fate. A brig that put into Beaufort, South Carolina, reported that the *Wasp* had boarded her near Turk's Island on 19 December, but had no information as to her destination or activities. Firing heard off the Charleston bar was reportedly the frigate *Lacedemonian* and two schooners attacking the *Wasp;* had this been true, however, the British would have been only too happy to have reported their success. John C. Calhoun cited certain naval officers who thought the *Wasp* was in the Pacific, discounting a reported engagement between a frigate and the *Wasp* near Lisbon, Portugal. A year elapsed before hope was finally abandoned; as J. C. Gilleland said, "the Wasp was for a long time fondly expected home: but alas! her fate is now but too certain; our gallant seamen are covered by the mountain waves of the ocean." A privateer was built in Boston and named for Blakeley; he was promoted, posthumously as it developed, to the rank of post captain; the North Carolina legislature voted him a sword to be sent to his widow, and pledged itself to educate his only child, a daughter Udney Maria Blakeley. His heirs were paid $50,000 for his share of the prize money for the defeat of the *Reindeer* and the *Avon*, plus his pension of $50 per month and his back pay.[20] Blakeley

---

Register, 10 Dec. 1814, and citations from British newspapers in ibid., 19 Nov. 1814.

19. Johnston Blakeley to William Jones, 22 Sept. 1814, RG 45, M 124; appointment of David Geisinger as prize master, 22 Sept. 1814, RG 45, M 625; Coggeshall, *American Privateers,* pp. 214-15; *American,* 17 Nov. 1814; Niles' *Weekly Register,* 19 Nov. 1814.

20. Raleigh *Minerva,* 3 Feb. 1815, 2 Dec. 1814; Niles' *Weekly Register,* 3 Dec. 1814; Johnson, "Biographical Sketch of Capt. Johnston Blakel[e]y,"

was the most illustrious naval officer from North Carolina in the history of the United States under the Constitution.

Privateers played a much more important role in North Carolina sea warfare than did the American navy. In fact, they were vitally significant in the nation. Cities such as Baltimore, New York, and Salem, Massachusetts, sent out so many privateers that they far outnumbered the little navy. It has been calculated that 526 American ships received letters of marque under an act of Congress dated 26 March 1812, which authorized the president to send blank letters to various ports for issuance by the collectors of customs. An estimated 1,334 British merchantmen worth some $7,750,000 were captured or destroyed by American privateers. So successful were these raiders that the governor of British Barbados, George Beckwith, asked Admiral Warren for greater protection, saying that "these Seas [are] infested with American Privateers, fully manned, and superior to His Majesty's Cruizers in point of Sailing." Warren reported to the admiralty that from 18 June 1812, the date of the American declaration of war, to 5 November of the same year, 156 merchant ships had been captured by the Americans. As Glenn Tucker so neatly put it, this occurred "almost before Great Britain was aware of the existence of the war."[21] Of these privateers, North Carolina supplied four, one each from Washington and Wilmington, and two from New Bern. In addition to commissioning their own privateers, North Carolina ports played host to many others and their prizes, especially toward the end of the war when the blockade was tightened on the more northerly ports.

Wilmington received an immense number of privateers because of its ready access from the ocean. Businessmen had

p. 13; *Raleigh Register*, 23 Dec. 1814; John C. Calhoun to Patrick Calhoun, 4 Jan. 1815, *Calhoun Papers*, 1:274; J. C. Gilleland, *History of the Late War, between the United States and Great Britain* (Baltimore, 1817), p. 92; Coggeshall, *American Privateers*, p. 387; Niles' *Weekly Register*, 26 Nov. 1814; *Raleigh Register*, 2 Dec. 1814; *N.C. Senate Journal, 1816*, p. 55; Ingersoll, *Historical Sketch of the Second War*, 1:441; pension award to Jane Ann Blakeley, RG 45, M 625.

21. Jacobs and Tucker, *War of 1812*, p. 170; Sir John B. Warren to Admiralty, 6 Oct. 1812, Adm 1/502; Seybert, *Statistical Annals*, p. 395, the figure of $7.75 million being arrived at by calculation; George Beckwith to Warren, 22 Nov. 1812, Adm 1/503; Warren to Admiralty, 5 Nov. 1812, ibid.; Jacobs and Tucker, *War of 1812*, pp. 169-70.

trouble attending to any other kind of business because there was such great enthusiasm for privateering. The men who captained these vessels were, according to one report, extravagant, corrupt, and dissipated, but they were also jovial, sociable, and generous in their attentions to strangers. The *Lovely Lass* was Wilmington's own privateer. How successful she was is not clear, because only one capture, a schooner carrying a cargo estimated at $10,000, was reported. She herself was captured by the British vessel the *Circe* off Montego Point on 15 May 1813, after a nineteen-hour chase. The *Lovely Lass* threw two of her five guns overboard during the chase but this did not save her. Although she and her crew of sixty men, commanded by John Smith, an officer in the American navy, had been out forty-four days on a hunting expedition and claimed they had made no captures, the British Captain Woolcombe doubted the truth of this statement because part of the log book had been torn out. The crew were held prisoners in Nassau, from whence William L. Robeson wrote to his brother Captain Thomas J. Robeson of the Rifle Corps asking that he not be forgotten when the time came for exchanges.[22]

During 1812 three captured British ships were sent into Wilmington for disposal. In 1813 the count increased, with five vessels being sent in, laden variously with dry goods, coffee, rum and sugar, and molasses; plus a tender to the British naval vessel *Admiral*. The privateer *Saratoga* came into port with the cargoes of four prizes and a large sum in specie which it disposed of there. The peak year was 1814, during which fifteen captured vessels and the cargoes of several others came into Wilmington. Newspapers advertised the sales of goods from prizes, conducted at auction, sometimes including the vessel itself, as the cargo of the *Prince Regent* plus the schooner that was advertised for sale on 1 January 1815.[23] Occasionally, in the zeal of the chase, the Americans

22. Myer Myers to Samuel Mordecai, — Nov. 1814, Mordecai Papers; Coggeshall, *American Privateers*, p. 68; Edward Woolcombe to Charles Sterling, 15 May 1813, Adm 1/503; William L. Robeson to Thomas J. Robeson, 27 Nov. 1812, *American State Papers: Military*, 1:342; the other prisoners were Autine Lambert, William Thomas, John Crandel, David Ashton, John Gamache, John Hynes, Darius Swain, and John M'Kenzie.

23. Coggeshall, *American Privateers*, pp. 59, 98, 120, 156, 170, 226, 227, 231, 298, 304, 313-15, 317, 324, 328, 355; Raleigh *Minerva*, 18 Nov. 1814;

captured vessels that were not British, or at least that had a substantial claim to another country's flag. The owners appealed such captures to the courts in an effort to regain their ships and cargoes. Several such cases originated in Wilmington, in the Cape Fear district of the federal judicial system, and three were eventually appealed to the United States Supreme Court. One such case was that in which the privateer *Roger* from Norfolk captured the *Fortuna* on 19 April 1814, en route from Havana to Riga with 1,520 boxes of sugar, and brought it in to Wilmington. The owners claimed to be Russian, but secret papers were found in a cannister sealed in a block of wood in the captain's cabin that showed the cargo to be British. The owners appealed to the circuit court, which, with Chief Justice John Marshall presiding, upheld the decision of the district court with the exception that the captain, who was a citizen of Sweden, might have back his personal property. Appealed once again, the United States Supreme Court upheld the circuit court. The energetic crew of the *Roger* was responsible for two more cases before the federal courts, one involving the *Amiable Isabella* that claimed to be Spanish, and the other the *Contract*, laden with salt. The *Roger* won both cases.[24]

National Intelligencer, 12 May 1814; List of British Vessels Captured, 5 Nov. 1812, Adm 1/503. The *Perry* of Baltimore had to fight the *Bulaboo* to effect its capture (Coggeshall, *American Privateers*, p. 239). The *Globe* of Baltimore limped into Wilmington after being defeated by two British vessels; two lieutenants and five seamen were killed, the captain and 17 men wounded (Raleigh *Minerva*, 28 Jan. 1814). None of the captures brought into Wilmington were made by North Carolina privateers.

24. Case of the *Roger* v. the *Fortuna*, in J. W. Brockenbrough, ed., *Report of Cases Decided by Hon. John Marshall in Circuit Court of the United States for the District of Virginia and North Carolina, 1802-1833*, 2 vols. (Philadelphia, 1837), 1:299-315; Stephen K. Williams, ed., *Cases Argued and Decided in the Supreme Court of the United States*, Lawyers' Edition, Book 4 (Rochester: Lawyers Co-operative Publishing Co., 1926), 16:160 (hereafter cited as 4 Law Ed. U.S.); ibid., 17:234. Case of the *Roger* v. the *Amiable Isabella*, Minutes of the Federal Circuit Court of North Carolina, Raleigh, May Term 1816, Records of the United States District and Circuit Courts for the Eastern District of North Carolina, 1801-16, Record Group 21, National Archives and Record Service, Regional Archives Branch, Federal Records Center, East Point, Ga. (hereafter cited as RG 21). The *Contract* v. the *Roger* may be found in ibid. Other cases were: the *Caridad* v. the *Harrison*, 4 Law Ed. U.S. 17:494; the *Herald* v. the *Friendschaft*, Federal Circuit Court at Raleigh, May Term 1815, RG 21, and 4 Law Ed. U.S. 16:12-52, 17:102; the *Caroline* v. the *Osiris*, Federal Circuit Court at Raleigh, May Term 1814, and Executive Docket, May Term 1815, RG 21; the

The *Hawk* was a privateer out of Washington. It was reported as capturing one schooner, the *Phoebe*, laden with rum and molasses, which was sent in to Wilmington. Occasionally a captured vessel was sold at Washington, as the brig *Morton*, prize to the *York Town*, in 1813.[25]

The port of Beaufort supplied no privateers, but was a port into which came four well-laden prizes. The schooner *Ellen*, a prize to the *Herald* of New York, en route from Belfast to Lisbon, was loaded with pork, beef, hams, lard, and herring. The *Chasseur* of Baltimore captured two prizes that it sent into Beaufort; one was the *Galatea* bound for Pensacola with crockery, hardware, dry goods, and white lead; the other was an English brig laden with Teneriffe wine. The fourth vessel was the schooner *Nimble*, laden with log wood, captured by the *Saucy Jack*.[26]

At Ocracoke, which supplied no privateers, prizes to other vessels sometimes came into port. The *Anaconda*, which was captured by Admiral Cockburn at Ocracoke, had come in with the profits of a prosperous cruise, mostly in the form of specie, which it had thoughtfully sent to Edenton for transmission to the bank vaults at Tarboro before Cockburn arrived. The gold bullion and diamonds were sold in Raleigh for $65,000. The privateer *Globe* from Baltimore brought in the *Kingston Packet* laden with rum, and despite a court suit, was allowed to keep the proceeds. Two valuable prizes were lost on one of the bars, a three-masted schooner, captured by the *Warrior* of New York, lost on New Inlet bar, and the schooner *John & Ann*, captured by the *Young Wasp* of Philadelphia and lost on Ocracoke bar. The same *Young Wasp* also sent into Ocracoke a schooner, possibly the *Goldfinder*, laden with salt. The capture of the brig *Malvina* by the armed schooner *Ned* of Baltimore led to a court suit in the Albemarle district of the federal judiciary, the decision being in favor of the *Ned*. One other vessel is reported to have been

Herald v. the *Antonio Johanna*, Federal Circuit Court at Raleigh, May Term 1815, RG 21; the *Rattlesnake* and the *Enterprize* v. the *Isabella*, Federal Circuit Court at Raleigh, May Term 1814, RG 21.

25. Coggeshall, *American Privateers*, p. 232; *Carolina Federal Republican*, 11 Sept. 1813.

26. Raleigh *Minerva*, 22 July 1814; *National Intelligencer*, 7 Mar. 1814, 11 June 1814; Coggeshall, *American Privateers*, pp. 169, 225, 239-40.

sent as a prize to Elizabeth City, captured by the *Caroline*. The brig *Peter* arrived as a prize at an unidentified North Carolina port, and the privateer *Kemp* of Baltimore arrived from Nantes with what was described as valuable cargo, port not given. The *Comet* of Baltimore was reported to have sent two captured vessels into North Carolina, one of whose cargoes sold at New Bern for $25,558.[27]

A French privateer involved the United States in some trouble. This vessel had been fitted out illegally at Washington so that a prize it had captured and sent into Beaufort under a new name caused great efforts to discover the purchasers of her cargo in order to make restitution to the true owners.[28]

New Bern was the only North Carolina port whose citizens outfitted two privateers. Both the *Hero* and the *Snap Dragon* were from New Bern, and all prizes sent into New Bern except a brig laden with gum from Africa were taken by one or the other of these two vessels. On a cruise from L'Orient, France, to North Carolina, the *Hero* under Captain Thaddeus Waterman captured five prizes, one of which came to New Bern with a cargo of sugar and molasses valued at $20,000. It is possible that the schooner *Funchall* was captured on this same cruise. A sloop, a brig, and a "fine copper bottom British schr.," were also credited to the *Hero*.[29]

Best known of all the North Carolina privateers was the second one from New Bern, the *Snap Dragon*. The vessel was originally built in 1808 on West River, Maryland, and was in

27. *National Intelligencer*, 13 July 1813, 8 Sept. 1813; Niles' *Weekly Register*, 17 July 1813; the *Anaconda* was reported in the *National Intelligencer*, 8 Dec. 1813, lost in a storm at Halifax, Nova Scotia, following its removal there; Coggeshall, *American Privateers*, pp. 119, 324, 358, 312, 320; Niles' *Weekly Register* 15 May 1813; Trial Docket of Albemarle District, Federal Court, June Term, 1813, RG 21; other cases included the *Globe* v. the *Kingston Packet* in June Term, 1813, *Kemp* v. the *Thomas J. William* in April Term 1814, the *Young Wasp* v. the *Modesty* in April Term 1814, and the *Young Wasp* v. the *John & Ann* in April Term, 1815, ibid., Coggeshall, *American Privateers*, pp. 159, 324, 247, 170, 226; Raleigh *Minerva*, 6 May 1814.

28. Thomas Trotter to Ebenezer Pettigrew, 1 June 1813, Pettigrew Papers, NC Archives; Raleigh *Minerva*, 3 Sept. 1813.

29. Coggeshall, *American Privateers*, pp. 236, 307; *National Intelligencer*, 11 June 1814, 16 June 1814; *Carolina Federal Republican*, 4 June 1814; *Raleigh Register*, 11 Nov. 1814, 30 Dec. 1814; *Carolinian* (New Bern, N.C.), 31 Dec. 1814.

New York at the time she was purchased for the privateering service.[30] The total number of owners is not known, but from New Bern, Colonel Edward Pasteur, John H. Bryan, James Harvey, and William Shepard; and from Tarboro, Theophilus Parker, Randolph Cotten, and Spencer D. Cotten were shareholders. Bills for the purchase of nails, coffee, sugar, and rope may still be found in account books both from New Bern and from the rope walk at Edenton.[31] Although the *Snap Dragon* had at least two captains, the best known is Otway Burns of Beaufort who has had a colorful mythology woven around his name.[32] Purportedly a journal kept by one of the crew members, an old magazine article has described some of the hair-breadth escapes from the British that succeeded because of Burns's superior navigational and sailing ability. Once, when a British ship gave chase in the Caribbean, the crewman wrote that "it was pretty tight times; the wind blowing big guns, the sea breaking over us, and a dangerous looking stranger walking right in our wake." The *Snap Dragon* passed ahead of the other by three hundred yards, and by sunset was

30. Theophilus Parker, conveyance of one Share [1/50] in the privateer *Snap draggon [sic]*, 7 Oct. 1812; photocopy (original in possession of Mrs. Pembroke Nash, Tarboro, N.C.) describes the origin and size of the vessel. Originally named the *Zephyr*, she had one deck and two masts, was 85 feet 6 inches in length, 22 feet 5 inches in breadth, and 8 feet 8 inches in depth, 147 40/95 tons, square stern, and round truck. The share was purchased for $260.00.

31. To owners of the *Snap Dragon*, William Hollister Account Books, New Bern, N.C., 1808-18, Acct. #88, 3:147, 148, 149, 153, microfilm, NC Archives; balance due Edenton ropewalk, 3 Aug. 1816, from Otway Burns and William P. Ferrand, Josiah Collins Papers, Box 9, loose pages, NC Archives, although this may represent Burns's own business and not that of the *Snap Dragon*.

32. In an oration on Burns, North Carolina Chief Justice Walter Clark expressed the belief that two logs of Burns's three voyages were destroyed during the British raid on Washington in 1814. Clark said he had seen the one remaining; he further expressed the belief that the "log" of the first voyage published in the *University Magazine* (cited below) was actually written by the University of North Carolina's president David Swain, who possibly had seen copies of the other logs made by members of the *Snap Dragon* crew. Walter Francis Burns, *Captain Otway Burns, Patriot, Privateer and Legislator* (New York, 1905), p. 27; "Otway Burns and the Snap Dragon," *North Carolina University Magazine*, 2d ser. 4 (1855): 407-13, 461-67; 5 (1856): 126-31, 205-8. A detailed article in the *Carolina Federal Republican*, 18 Sept. 1813, is referred to by its editor as an abstract of the journal of the privateer on its second voyage under Burns. Enough items have been found in contemporary newspapers to piece together a fairly accurate account without too much reliance on the secondary sources, some of which contain demonstrable errors.

two miles safely ahead.[33] The *Snap Dragon* made three cruises, two to the Spanish Main and one in between those two up to Newfoundland waters. Gone six months off the Spanish Main in 1812-13, she returned to Beaufort on 10 April having captured eight vessels, three of which she divested of their most valuable cargoes and burned, three also divested of cargo and filled with prisoners to be released, and one fine copper-bottomed sloop turned into a tender and storehouse for the *Snap Dragon*. The sloop *Fillis* was captured 19 January 1813, and sent into New Bern as a prize, loaded with three thousand goatskins, ten hides, fifty mats, and thirty bushels of yams; she also brought the message that the vessel was bound for "Carthagena to victual for another cruise, all well and in good spirits on board." Two sloops and a schooner were relieved of their cargoes, including eighteen male Negro slaves.[34] Returning to Beaufort for a brief rest, the *Snap Dragon* then sailed, on 3 June 1813, for Nova Scotia and Newfoundland from whence she returned in the late summer with cargoes worth a half million dollars taken from nine prizes, and a battle with the fourteen-gun *Adonis* to her credit. Upon her arrival at Beaufort she was so laden with valuable goods that the captain and crew were sleeping on deck. The goods were auctioned at New Bern on 11 October at William Shepard's warehouse, a sale that attracted some three hundred buyers from Boston to Augusta. Realized from the sale was nearly $400,000. A brig was also sold. Prize money was paid to the original investors only, and $3,000 went to each member of the crew.[35] The *Snap Dragon* made a foray

33. "Otway Burns and the Snap Dragon," 2d ser. 4, p. 463.

34. *Edenton Gazette,* 9 Mar. 1813; *Raleigh Register,* 30 Apr. 1813; Coggeshall, *American Privateers,* p. 115; Buckner Hill to William Hawkins, 17 May 1813, Hawkins Letterbook 19, p. 219; *Carolina Federal Republican,* 27 Feb. 1813, 20 Mar. 1813, 17 Apr. 1813, 1 May 1813.

35. *Carolina Federal Republican,* 5 June 1813, 4 Sept. 1813, 11 Sept. 1813, 18 Sept. 1813; *National Intelligencer,* 28 Sept. 1813, 8 Sept. 1813, 27 Oct. 1813; *Raleigh Register,* 17 Sept. 1813; Edgar Stanton Maclay, "The Exploits of Otway Burns, Privateersman and Statesman," *United States Naval Institute Proceedings,* 42 (May-June 1916): 876, Coggeshall, *American Privateers,* pp. 126, 127, 147, 150. One William Johnson, on this cruise, was put on board a prize which was afterward recaptured by the British, and was carried to Halifax as a prisoner. There he was seen a year later by Thomas M. Barker, himself captured on the fatal cruise of the *Snap Dragon* and also carried into Halifax (Deposition by Barker, 21 June 1815, in the case of Jacob Henry, administrator of William Johnston, v. Edward Pasteur

from 20 January to 11 April 1814 to the West Indies, capturing a Swedish schooner and fighting an engagement with a British privateer of eighteen guns and seventy men; but before she could board the other vessel, an accident caused her to sheer off and the Britisher escaped.[36] The final cruise of the *Snap Dragon* began on 26 May 1814, under Captain W. R. Graham, with the citizens of New Bern expressing the fervent wish that "success attend her." Whether three schooners captured by her belong in this period or whether they were taken on the immediately preceding cruise cannot be ascertained, but the good luck did not continue. On 30 June the cruise of the *Snap Dragon* came to an abrupt end. That day she, her six guns, and her eighty men fell victim to the British sloop *Martin*, commanded by H. Flunf-Senhouse, who unfortunately did not report whether he destroyed her or carried her to port as a prize. The crew, however, was taken to Halifax, Nova Scotia.[37]

North Carolina's lack of deep-water ports had prevented her from developing into as strong a commercial state as her sisters to the north, or even South Carolina. She therefore provided fewer naval officers and fewer privateers, but a safe refuge for many small coasting vessels, open ports for privateers whose home bases were blockaded, and four privateers, the two from New Bern being especially successful. Otway Burns became a hero in some portions of the state; the town of Burnsville in the mountains is named for him; his tombstone in the cemetery at Beaufort carries a cannon barrel on it and a memorial plaque in tribute to his colorful career.

and William Shepard, Craven County, N.C., Estates Records [Johnson], NC Archives).

36. *National Intelligencer*, 27 Apr. 1814.

37. *National Intelligencer*, 16 June 1814; Coggeshall, *American Privateers*, pp. 229, 240, lists the capture by the *Snap Dragon* in 1814 of a schooner laden with mahogany, the schooner *Linnet* with fish and oil, and a third schooner which was burnt, but he does not indicate which of the two 1814 voyages accounted for these captures; *Raleigh Register*, 5 Aug. 1814. Both Walter Clark and Maclay state that the *Snap Dragon* was captured by the British frigate *Leopard*, 54 guns; Burns, *Captain Otway Burns*, pp. 52-53; Maclay, "Exploits of Otway Burns," p. 910, probably taking his information from the earlier Clark statement. However, Captain H. Flunf-Senhouse [?] of the British sloop *Martin* reported her capture to Admiral Edward Griffith, 30 June 1814, Adm 1/507, p. 63. It can only be supposed that certain persons felt it more honorable for the prestigious privateer to have necessitated a frigate to halt her career than a mere sloop carrying no more than 16 guns; probably a sailor began what later became a legend.

8 THE POLITICS OF WAR

Politics did not disappear during the war. Pleas for unity, made chiefly by the Republicans, went unheeded as far as the Federalists were concerned, both in the nation and in the state, although a few party members crossed party lines in the Congress on certain issues for specific reasons. At the state level, the pro-Madison group had such strong control of the legislature that the Federalists could chiefly engage only in sound and fury.

The elections for the Twelfth Congress seated twelve men from North Carolina, some of whom were extremely colorful personalities.[1] Only two, Macon and Stanford, had national reputations; both had been members of the anti-Madison Quids and were devoted to John Randolph of Roanoke.

Willis Alston, of Halifax, a Republican, was a nephew of Nathaniel Macon. A farmer and planter, he had attended Princeton College. His congressional career began when he was elected in 1799 as a War Democrat and he continued to be such throughout the War of 1812. During the war, he was a member of the important Ways and Means Committee. Although his uncle was a dear friend of John Randolph's, Alston

1. All general biographical information for the members of Congress in the 12th and 13th congresses may be found in U.S., Congress, House, *Biographical Directory of the American Congress, 1774-1949*, H. Doc. 607, 81st Cong., 2d sess., 1950.

feuded with Randolph from 1804 on, when they had had an altercation at the dinner table in their boardinghouse during which they threw decanters and glasses at each other. Then, in 1810, Randolph attacked Alston verbally with his notorious slashing tongue, and a year later when Alston made a remark about a "puppy" that offended Randolph, the latter attacked him with his cane and an ugly brawl ensued. Randolph wrote a friend that he was sorry about the affair for Macon's sake, although reportedly Macon too despised him.[2]

William Blackledge, Republican from Craven County, defeated Federalist John Stanly of New Bern for his post. A lawyer and a friend of John Gray Blount, Blackledge was interested in naval increases by Congress. He had served as one of the managers in 1804 to conduct the impeachment proceedings against Federalist Judge John Pickering, which indicates the depth of his political commitment to the Jeffersonian party. Blackledge was an anomaly in Federalist New Bern, and was defeated by William Gaston in the elections of 1813 after serving only one term.

General Thomas Blount, member of the large and wealthy Blount clan, and veteran of the Revolutionary War, was a merchant in Tarboro. After serving several different terms in Congress, he defeated Federalist William Kennedy for the seat in the Twelfth Congress, but died before the war vote was taken. Since a death in office had not occurred before in the state, Governor Hawkins was uncertain as to his powers of appointing a successor. Deciding that he could not, he declined and the post remained vacant until the next regular election.[3] Thus no vote was cast in Congress from this district on the declaration of war. William Kennedy, who lived in Nash County and had been defeated by Blount, was chosen his successor and immediately took his seat, thus serving a short time in the Twelfth Congress. Kennedy had attended the University of Pennsylvania and had served two previous terms in Congress.

James Cochran, a farmer who lived near the present Roxboro, North Carolina, was elected as a Republican to two

2. William Cabell Bruce, *John Randolph of Roanoke, 1773-1833,* 2 vols. (New York, 1922), 1:362-64.

3. *National Intelligencer,* 11 Feb. 1812, 30 Jan. 1813; William Kennedy to William Hawkins, 23 Jan. 1813, Hawkins Papers.

terms in Congress and died at the end of his second term, in 1813. He spoke little in the war Congress, possibly because of failing health. Meshack Franklin also was a faithful party member, voting regularly and attending at all times, but he was not effective. A Republican from Surry County, he served in Congress from 1807 to 1815, and was then succeeded by another member of his party.

William Rufus King, a Republican from Sampson County, had attended the University of North Carolina and served as city solicitor in Wilmington. After serving in Congress from 1811 to 1816 as a strong supporter of the war, he moved to Alabama where he became United States senator and in 1852 was elected vice-president of the United States, an office he did not live to fill. Mrs. William Winston Seaton recalled his appearance in 1812 when he attended one of President Madison's dinner parties in Washington. Mr. King, she said, "came to our side *sans ceremonie,* and gayly chatted with us until dinner was announced." Dinner was "certainly very fine" but did not surpass "some I have eaten in Carolina." The menu included several French dishes, wine, ice cream, macaroons, preserves and cakes, almonds, raisins, pecans, apples, and pears.[4] Presumably King was quite well fed by the end of the dinner.

Archibald McBryde, a native of Scotland, was a farmer who also practiced law in Moore County. Although he served two terms in Congress as a Republican, he was against the war, voted with the Federalists, and was a leader of the Peace party movement. Seeing that he could make no impression on the war-minded House of Representatives, he declined to run in 1813 and instead was elected to the state senate for two terms. Here he was a mastermind of the antiadministration forces.

Nathaniel Macon was a student at Princeton when the Revolutionary War began. Along with other students, he served briefly as a private and then returned to North Carolina where he served in various brief military positions until the end of the war. A member of Congress from 1791 until 1828, he was a planter in Warren County who preferred to

4. Mrs. Seaton's Diary, 12 Nov. 1812, quoted in Allen Culling Clark, *Life and Letters of Dolly Madison* (Washington, D.C., 1914), pp. 138-39.

call himself a farmer, and was the political pundit of the state chiefly from sheer length of service. Jefferson consulted him on patronage, and even after he left the halls of Congress, he was revered by politicians including Martin Van Buren as well as those of his own state. Macon served seven years as Speaker of the House, but he was not caught up in the war fever, was a strict constructionist, and eventually was ousted as speaker when Madison became president. According to Mark Alexander, who knew him, Macon had no literary attainments, "being bred in the Revolution." His speeches were always "in plain language and to the purpose, with no pretension to eloquence"; but he earned a high reputation "for sound judgment and purity of character—a second George Mason."[5] He seems to have been an excellent example in American politics of "homespun wisdom, natural dignity, and the elementary virtues of courage, truthfulness, and honesty."[6] Physically of middle stature, he had "a round, shining, playful countenance, bald and gray, always dressed in the same plain but not inelegant manner, and so peculiar in his ideas and conversation, that one of the Jersey members, told him, that if he should happen to be drowned, he shoud look for Macon's body up the stream instead of floating with the current." He did not, as did Gaston and Pearson, his colleagues, attempt to persuade others to his antitaxation views, but nevertheless often cast his votes in favor of a stingy purse. As Ingersoll said, he was a "passive, not active, radical, except by example." His views were arrived at through his Old Jeffersonian philosophy of government and no argument persuaded him otherwise. Because he did not attempt to manipulate votes, he has been called a "leading follower, not a summit, but part of the mass of Congress."[7] While this may have been true for members from other parts of the Union, for North Carolinians Macon was a leader because of his great length of service and his Jeffersonian views. His influence, although often quiet, was undoubtedly strong. The editor of the *National Intelligencer* pertinently noted that his speech on the loan bill in 1814, "emanating from a man, the purity of whose motives

5. Mark Alexander to Hugh Blair Grigby, quoted in Bruce, *John Randolph*, 2:595.

6. Ibid., 1:167.

7. Ingersoll, *Historical Sketch of the Second War*, 1:209, 211, 215.

has never been seriously questioned, whose independent course, during a long term of public service, has secured to him the confidence of all parties, is entitled to the perusal and respectful attention of every man in the nation."[8]

Joseph Pearson served three terms as a Federalist from Rowan County, being turned out at the end of the war by Republican William C. Love. The son-in-law of John Steele,[9] a noted Federalist and supporter of a strong banking system, Pearson was hot tempered and controversial. He fought a duel with Representative John George Jackson of Virginia and was wounded on the second fire. When certain citizens of Mecklenburg County, a hotbed of Republicanism located in his congressional district, met to chastise him, he was extremely insulted, although his friends in Rowan County held a meeting to praise him. The Rowan resolutions were adopted and declared, over the signature of E. Frost, chairman, that Pearson should be commended for "opposing a system of injudicious and ruinous measures," for "his continued affection for and zealous support of the liberties and welfare of his country" and for his "unqualified attachment to the constitution and form of government under which we live."[10] Perhaps because of his temper and his somewhat flamboyant actions, he had less influence in the Congress than did Gaston. Colonel Jesse Pearson of the Seventh Regiment of the detached militia that participated in the Creek Indian campaign was his brother.

Israel Pickens represented the northwestern portion of the state, he himself being from Burke County. A Republican, he was the son-in-law of Revolutionary War hero and militia

8. *National Intelligencer*, 9 June 1814. Bruce compared him with Lincoln in his "goodness and tenderness of heart . . . ," *John Randolph*, 2:776. This may be illustrated in a letter from John Randolph to J. M. Garnett, Jr., 31 Dec. 1822, ". . . our old friend Mr Macon, whom I have now known for more than thirty years, grows every day upon my esteem and my affections. His innumerable, nameless little attentions and kindnesses, springing directly from the heart, shew that age has had no power in chilling his benevolent feelings" (J. M. Garnett, Jr., Manuscripts, LC). Ingersoll noted that Macon's views against banks and tariffs had prevailed by 1845 (*Historical Sketch of the Second War*, 1:217).

9. William Thornton to John Steele, 18 Apr. 1812, Steele Papers. Apparently a second marriage, Pearson wed Eleanor Brent of Washington, D.C. (Raleigh *Minerva*, 13 Dec. 1811).

10. *Raleigh Register*, 6 Nov. 1812; Raleigh *Minerva*, 6 Nov. 1812.

Major General Lenoir. A lawyer, he had attended Jefferson College in Pennsylvania. After serving three terms in Congress, following the war he moved to Alabama where he was elected governor and later United States senator. A strong supporter of the war, he wrote to his father-in-law that his policy was always to vote for the strongest measure on the floor; if that failed, to vote for the next strongest, and so on down the list until finally he would vote for the weakest rather than for no measure at all. He supported the raising of men and money to such an extent that he anticipated being defeated in the election of 1816; perhaps this influenced his decision to move to Alabama.[11] Pickens spoke frequently and forcefully on the floor of Congress; it was North Carolina's loss when men like Pickens and King moved to the newer states of the Southwest.

Lemuel Sawyer of Camden County was a Republican who served three terms in Congress. Although he has been recorded as a supporter of the war because of "national spirit," there is little basis on which to judge because his ill health forced him to obtain a leave of absence from Congress in November 1811 for the remainder of the session.[12] When he did not run for the next Congress, his place was taken by another member of the same party.

Richard Stanford, "little Stanford" as a friend called him, a Republican who served in Congress from 1797 to 1816, and was still in Congress when he died, was a schoolteacher from Orange County, a bosom friend of John Randolph even when Randolph and Macon had temporarily parted company. Of the Old Jeffersonian school, he had opposed every warlike action from 1798 on. Somewhat eccentric, he was faithful and conscientious to what he regarded as his public duty. At his death a friend wrote "that no one ever continued so long in public life less contaminated by its numerous temptations and corruptions." He literally hated war and hated any restraint upon the human mind. Gaston esteemed him highly and the two men, of opposite parties, found themselves voting together throughout the war.[13]

11. Israel Pickens to William Lenoir, 10 Jan. 1815, Lenoir Papers.
12. Adams, *History of the United States*, 5:184; *National Intelligencer*, 28 Nov. 1811, 6 Feb. 1812.
13. Bruce, *John Randolph*, 2:596-97; William Gaston to Mrs. Mary Stanford, 10 Apr. 1816, Gaston Papers, NC Archives.

The two senators were Jesse Franklin and James Turner. Franklin, a Republican from Surry County, was a good friend of William Lenoir; both men had fought together at Kings Mountain and at Guilford Court House during the Revolution. Franklin served two separate terms as senator, but following the end of his term in 1813 he did not run again, although he later became governor of the state. Although Franklin described politics in Washington to his old friend Lenoir in a number of letters, he did not express many opinions nor did he take an active part in the Senate other than to make several motions regarding Indian treaties, public lands, and similar questions unrelated to the war.[14] James Turner was from Warren County, the home of Macon, and like Macon had served as a private in the Revolutionary War. Following three years as governor of the state, he served two terms as United States senator and then resigned because of ill health. His replacement was Nathaniel Macon. Turner, like Franklin, made little mark in the Senate, although both men voted in favor of the declaration of war and of war-supportive measures.

In the Thirteenth Congress, five old faces disappeared and six new ones appeared, the state having gained one representative because of reapportionment. Only one of these, however, was a contest against an incumbent. Cochran died, Sawyer did not run because of ill health, Franklin did not run, and McBryde preferred state to national politics. The new senator was David Stone, a Republican from Bertie County, who had a distinguished record of public service. After attending Princeton, he served one term in Congress followed by a term as United States senator; governor for two years, he was elected senator in 1813 but resigned because of a violent political clash with the state legislature in 1814. The clash was one of theory: should a senator vote his best judgment or should he vote as instructed by the state legislature that had elected him? Stone trusted his own judgment and refused to conform. Having been a Federalist prior to 1798, then a Republican until 1813, Stone was so independent of spirit that he finally abandoned politics entirely rather than conform to a party platform. His votes were contrary to the wishes of his con-

14. *National Intelligencer,* 1 Jan. 1813.

stituency, yet as the *National Intelligencer* said, one could not impugn his integrity and character.[15]

One of the new faces in the House of Representatives was that of John Culpepper, a Federalist of Montgomery County who had served one term in the Tenth Congress. A replacement for McBryde, he was a country preacher who loved to make speeches and made several good ones in Congress, even though the members walked off the floor when he began to orate. An aristocratic Federalist in Fayetteville regretted that John Cameron was not elected instead, for Culpepper was good only for "log-rolling or corn shucking" in his opinion.[16]

Peter Forney, a Republican and ironmaster from Lincoln County, had served as a captain in the Revolutionary War, and was a presidential elector for Jefferson, Madison, Monroe, and Jackson. Not liking Congress particularly, he served only one term and then relinquished his seat to his son, Daniel M. Forney, who served as an officer in the regular army during the War of 1812.

William Hardee Murfree, a Republican from Chowan County, replaced the ailing Sawyer. A lawyer who practiced in Edenton, he had attended the University of North Carolina and had been a presidential elector for Madison in 1812. After two years in Congress, he declined to run, eventually moving to Tennessee where other relatives had already gone to settle.

Bartlett Yancey, a Republican from Caswell County, was also an alumnus of the University of North Carolina. A hard-working candidate for office, he left at least two interesting letters depicting campaign methods of the time. Since he replaced Republican Cochran who had died, the political representation did not change, although Yancey was a more vigorous man than Cochran had been. Yancey, later declining both a presidential appointment to serve as minister to Peru, and a seat on the state supreme court, died in 1828.

The contested seat was from the New Bern district, the race being between William Blackledge and William Gaston. The victory by Gaston changed the vote in Congress from that district, and probably more nearly represented the feelings

15. Melonie Johnson Taylor, "David Stone: A Political Biography" (Master's thesis, East Carolina University, 1968), pp. 99, 101; *National Intelligencer*, 27 Aug. 1813.

16. W. B. Grove to William Gaston, 8 July 1813, Gaston Papers, SHC.

of its leading citizens toward the administration. Gaston, a Federalist, had attended Princeton and retained his connections with fellow students for many years. His election brought congratulations from John Devereux in New York, and praise from John Randolph who said that Chief Justice John Marshall had "taught me to think highly of his abilities."[17] He did not, however, care for a legislative career, although he was reelected after the war; his greatest reputation in North Carolina was in the field of jurisprudence. A "handsome man of pleasing address and speech," he was chosen by Daniel Webster as a member of the steering committee in Congress to oppose the administration party, a committee of thirteen including Webster himself, Timothy Pickering, and Richard Stockton besides Gaston.[18] His lengthy speeches on the floor of Congress were masterpieces of learning and rhetoric. One of his opponents, John Forsyth of Georgia, once said of him, "His language is correct, gentlemanly and polished. No harsh terms deform the smoothness of his periods. It matters not, though, whether the victim is struck down by the butcher's cleaver or a glittering Spanish blade." William C. Preston recalled that after Gaston's speech refusing to assume the reins of government unless the Republicans would hand them over as they had received them from the Federalists, Madison remarked on hearing of it, "The damned rascal, I wonder how he would conduct the Government. It is easy for them to make speeches."[19] Gaston was easily the strongest Federalist in the North Carolina delegation and a tower of strength in the national party against the encroachments of war on personal rights and constitutional restraints. He possessed the greatest ability of any, either Federalist or Republican, from North Carolina; although he was unable to change anyone's

17. John Devereux to William Gaston, 27 May 1813, Gaston Papers, SHC; John Randolph to Francis Scott Key, 17 July 1813, quoted in Hugh A. Garland, *The Life of John Randolph of Roanoke*, 2 vols. in 1 (New York, 1860), 2:17.

18. Daniel Webster to Ezekiel Webster, 4 Aug. 1813, *The Private Correspondence of Daniel Webster*, ed. Fletcher Webster, 2 vols. (Boston, 1857), 1:237 (hereafter cited as *Webster Correspondence*). Schauinger, *William Gaston*, p. 70, claims too much for Gaston by calling him the leader of the Federalists in the House; he also says that Gaston served in the 2d session of the 12th Congress, whereas he was elected to the 13th Congress.

19. Schauinger, *William Gaston*, p. 75; *The Reminiscences of William C. Preston*, ed. Minnie Clare Yarborough (Chapel Hill, 1933), p. 9.

votes on the floor of Congress, he was a capable, dignified, and dynamic contender. Only Pickens and King for the administration are comparable; it would have taken a Clay or a Calhoun to have equalled him.

These were the men who fought the financial and diplomatic battles of the war in Washington as representatives of the state of North Carolina. Their struggles were almost as frustrating as were those of the military and naval forces, for the Republicans could not seem to win the war and the Federalists could not halt it.

During the months from November 1811 to June 1812 the majority of delegates to Congress from North Carolina supported war preparations, as they also did for the nearly three years of fighting. The creation of a standing army was so un-Jeffersonian that it is understandable that Old Republicans and strict constructionists should hesitate over such a reversal of philosophy. Macon preferred to raise troops in the same manner as in the Revolutionary War, a method he regarded as having been highly satisfactory. Too many new categories of troops with varying obligations and lengths of service would create discord and confusion, he rightly pointed out. An army should be "but one body, and ought to be moved but by one soul," he maintained. It also troubled him, even before a military campaign was begun, that no leader of the caliber of Washington or the Old Testament Joshua was on the scene. Before the nation went marching off to Canada, he warned, a general should be found.[20] Pickens, on the other hand, while granting that it would take a long time to prepare because of dependence on the militia, a scattered population, and freedom of discussion, replied that a military leader who could do the job would be found. King made his maiden speech in support of the army bill. As might be expected, the Federalist *Minerva* commented on King's address to the effect that "curiosity may be gratified if the understanding be not enlightened by its perusal." The *Minerva* also lamented that the administration was treating the country like a child, plunging it into the waves and letting it struggle to the shore the best way it could. Thus "it matters little whether we be

20. *Annals of Congress*, 12th Cong., 1st sess., 1811-12, p. 660; *National Intelligencer*, 21 Jan. 1812, 2 Jan. 1812.

prepared or not." When the vote was taken to create an army of 25,000 in addition to the 10,000 already in arms, and carried in the House by 94 to 34, Alston, Blackledge, Blount, Cochran, M. Franklin, King, and Pickens voted aye, and Macon, McBryde, Pearson, and Stanford voted nay.[21]

The next issue was the method of using the militia. Again, the strict constructionists believed that the militia was subject only to the call of the state authorities and could not, indeed must not, be handed over to the president. Since the duty of the militia was to protect the home state, it could not be ordered into Canada or indeed outside its own state borders. Macon promised to give the president all he asked for if the nation went to war to make that war "efficient" but he would never vote, he stated, for an unconstitutional measure. The federal government possessed the army, but the states had the militia, he said. If the states consented for the federal government to use the militia, then the states could raise no objection to any orders given to march anywhere in the world. The resulting discord between state and national authorities would break up the republic, he feared. "A nation," he concluded, "any more than a house, divided against itself cannot stand." Alston, disagreeing with his uncle, held that unless the militia could be marched out of the United States it would be "an inefficient force."[22] In the end no decision was written into the bill, with resulting conflicts when on occasion a militia unit refused to cross the boundary into enemy territory. Arms for the militia were to be assigned to the states, a logical move strongly opposed by Calhoun who wished to see arms placed directly into the hands of the militia lest certain anti-administration governors not distribute them.[23] An antiwar Federalist could see in this measure only a means of self-defense, which all approved; therefore only the most hawkish voted against it. Alston of North Carolina supported Calhoun's view, but the bill passed with all other North Carolinians voting for it, even McBryde, Pearson, and Stanford.

While the Jeffersonians could see the occasional need for

21. *National Intelligencer,* 16 Jan. 1812; Raleigh *Minerva,* 17 Jan. 1812, 31 Jan. 1812; *National Intelligencer,* 7 Jan. 1812.

22. *National Intelligencer,* 1 Feb. 1812, 6 Feb. 1812. See also Niles' *Weekly Register,* 15 Feb. 1812.

23. *National Intelligencer,* 22 Feb. 1812.

land forces to protect the nation against invasion, a navy had always been considered by them an aggressive arm and hence unsuited to the character of a republic. The resistance against building new frigates for the national defense was therefore too great to overcome. Blackledge was the only North Carolinian to take an interest in the navy; he moved the adoption of the section of the navy bill authorizing the construction of four ships of the line carrying seventy-four guns, but the question was defeated. When $200,000 was authorized to buy timber to be held ready for future use, Blackledge interested himself greatly in the quality of such timber, arguing that no provisions were included to guard against green timber, and that no basic large pieces such as the keel, stern, and beam were available. Repairs to ships improperly built would be exceedingly expensive, he noted.[24] But since North Carolina was not a great sea-faring state, and additionally was quite noticeably strict constructionist, her opposition to the naval bill was no surprise.

The party vote was more clearly evident on finances than on any other issue. Since Secretary of the Treasury Gallatin had no intention of resorting to issues of paper money to pay for war preparations and operations, only taxation and loans were available to meet the expenditures. Taxes were hard for the Republicans to swallow, for they had always preferred a parsimonious government. They had opposed the Adams administration in 1798 on the issue of taxation for a foreign war, and now found themselves in the position of having to ask for taxes for the very same purpose. Men like Stanford and Macon opposed taxes that were not clearly designed for defensive measures; Federalists objected because it was the Republicans' war and they did not wish to pay for it. While Pickens said that "I have only to regret that we have not quite promptness enough in providing efficient means" and continued by promising to persevere, saying that "by perseverance & firmness we must succeed in establishing our rights, which will make peace a real blessing," the *Minerva* pointed out that $100 each minute was being spent to run the government during the war. In only one year, the editor

24. *National Intelligencer*, 30 Jan. 1812, 21 Mar. 1812, 19 Mar. 1812, 5 Mar. 1812.

charged, was spent the entire amount that Washington and Adams had spent in twelve years. Wake County's taxes would last this voracious government only one hour, four minutes, and twenty seconds. William Thornton wrote to John Steele in doggerel:

> How we shall bear it all I cannot tell
> But this my Friend I really know full well
> We wish the War & tax-men all in hell.

Culpepper stated plainly his objection to paying taxes for any war not for the mutual benefit of the entire nation; this war was not for the purpose of repelling foreign invasion or maintaining domestic tranquility, and therefore the taxes to support it were unconstitutional. Macon found that he could not with good conscience vote for all the taxes, although most he did indeed support. A tabulation of votes in the House on sixteen items of war taxation reveals that three Republicans, M. Franklin, King, and Pickens, had perfect records in support, while one Federalist, Pearson, had a perfect record in opposition. Macon voted nay three times, as did Cochran; McBryde voted nay twelve times, and Stanford thirteen. Lack of a perfect voting record in support for Alston and Blackledge was due to absences.[25] The only proposed tax that produced a disagreement other than over the party line was that on salt. King, whose district included salt-producing Wilmington, moved to instruct the Committee on Commerce and Manufacturing to inquire into the expediency of a tax on imported salt, hoping that such a tax would encourage home manufacture. Blackledge also supported the salt tax on the same grounds, the encouragement of manufacturing. Both Stanford and Macon disapproved for that very reason: no tax should be levied for the purpose of encouraging infant industry, as this was discrimination and hence unconstitutional. Citizens on the coast would not be affected by the tax, said Stanford, whereas those in the interior would be hurt by higher prices; this was therefore a geographical tax and thus discriminatory. "People on the seacoast," said Macon, "would

25. Israel Pickens to William Lenoir, 20 Dec. 1814, Lenoir Papers; Raleigh *Minerva*, 8 Apr. 1814; William Thornton to John Steele, 8 Oct. 1813, Steele Papers; *Annals of Congress*, 13th Cong., 1st sess., 1813, pp. 410, 412; *National Intelligencer*, 29 Feb. 1812, 7 Mar. 1812.

not feel it. . . . The interior of the country would have to bear the weight of this tax." He was not willing to tax the North Carolina "sandhill" people to support King's "sandbank" constituents. Unwilling to engage in a struggle with Macon, King withdrew his motion. Following an initial defeat, the tax the next day was approved by the House, with Alston, Blackledge, M. Franklin, King, and Pickens voting in the majority and Cochran, Macon, McBryde, Pearson, and Stanford in the minority.[26]

Although Senator Turner and Senator Franklin supported the administration's war taxes, not so when Stone replaced Franklin. Stone opposed the war taxes of 1813 on distillers, sugar refined in the United States, sales at auctions, the direct tax, the retail liquor tax, and the import duties on salt.[27] Resident of a strongly prowar section of the state, as well as representative of the proadministration legislature of North Carolina, Stone found himself more and more the object of obloquy until his opposition to war measures culminated in a resolution of censure passed by the general assembly.

The second method of raising funds was through loans, more difficult to float since the Bank of the United States had expired than the task would otherwise have been. Three loan bills were passed: one each in 1812, 1813, and 1814; a final one was passed following the treaty of peace but not executed. The first loan, a bill for $11,000,000, was opposed by Pearson and Stanford, McBryde not voting, and that of 1813 opposed by McBryde, with Pearson and Stanford not voting. Most of the Republicans from the state recognized the necessity of raising funds and followed the administration's lead.[28] When Gaston joined Congress, however, the vitality of the opposition increased and others joined him in bitterly debating the loan bill of 1814. Pearson in a lengthy speech on the subject declared that it was impossible to raise the requested $30,000,-000 because the nation's credit was "a tottering fabric." Gaston, whose speech was eagerly awaited by Daniel Webster, de-

26. *National Intelligencer,* 23 Nov. 1811, 29 Feb. 1812; *Annals of Congress,* 12th Cong., 1st sess., 1811-12, pp. 113, 360-61; *National Intelligencer,* 3 Mar. 1812.

27. *Annals of Congress,* 13th Cong., 1st sess., 1813, pp. 58, 59, 65, 68.

28. *National Intelligencer,* 27 Feb. 1812; *Annals of Congress,* 12th Cong., 2d sess., 1812-13, p. 907.

livered a masterpiece of opposition to the war, presenting, according to one who heard it, "so much good sense, useful information, sound reasoning, and genuine eloquence. . . ." Both men ran the gamut from the invasion of Canada to the machinations of France and the stupidity of the Madison administration through the futility of dreaming that the United States could possibly defeat the mistress of the seas. Macon and Yancey replied, with Macon dwelling on the improved military picture on the Canadian front and Yancey delivering "a very neat speech of more than an hour in length" in support. Nine representatives from the state voted aye, with only Culpepper, Pearson, and Stanford present and voting nay. It was obviously useless for the Federalists and antiwar men to hope to stem the tide; unable to turn it prior to 18 June 1812, certainly they could not do so in the midst of a conflict, but they continued to speak and to vote as often as they could get the floor. Gaston was always listened to with respect and enthusiasm, even by his opponents, but Culpepper had his audience walk out on him at least once. His speech was not a poor one, but his subject had become one of tiresome reiteration by 1814. The administration paper, the *National Intelligencer,* asked attention to Gaston's remarks, saying that his speech against the loan bill had "plausibility and ingenuity, though we deny the claims of the orator to correctness either in his premises or his conclusions."[29]

Opponents of the war were unable to do more than provide foils against other wartime problems. The best of them, as Gaston, served in the role of a loyal opposition; the worst were self-interested politicians. As a resident of Iredell County remarked, the best talent was on their side, but they were no better than prisoners because "our modern majorities" would not listen to reason. Citizens of Lexington, North Carolina, toasted them in 1814: "The minority of the last Congress:—

29. *Annals of Congress,* 13th Cong., 2d sess., 1813-14, pp. 1,447-70, 1,542-76; Daniel Webster to Ezekiel Webster, 5 Feb. 1814, remarked that Gaston and Grosvenor were prepared to give "great speeches" on the loan bill (*Webster Correspondence,* 1:240-41); James Robertson to William Gaston, 24 May 1814, Gaston Papers, SHC; *Annals of Congress,* 13th Cong., 2d sess., 1813-14, p. 1,370, ". . . the House adjourned (38 to 38, the Speaker deciding in the affirmative) before Mr. Culpepper finished his speech, which is given entire"; *National Intelligencer,* 16 June 1814, 21 Feb. 1814, 4 Mar. 1814, 16 Mar. 1814.

Their conduct suited the times, decidedly superior in intellect and eloquence, their friends must admire their bold and manly exposition of the wickedness and imbecility of our rulers."[30] They attacked most strongly the invasion of Canada and upheld freedom of speech in wartime. Indeed the lack of the latter limited what they could say about the former, for freedom of speech was restricted by the majority. The use of the device of the previous question, first begun in 1810, was a powerful tool in the hands of Clay and the supporters of the administration. When Stanford, for instance, tried to debate the Senate amendments to the embargo, the previous question was called for and an affirmative vote prevented his speaking.[31] As the sessions of Congress wore on, more and more there was a refusal to debate issues. Gaston's resolutions in 1814 to consider repealing the wartime embargo were rejected by a vote not to consider. Stanford accused the war party of railroading its program through just as much as had the Federalists in 1798. All that was lacking for complete similitude was a Sedition Act. When petitions sent to Congress asking for greater protection by the general government became so frequent that Congress declined to hear them, Gaston raged. He hoped that "the time would never come when, to speak the language of truth, or to hear it spoken, would be incompatible with the respect due to the Legislature." Although he, together with Macon, Pearson, and Stanford, voted to print the Maryland petition which had provoked these remarks, the motion lost by sixty-eight to ninety-two. Felix Grundy of Tennessee strongly insinuated that any opposition to the war was equivalent to moral treason, to which Pearson and Gaston replied indignantly. The doctrine that, once war is declared, all must volunteer their aid or be guilty of moral treason was pernicious, said Pearson in one of his finest speeches. Such a view would destroy all our rights and could not be tolerated. "Let this doctrine be once established, an ambitious Executive, and a weak, a wicked, or interested majority of Congress have nothing to do but declare war, under any pretence, or for any cause or object, however unimportant, or however destructive of our best interests, we

30. Raleigh *Minerva*, 5 Feb. 1813, 22 July 1814.
31. *National Intelligencer*, 7 Apr. 1812.

will be bound to strengthen the arm lifted for our destruction
—join in acclaim of praise to our destroyers, or sit by, in silent
anguish, awaiting the death-blow to our Constitution, and
with it our liberties as a people." The *Minerva* cheered those
who "stood as a fence between the people and the oppressive
strides of their unworthy rulers."[32]

Pearson and Gaston joined other Federalists in criticizing
the invasion of Canada. What to do, asked Pearson, if Canada
is conquered? "Do they mean to plant their standard on the
walls of Quebec, apportion out the lands to the conquerors,
and sing a requiem to 'free trade and sailors' rights?'" Such
a conquest, Gaston pointed out, "is never finished; when nom-
inally effected, it is to be begun." On a less elevated level
newspapers descended to rough sarcasm in attacking the administration. Reporting an American defeat in Canada the
Minerva wrote: "General Van Rensselaer attacked Queenston
—pushed the enemy; fought well; won the battle; enemy's
reinforcements arrived; Militia read the Constitution: refused
to cross—victors fled—boatsmen run away—all was lost; all
surrendered but were soon paroled."[33]

On the other hand, while the majority listened politely to
men of integrity, it agreed with Pickens who told his constituents that "those brave soldiers have triumphed through
all the errors of their commanders; and, under better auspices,
must promise certain success."[34] Efforts by the Federalists to
initiate congressional investigations of the conduct of the war
in Canada hoping to discredit the administration failed to
achieve their ends because the committee appointed to investigate the atrocities of the war, of which Macon was chairman and Gaston a member, turned into a denunciation of
British and Indian atrocities rather than a two-pronged impartial investigation. Indeed, the Federalists should never have
supposed that there would be any other kind of investigation
during a war. The detached militia was considered a draft by

32. *Annals of Congress*, 13th Cong. 2d sess., 1813-14, p. 1,868; *National
Intelligencer*, 20 Feb. 1812; *Annals of Congress*, 13th Cong., 2d sess., 1813-
14, p. 1,220; ibid., 13th Cong., 1st sess., 1813, pp. 285-86; Raleigh *Minerva*,
13 Aug. 1813.
33. *Annals of Congress*, 13th Cong., 2d sess., 1813-14, pp. 1,453-54, 1,569;
Raleigh *Minerva*, 8 Jan. 1813.
34. Israel Pickens, *Letter to His Constituents* (Washington, D.C., 1813),
unpaged.

Gaston, a crime to free men further compounded by sending them "abroad as military machines, to wage a war of conquest!" Former North Carolinian William R. Davie, a member of the Constitutional Convention of 1787, corresponded with Gaston and others on this subject, suggesting that no state would have ratified the Constitution had such a power been specifically stated.[35]

Federalists also voted against the wartime embargo and the confirmation of Gallatin as a peace envoy, and further attempted to embarrass the administration by charging that Madison had concealed a letter from the French government that would have exonerated Britain and incriminated France. The greatest supporter of the embargo was Macon, who implicitly believed that this Jeffersonian device would have prevented war in the past and was the key to peace in the future. On principle Culpepper, Pearson, and Stanford opposed it, and gleefully joined in the motion to repeal in 1814. Hoping to embarrass the administration, they took delight in voting with Alston, Kennedy, and King to abolish the very embargo that only a year before had been laid. Macon and Yancey held to the principle of embargo and refused to compromise, but they were defeated. The editor of the *Minerva* laughed at the sight of the Republicans scampering to do the president's bidding, even if it meant that they must admit their embargo to have been a failure. Efforts by John Randolph in the Twelfth Congress and by the Federalists including Gaston in the Thirteenth Congress to involve Madison in a lengthy dispute over French influence failed; Blackledge moved to postpone consideration of Randolph's motion, and Gaston's was tabled. On the question of Gallatin's confirmation as an envoy extraordinary to the peace commission, Stone voted to reject; since Gallatin lost by one vote, eighteen to seventeen, it is obvious that had Stone supported the administration as the North Carolina legislature desired him to do, Gallatin

35. Barlow, "Congress during the War of 1812," p. 27; Raleigh *Minerva*, 6 Aug. 1813; the *Minerva* editor, 20 Aug. 1813, charged Macon with using every newspaper report and rumor for electioneering purposes; Ingersoll, *Historical Sketch of the Second War*, 1:205-8; in *Annals of Congress*, 13th Cong., 2d sess., 1813-14, p. 1,559, Gaston condemned atrocities of the Canadian invasion, and the principle of retaliation; ibid., pp. 1,567-68; William R. Davie to William Gaston, 27 Nov. 1814, William R. Davie Papers, typescript, 2:98, NC Archives.

would have been confirmed.[36] In summation, the opposition from North Carolina produced some excellent arguments and fine speeches, but influenced no important measures except the confirmation of Gallatin.

In North Carolina two important national elections were held during the war: the presidential election of 1812 and the congressional election of 1813. As soon as it was evident early in 1812 that war would come, Federalists and antiwar men began to construct a Peace party in the state. John Steele, in February 1812, prophesied a new president in the November election. Vigorously corresponding with those of like mind, he promoted DeWitt Clinton as a replacement for Madison, believing that the Federalists in North Carolina would support him even though he was a Republican. William R. Davie used his influence in North Carolina in favor of Clinton, not only because of the war but because he wished to break the Virginia monopoly on the presidency. The *Minerva* too was pro-Clinton. An invitation to attend a pro-Clinton caucus in New York was received by William Boylan of Raleigh, but apparently no North Carolinians attended. Benjamin Stoddert, however, urged Steele to consider John Marshall instead; he thought North Carolina would vote for a southerner in preference to Clinton even though he might be a Federalist, and he believed Marshall would be personally more acceptable. Boylan advised Steele to consider carefully the consequences of nominating a Republican like Clinton who would draw from Madison votes of people who would never vote for a Federalist, as against the personal dislike for Clinton held by such Orange County leaders as Archibald D. Murphey and Duncan Cameron who might prefer to support a Federalist. Optimistically Boylan estimated the Peace party's strength in the state legislature at eighty-seven votes, possibly ninety-nine; had he been correct, the Peace party would have controlled the legislature if he meant the House of Commons. If he meant both House and Senate, it would have constituted a sizeable block; however, he had sadly overestimated. Such discussion led Madison to evaluate the North Carolina sit-

36. *Annals of Congress*, 13th Cong., 1st sess., 1813, pp. 85, 86, 89, 100-101, 1,364, 1,369; ibid., 2d sess., 1813-14, pp. 510-11, 920, 1,130-31, 1,167; *National Intelligencer,* 21 Dec. 1813, 23 Dec. 1813, 8 Apr. 1814; Raleigh *Minerva,* 15 Apr. 1814.

uation as "in considerable vibration." Madison, however, safely won the state's electoral votes and the prowar governor, William Hawkins, was reelected. Unable to accept the defeat gracefully, the *Minerva* accused the Republicans of buying votes, gave publicity to a charge that the military interfered in the election in Edenton where the Republicans won by only four votes, and described election day symbolically as gloomy and overcast.[37]

Congressmen were not elected at this time, however, except for Blount's replacement. Since the Thirteenth Congress was not scheduled to convene until December 1813, unless a special session were to be held, North Carolina set the election for August 1813, thus separating it from the presidential election. When Madison called for a special session to meet on the fourth Monday in May 1813, the elections were then held in April. The Peace party attempted to put candidates in the field against each of the administration's supporters where there was a chance of defeating him, and to support men like Stanford whom the Republicans hoped to oust. McBryde, choosing not to run for reelection, suggested that party did not matter as long as the candidate was for peace. William Polk asked Gaston to find opponents for King and Sawyer. Polk also urged Steele to get out the vote for the peace candidate running against Yancey in Stokes County. "Do for Gods sake & our countries write to some of our friends in Guilford & Rockinham [*sic*] who have it in their power, to bestir themselves in [James] Martin's favor," he pleaded. Duncan Cameron and Archibald Murphey supported Stanford against the "War-party" in Raleigh; Stanford did not carry Raleigh and Wake County, but was reelected in the district by a margin of 918 votes. Yancey was chosen from Rockingham, "which is far gone with the war fever," noted the *Minerva*. Pearson squeaked by with a majority of 417; Culpepper defeated another Federalist by 300; the big victory was that of

37. John Steele to ———, first draft, 23 Feb. 1812, Steele Papers; Steele to Joseph Pearson, 31 Aug. 1812, *Steele Papers*, 2:679-82; William R. Davie to ———, 15 Oct. 1812, quoted in Hamilton, *William Richardson Davie*, p. 73; Raleigh *Minerva*, 11 Sept. 1812; William Boylan to Steele, 5 Sept. 1812, Steele Papers; Benjamin Stoddert to Steele, 3 Sept. 1812, *Steele Papers*, 2:682-86; James Madison to Thomas Jefferson, 14 Oct. 1812, *Madison Writings*, 2:550; Adams, *History of the United States*, 6:414; *Raleigh Register*, 27 Nov. 1812; Raleigh *Minerva*, 11 Sept. 1812, 4 Dec. 1812.

Gaston who won over Blackledge by 1,000 votes.[38] The administration supporters lost one vote in Congress, but this was offset by the addition of a new district that returned a Republican. There was still hope expressed by the Federalists in 1814 and 1815 that they could win control of the state. Gaston and John Stanly were urged by A. C. Hanson to "brush up the N. C. Fed. Rep. By taking advantage of circumstances & the times [the first defeat of Napoleon] you may get the State with you." Murphey was likewise urged to get some good Federalists to run for office. "With proper exertions there must be a Federal majority in the Legislature. In Edenton & Halifax Districts there will be a considerable addition of Federalists," thought P. Browne. Davie's hope that the disasters of the war would turn the people against the Republicans was dashed, however, by the victories in the late fall of 1814 and especially by Jackson's victory at New Orleans.[39] The Federalists never gained control of the state.

The state legislature was also a battleground of politics, revolving chiefly around two arguments: to what degree the state should spend its own money in defense, and whether the legislature had the power to censure its elected senator.

A tabulation of persons voting consistently in opposition to financing the war, expressing confidence in the national government, and censuring Senator Stone, reveals that a hard core of fourteen men in the state senate and thirty-nine in the house were opposed to the national and the state administrations. Among the leaders of this opposition were Archibald McBryde, William Bodenhamer of Rowan County, John Hinton, Jr., of Wake County, and Archibald Murphey of Orange County in the senate, and Jesse Pearson in the house. Gaston in the session of 1812, Thomas Ruffin in 1813,

38. *National Intelligencer,* 2 Jan. 1813; James Turner to William Hawkins, 26 Feb. 1813, Hawkins Papers; Israel Pickens to Hawkins, 25 Feb. 1813, ibid.; Jesse Franklin to Hawkins, 25 Feb. 1813, ibid.; William Polk to William Gaston, 23 Mar. 1813, Gaston Papers, SHC; Polk to John Steele, 27 Mar. 1813, *Steele Papers,* 2:706-8; Duncan Cameron to Archibald D. Murphey, 1 Apr. 1813, *Murphey Papers,* 1:68; Bartlett Yancey to Thomas Ruffin, — Mar. 1813, 2 Apr. 1813, Ruffin Papers, contains a description of campaign techniques; Raleigh *Minerva,* 7 May 1813.

39. A. C. Hanson to William Gaston, 12 June 1814, Gaston Papers, SHC; P. Browne to Archibald D. Murphey, 11 Apr. 1815, Murphey Papers; Blackwell P. Robinson, *William R. Davie* (Chapel Hill, 1957), p. 389.

and John Stanly in the sessions of 1814 and 1815 were other outstanding figures.[40] Such was their strength that a resolution supporting the president but requesting greater coastal protection could not be passed in 1813 until the statement of support was greatly watered down. Both the house and the senate in 1812 refused to authorize the governor to purchase arms and munitions to defend the state. The following session was able by a narrow majority to permit a loan of $50,000, if needed, to supply the defense needs of the militia. By 1814 the depressing situation persuaded the legislature to supply money for tents, arms, and clothing for the militia on duty, although an attempt was made to table the bill. Criticism of a brigadier general of the militia on active service in the form of a petition for his removal was indefinitely postponed.[41] The gradual growth of support for the prosecution of the war at the state level reflects the dissipation of an initial fear that the governor might become a tyrant if granted too much power; the needs of a desperate situation finally overcame a reluctance dating from the colonial period and reflected in the constitution of the state.

The case of Senator David Stone was the most spectacular conflict between the pro- and antiadministration forces. Because of Stone's adverse votes in the United States Senate, a memorial was presented to the North Carolina senate to question his political behavior. By a vote of only thirty to twenty-five, a committee was appointed to investigate his conduct. This committee brought in a resolution that " the said David Stone hath disappointed the reasonable expectations, and incurred the general disapprobation of this General Assembly." A motion to recommit failed; a motion to postpone indefinitely failed; the senate thereupon adopted the resolution by a vote of forty to eighteen. But the struggle was not over, for Murphey brought in a protest signed by fourteen senators charging that the legislature had no right to censure Stone. The protest

40. *N.C. Senate Journals, 1811-15, passim; N. C. House Journals, 1811-15, passim.*

41. Key votes may be found in *N.C. Senate Journal, 1812,* p. 49; ibid., *1813,* pp. 15, 40; ibid., *1814,* pp. 21, 39; and in *N.C. House Journal, 1812,* pp. 56, 59, 62, 65; ibid., *1813,* p. 20. See also John Stanly, *Speech in the North Carolina House of Commons, December 1815* (Privately printed, 1816).

was rejected.[42] In the house the pro-Stone leadership of Jesse Pearson marshaled thirty-nine votes in Stone's favor against seventy-six for censure. A petition was also brought to the house maintaining that the assembly had no right to censure, bearing many distinguished names including John Stanly, Duncan Cameron, James Iredell, Jr., William Boylan, and John Steele. The petition, like that in the senate, was overridden. The basic argument in favor of censure was that the people had a right to approve or disapprove the conduct of their public servants. Since Stone's votes were "in direct submission to the enemy and in countenance of those who fed the British ships on our coast," the assembly felt it was justified. The argument against the right to censure was that the United States Senate was intended as an anchor and a ballast against the storms of public opinion. A senator represented the entire nation, and must vote for the good of all, not for one state alone. Therefore it was "neither constitutional nor expedient" to censure Stone. The Senate, said Steele, must be independent and beyond the passions of the moment.[43] Although censured, Stone declined to resign his seat, waiting instead until another election in the hopes that the general assembly would reflect a change of viewpoint. When it appeared, after the 1814 election, that such an event had not occurred, Stone resigned on 21 November. His letter of resignation explained that he had not been so much opposed to the war as to the extravagant way in which it was waged and the taxes that were levied therefor. His resignation was accepted promptly, followed by a struggle to replace him. At the beginning the chief candidates were John Stanly, Jesse Franklin, and Israel Pickens. But as ballot after ballot was taken with no majority, other names were offered until finally, three days before the end of the session, Francis Locke was elected to the unexpired term.[44]

The language of politics was extremely colorful. Appeals for unity, although appropriate, were seldom heeded. The

42. *N.C. Senate Journal, 1813,* pp. 16, 27-28, 45-46.

43. *N.C. House Journal, 1813,* pp. 42-44, 52; Raleigh *Minerva,* 3 Dec. 1813, 10 Dec. 1813; Niles' *Weekly Register,* 29 Jan. 1814.

44. *Raleigh Register,* 9 Dec. 1814; *N.C. House Journal, 1814,* pp. 19-20; *N.C. Senate Journal, 1814,* p. 40; Montfort Stokes to Israel Pickens, 12 Dec. 1814, RG 94, M 566.

editor of the *Star*, who attempted to steer an impartial course, asked that every citizen contribute to the success of the war, "whatever may be his opinion of its policy." However, bitterness was only too common on both sides of the political fence. As John Randolph wrote to Stanford, "This war, my old comrade, has been, in most of its features, *a civil war—* . . . It has rent the nation in twain,—it has dissolved the oldest friendships,—it has severed the ties of blood." The administration, Sam Mordecai told his sister, had "deeply tarnished the honor of the nation and now they are endeavouring to wash out the stain with blood." A "war prayer" that appears to be a forerunner of the famous prayer by Mark Twain at the time of the Civil War was written for "Porteus" to the *Minerva*: After asking God to help America tear down and destroy, to slaughter the enemy, it concluded: "Thou, who has made of one blood *all* the dwellers upon the earth, we trust *thou* wilt view us *alone* with partial favor, and enable us to bring misery and destruction upon our fellow-creatures!" With ridicule a fictitious Atlas Jones laughed at the militia that rushed to the defense of New Bern in July 1813. "I hope 'ere this reaches Raleigh, Most Redoubted Warriors, you will have made your triumphal entry into that capital. The very terror of your names has compelled the enemy to retire. . . . Now O Warriors! will your return to Raleigh be celebrated by all the Notable Housewives in 5 miles round the city; for by the terror of your names, the sound of hostile arms will not disturb the repose of henroosts of Raleigh." Pearson called the war "impolitic and disastrous," spoke of Madison's "high toned despotism," and claimed that the "alleged objects" of the war were not won by the peace treaty. When Gaston was charged with being an opportunist, he retorted that he had always been anxious "to discover some measure of the majority, which a regard for the welfare of his country, and a respect for the dictates of his conscience, would permit him to support." He feared, however, that there were no such measures. The army was "hastily collected, badly equipped, and under the guidance of weak and distracted councils," he correctly charged.[45] Invective was not the sole property of the Fed-

45. Raleigh *Star*, 26 June 1812; John Randolph to Richard Stanford, 9 Apr. 1814, Garnett Manuscripts; Samuel Mordecai to Rachel Mordecai, 4

eralists, however. To John Gray Blount, James Taylor wrote from Washington, D.C.: "What a War!! Poisoning of Wells—is nothing to this—Yet the New Bern Gentry—the factious Bostonians—and all the rest of the chaste Regents subjects—will say tis a Glorious thing—G—damn them—." Israel Pickens attacked the New Englanders' attitude against the war in a letter to Lenoir: "A majority of them would sell their birthright independence, if not for a *mess of pottage,* at least for its value in cash; so entirely have they degenerated into a nation of pedlars & speculators."[46]

There was more opposition to this war than to any other in the history of the nation prior to 1960. Approximately one-fourth of the North Carolina congressional delegation and one-third of the state legislature were antiwar. Partly this was due to the fact that, for the first time, a war was being waged by the republic under its untried Constitution, so that neither Congress, the executive, nor the army knew exactly how it might be carried on. Partly it was due to the change from a Jeffersonian states' rights attitude to the beginnings of a strong nationalistic spirit, from the old Revolutionary generation that feared executive power to the new generation that saw means to utilize such power for the benefit of a growing country and sometimes, to be sure, for its own benefit as well. Party lines were crossed by individuals, but for the most part the opposition was engaged in a losing battle against the new nation, until, worn and frustrated, it collapsed.

Aug. 1814, Mordecai Papers; Raleigh *Minerva,* 27 Aug. 1813; Atlas Jones to the editors of the *Star,* 13 Aug. 1813, Calvin Jones Papers; Joseph Pearson, *Circular* (Washington, D.C., 1815), pp. 1-16; *Annals of Congress,* 13th Cong., 2d sess. 1813-14, p. 1,136; William Gaston, *Circular* (Washington, D.C., 1815), pp. 1-11.

46. James Taylor to John Gray Blount, 8 June 1813, Blount Papers; Israel Pickens to William Lenoir, 20 Feb. 1814, Lenoir Papers.

9 *THE HOME FRONT*

The home front during the war was unorganized and in many instances untouched by the war. Those who lived near army camps, the capital city, or the coast, of course, were only too well aware that a war was going on; but far away events hardly touched the people until many weeks after their occurrence because of the slowness with which news traveled. As Israel Pickens reminded his constituents, North Carolina was remote from the fighting, and he might well have added, from other impacts of war. "And although our brave yeomanry would anxiously share with their fellow-citizens of other parts in the glory of resisting their country's foes, their situation will probably exempt them from any other participation in the evils of war than their portion of its expense."[1]

Vicariously, however, the citizens shared in the glories and the defeats of their armies and navies. Following Hull's surrender at Detroit, the citizens of Greensboro burned him in effigy. The slightest victory brought rejoicing to counteract the blow of Hull's crushing defeat, so that raids by Forsyth's riflemen were treated by Carolinians as if they were great conquests. Real victories were to come, however, both on land and on the sea. The *Minerva* exulted over naval victories especially because the officers were often Federalists. The editor toasted

1. Pickens, *Letter to His Constituents,* unpaged.

the infant navy on 4 July 1813 thus: "It has astonished, and will continue to astonish the World, by its unexampled Intrepidity and Valour." Perry's victory on Lake Erie produced great rejoicing, both in Raleigh and in Salisbury, among other places. Salisbury staged a parade, applauded Wellborn's Tenth Regiment encamped there, and "handsomely illuminated" the town with a transparency near the center decorated with emblems and mottoes. When William Henry Harrison defeated Brigadier General Thomas Proctor and his Indians, Fayetteville illuminated until 10:00 P.M. and also discharged eighteen rounds of artillery. A dinner at Casso's Tavern in Raleigh brought together a number of men to celebrate victories, with no politics allowed. "Accompanied with appropriate songs and music," toasts were offered. Macdonough's defeat of the British on Lake Erie brought forth at Raleigh a federal salute (one gun for each state in the union) in honor of the news. When the Baltimoreans at Fort McHenry repulsed the British assault, even the *Minerva* praised the coolness, reliance on each other, and faith in their officers of the citizens of that city. It was satisfactory, indeed, wrote Rachel Mordecai to her brother, "to find that *all* Americans have not totally degenerated." Large headlines announced the "GREAT VICTORY" over the Creek Indians and the "GLORIOUS NEWS!" of Jackson's achievement at New Orleans.[2]

Despondency was a darker thread, however, which wove in and out of the optimistic attitudes displayed. The British occupation of Washington and the destruction of the Capitol seemed a blow from which the young nation could hardly recover honorably. "We have the painful duty of informing our readers . . . ," began the *Raleigh Register* on 2 September 1814. "Oceans of Blood can hardly Wash out the foul stain upon our character," grieved Lieutenant Colonel Hamilton, "can hardly compensate for the shameful abandonment of our Capitol—." Ellen Mordecai was "thunderstruck" by the "distressing information." She hoped that President Madison

2. *Raleigh Register*, 2 Oct. 1812; Raleigh *Minerva*, 8 Jan. 1813, 9 July 1813; *Raleigh Register*, 1 Oct. 1813; *North Carolina Magazine* 1, no. 3 (October 1813): 96; *American*, 22 Oct. 1813; *Raleigh Register*, 29 Oct. 1813; Raleigh *Minerva*, 24 Sept. 1814; Rachel Mordecai to Samuel Mordecai, 19 Sept. 1814, Pattie Mordecai Collection, NC Archives; *Raleigh Register*, 15 Apr. 1814, 10 Feb. 1815.

was not "reclining on his velvet couch" when the British came, to which her sister Rachel added, "Shame, grief, and indignation." Either "our rulers" were traitors, or they trusted the British to be cowards or clement. She urged her country "to repulse the foe, to bury them in our sands, or drive them back into the ocean." Viewing the city upon his return to it on 5 September, Israel Pickens told Lenoir that the nation must keep on fighting "with increased energy." While Virginia ladies refugeed to Warrenton to escape the anticipated British assault, James Vaughan of Williamsboro proposed that six thousand men over forty-five years of age be formed into a home guard to protect North Carolina. Colonel Wellborn hastily wrote to the adjutant general from Wilkesboro asking to have an active share in repelling the enemy, if it were true that the capital city had been captured; while Colonel William Polk, who had previously declined a federal commission as brigadier general, offered his services.[3] The burning of the Capitol was a catalyst that produced greater enthusiasm for the war than had existed at any time before in North Carolina.

The loss of the federal city was quickly followed by news of the Hartford Convention and of unacceptable British terms at the peace negotiations in Ghent. The clouds of gloom deepened for many, with desperation setting in. Archibald Murphey believed that "the Government is upon the Brink of Dissolution. . . . The Public Credit is gone, and I fear there are not Talents in the Administration or in Congress to revive and reestablish it. . . . My Spirits are depressed. I see nothing but Ruin and Confusion before us." Wrote Stanly to Gaston, "Many of our most enlightened and patriotic friends I find affected by the despondency, almost *despair* of our national concerns which so deeply fastens on your mind." "I admit you are not alone," Pickens replied to Lenoir in January 1815, "in your fears for the annihilation of our government; many of our men here [Washington, D.C.] are almost despairing."

3. *Raleigh Register*, 2 Sept. 1814; William S. Hamilton to T. J. Robeson, 9 Sept. 1814, Hamilton Papers; Ellen Mordecai to Samuel Mordecai, 28 Aug. 1814, Mordecai Papers; Israel Pickens to William Lenoir, 25 Sept. 1814, Lenoir Papers; Ellen Mordecai to Samuel Mordecai, 30 Aug. 1814, Mordecai Papers; Raleigh *Minerva*, 16 Sept. 1814; James Wellborn to Adjutant General, 8 Sept. 1814, RG 94, M 566; Niles's *Weekly Register*, 29 Oct. 1814.

"*If* 'out of evil cometh good,'" wrote Rachel Mordecai to her brother, "how happy we shall be when this heavy cloud passes over." The *Minerva* referred to the "odious propositions of the enemy" and demanded that "a vigorous and determined prosecution of the war" be made by way of reply. The peace terms offered by Britain would negate everything the United States had asserted it was fighting for. The editor continued to hope, however, that the Democrats would receive the blame for the unacceptable peace terms and that the Federalists would return to power on a wave of disillusionment with the pusillanimous, arrogant, miserable, futile administration. Pickens, too, although of opposite party, thought hardly of the British demands. They were equal, in his opinion, to "*unconditional submission*." America would never agree, but would "rise in its undivided strength."[4]

Although the *Minerva* declared that the war was not popular in North Carolina, asserting that it could "certainly not be said to be inflamed with the war fever," it seemed that Raleigh at least was so inflamed. When war was declared, some Raleigh citizens fired off seventeen shots from a field piece to mark the occasion. Days of prayer when called for by the president were observed in the state capitol in becoming and proper manner. Young ladies of Scotland Neck formed a knitting circle to make stockings for the troops in Canada, even though no Red Cross existed to organize them. The students at the state university at Chapel Hill were so warlike that they decorated the pro-Federalist president's gatepost with tar and feathers and sent him a fiery note signed by "an Enemy to Hypocrisy."[5] The Moravians in Wachovia, pacifists by religion, maintained an attitude of prayerful seeking for peace. On days of humiliation and prayer they "urgently besought the Ruler over all to bring peace again to the

4. Archibald D. Murphey to Thomas Ruffin, 24 Nov. 1814, *Murphey Papers*, 1:76; Israel Pickens to William Lenoir, 10 Jan. 1815, Lenoir Papers; John Stanly to William Gaston, 11 Nov. 1814, Gaston Papers, SHC; Rachel Mordecai to Samuel Mordecai, — Sept. 1814, Pattie Mordecai Collection; Raleigh *Minerva*, 21 Oct. 1814, 4 Nov. 1814; Pickens to Lenoir, 12 Oct. 1814, Lenoir Papers.

5. Raleigh *Minerva*, 4 Sept. 1812, 26 June 1812; *Raleigh Register*, 10 Sept. 1813; Raleigh *Minerva*, 5 Nov. 1813; Kemp Plummer Battle, *History of the University of North Carolina from Its Beginnings to the Death of President Swain, 1789-1868*, 2 vols. (Raleigh, 1907-12), 1:235.

entire world." Their petitions for peace were "offered publicly and solemnly for the United States." Included in their prayers were their brethren in Europe who suffered under the invasions of the French emperor's troops. Acknowledging that as Moravians they had been spared the horror of war, they noted that "on the contrary many thousands of our fellow men have found this a year of death, of terror, of distress, of anxiety and need, of the loss of their goods and houses; a year in which the borders of our country by sea and land have felt the evil effects of war. Surely these thoughts arouse in our hearts the deepest sympathy for the distress of our fellow men, and the warmest thanks that despite our unworthiness we have had the favor of unbroken peace." They thanked God for "the mercies which have been enjoyed by this land during this time of war in contrast to conditions in other countries," and besought an end to the war in Europe "which has been going on so long." Applying their principles of love for one's fellowman, they gave food and drink to small parties of soldiers who were marching through Wachovia en route to the battlefields.[6] Although a hotbed of Federalism, Fayetteville was divided in opinion and gave a qualified support to the war. At a town meeting held in June 1812 a resolution was adopted to aid and support the government in the prosecution of the war but not if suppression of freedom of speech and press were involved. "We shall fervently pray for success to the arms, of the United States," read the resolution, "but we shall nevertheless not give up one jot of our freedom of opinion or right of remark." The Wilmington *Gazette* proposed such a town meeting to discover the views of its citizens on the war. The southern states had been "declared on the floor of Congress: to be in favor of the war, which might not be true"; hence a town meeting should be called. Congress should be informed if Wilmington did not approve of the war; citizens must "undeceive our government, to inform them how seriously and earnestly a war is deprecated by us, if it can be avoided without disgrace, that it can be avoided without disgrace to the *people* as we verily believe, so we confidently assert." In the recruiting service, Wellborn noted that the people at Anson Court House were

6. *Moravian Records*, 7:3,164, 3,191, 3,198, 3,190, 3,197, 3,214, 3,202.

opposed to the war; oddly enough, however, Fayetteville with more Tories and Federalists than any other part of the state was also one of the best recruiting areas. At Salisbury, the rendezvous for the Tenth Regiment, the troops found themselves in the midst of a strongly Federalist population, for this was the home town of Joseph Pearson. Bitterly Wellborn decided that the only good done by stationing the troops there was to "circulate money amongst those who dispise the administration and appear to enjoy our misfortunes. You may see there [sic] countenances glow," he told the adjutant general, "when they hear of our armies being defeated and uncommon to circulate bad news." It was noted by Dr. James Stuart when he traveled through Salisbury in 1814 that most of the people were Federalist and quite tired of the war.[7] Perhaps this explains Wellborn's removal of his rendezvous to Wilkesboro, his home town.

Trade and commerce were adversely affected not so much by the declaration of war as by the preceding embargo. Prices were depressed because European markets were closed to American vessels and the consequent accumulation of unsold produce hurt the farmers. The announcement in 1813 of the British blockade caused a further drop in the price of produce. These events placed many farmers and debtors in serious straits, so much so that the legislature passed a law postponing payment of debts and damages for two years if two persons would go surety for the debtor. The law was appealed to the state supreme court and held unconstitutional in 1814, but it had already been in effect for its intended duration by the time Chief Justice John Louis Taylor wrote his opinion.[8]

While prices obtained by farmers were going down, prices on goods transported from a distance went up. Retail prices quoted in newspapers for such towns as Fayetteville and New Bern show that coffee, rice, sugar, flour, and salt cost more per unit than in Baltimore, Charleston, and New York, the source of imports and distribution through the coasting trade. Almost the only item that was cheaper in North Car-

7. Raleigh *Minerva,* 3 July 1812, 22 May 1812; James Wellborn to Francis R. Huger, 7 Sept. 1813, RG 94, M 566; Wellborn to Thomas Cushing, 22 Feb. 1813, ibid.; Journal of Dr. James Stuart of Beaufort, S. C., 1814, *passim,* SHC.

8. Raleigh *Minerva,* 24 Sept. 1813, 28 Jan. 1814.

olina was whiskey. The price of sugar, in fact, nearly doubled; while conversely that received for tobacco, cotton, and beeswax dropped by half.[9] Bread in Salem was reduced in weight to offset "the considerable advance in the price of wheat." Petersburg, a main distribution point for central North Carolina, had no brown sugar available in 1813, while the price of groceries there was "*very* high!" A ship from Baltimore with groceries on board had not been heard from; "we begin to think they are lost; or taken by the English Squadron now in the Chesapeake Bay," wrote the merchant in response to an order. Yet some localities prospered because they were on inland freight routes. One such was Salem, which experienced an "unusually lively" year in 1813 because of "the large number of visitors, travelers, and freight wagons which have taken their way through this town, not to speak of the increase in barter and trade."[10] Use of these inland routes in order to replace coastal travel and exposure to the British blockade often required a six-weeks' trip from South Carolina to Philadelphia, with wagons piled up for miles at the ferries. Other complicating factors in the economic picture were bad weather conditions. In 1813 a severe drought caused widespread hunger. The water in the Cape Fear River was so low that vessels could not come from the interior down to the port city, creating a scarcity of new flour. David Jones in New Hanover County reported that people were going hungry yet provisions were being shipped out of Wilmington. Could something be done, he asked Governor Hawkins, to make food available to the people? Wake County also experienced such a drought that the oats were not worth harvesting and corn would be scarce even with a providential rain. The drought continued into 1814 so that when troops marched from Gates Court House to the relief of Norfolk, they chose different routes in order not to consume all the drinking water. The fact that the federal government did not pay its bills promptly, if it did at all, worked a hardship both on soldiers without pay and on their families. Even a wealthy man like

9. Price lists for comparative purposes may be found in Raleigh *Star*, 19 Oct. 1809, 1 Nov. 1811; Raleigh *Minerva*, 4 Feb. 1814, 18 Feb. 1814, and others.

10. *Moravian Records*, 7:3,205; William Gilmour to Calvin Jones, 26 Feb. 1813, Calvin Jones Papers; *Moravian Records*, 7:3,193.

John Steele who rented houses to officers in the army did not receive his money and wrote to Secretary of the Treasury Gallatin trying to collect it. One of the many minutiae indicating a declining economic situation is that the number of carriages owned in North Carolina dropped by a thousand between 1814 and 1815.[11]

North Carolina did not benefit from increases in war-related industries. Jefferson's embargo in 1807 caused some effort to develop the textile industry in the state, sufficient to clothe the local population "without being put to any non plus for supplies from any nation on earth." A new kind of spinning machine was noted by the *Star;* a society was formed in Caswell County and Person County to encourage the manufacture of cloth by awarding prizes. Dr. John Umstead and John Taylor in Hillsborough attempted to organize a company to raise $10,000 for the construction of a cotton and wool factory, as did another group of citizens in Mecklenburg County, in order "to render a section of our country measurably independent of foreign supplies." Among the leaders of the latter movement was John McKnitt, perhaps the son of the revolutionary veteran of the same name. That some success was achieved in a cottage-type industry is shown by the fact that in 1810 North Carolina ranked fourth in the nation in the number of yards of cloth woven, and first in the number of looms.[12] While the number of types of manufactured articles is large, as revealed by the wartime levies on certain goods, North Carolina ranked in seventh place or lower in every instance except in the manufacture of beer, ale, and porter. Salt was refined at establishments along the coast, but how much and by whom is hard to determine. In 1809 two companies were reportedly organized, one in Edenton by doctors Sawyer and Norcom, and one in Wilmington by

11. Jacobs and Tucker, *War of 1812,* p. 86; Myer Myers to Samuel Mordecai, — Nov. 1814, Mordecai Papers; David Jones to William Hawkins, 13 July 1813, Hawkins Letterbook 19, p. 289; Raleigh *Minerva,* 9 July 1813; Calvin Jones to Hawkins, 1 Oct. 1814, Hawkins Letterbook 20, pp. 388-89, adding that a "brisk fall of rain" had begun to break the drought; John Steele to Albert Gallatin, —— 1813, *Steele Papers,* 2:720-22; Seybert, *Statistical Annals,* pp. 490-93.

12. Louis Martin Sears, *Jefferson and the Embargo* (Durham, N.C., 1927), p. 67; Raleigh *Star,* 12 Jan. 1809, 16 Feb. 1809; Raleigh *Minerva,* 18 June 1813, 3 Dec. 1813; Pitkin, *Statistical View,* p. 473.

Samuel B. Jocelyn and others. During the war the salt works
at Wilmington were evidently in operation because there was
mention of British ships hovering in that vicinity that were
assumed to be searching for the salt works. One reference to
a supposed salt works in Rowan County was made by William
R. Davie to a friend, who reported that he was unable to learn
anything about it.[13] Iron was cast at furnaces in Lincoln and
Burke counties. Peter Forney, Joseph Graham, and the firm of
Brevard and Fulenwider had foundries. Graham furnished
balls, shot and shells of all sizes, selling 30,000 pounds of
shot to the United States government at Charleston during
the war and delivering anywhere desired by wagon teams.
The only rolling mill was that of Brevard and Fulenwider,
which supplied sheet iron for nail factories in Columbia and
Augusta; apparently there were no nail factories in North
Carolina. David Kennedy was desirous of establishing a
munitions factory for muskets and rifles on Bear Creek in
Moore County but apparently did not succeed.[14] Lead mines
were in operation in Warren County as early as 1808. General
Pinckney suggested the purchase of lead from these mines to
be delivered to Charleston, or the sending of an agent there
to purchase directly.[15] Mention of gristmills, sawmills, and

13. Seybert, *Statistical Annals,* pp. 494-95; John F. Smith established an
oil manufactory as reported in *Raleigh Star,* 12 Jan. 1809; a Mr. Gules
[Gales?] of Raleigh established a paper mill, possibly the first in North
Carolina, according to the *Washington Expositor,* 8 Oct. 1808, quoted in
Sears, *Jefferson and the Embargo,* p. 235; Raleigh *Star,* 23 Feb. 1809, 12
Jan. 1809; *Raleigh Register,* 3 June 1814; William R. Davie to John Steele,
4 Feb. 1814, quoted in Hamilton, *William Richardson Davie,* p. 75.

14. Raleigh *Minerva,* 21 Jan. 1808; Joseph Graham to William Hawkins,
4 Jan. 1814, Hawkins Papers; Graham to Hawkins, 17 Feb., 27 Feb., 1814,
ibid.; "Peter Forney," *Biographical Directory of American Congress,* p. 1,173;
Raleigh *Minerva,* 9 Apr. 1813, 5 Mar. 1815.

15. Thomas Pinckney to Secretary of War, 30 Oct. 1813, RG 107, M 221.
One David Penn wrote to Archibald D. Murphey, 22 Aug. 1808 (Murphey
Papers), asking legal aid in clearing the title of the lead mines which he
was working. He wished to complete their purchase from his former partners,
Davie Sheffee and John Mangram. The address given, unfortunately, was
only "Leadmines." An undated news clipping headed "Lead Mines" and
describing Panacea Springs was discovered by William S. Powell at the
North Carolina Collection, The University of North Carolina Library, Chapel
Hill. This article described the author's walk near Brinkleyville, along the
banks of Little Fishing Creek, on land belonging to Jones Lee, Sr., where
he observed the remains of a lead mine dating back, he thought, to the
Revolution. Another mine existed, he said, six miles south on Big Fishing
Creek at Ward's Mill, six or eight miles below Ransom's Bridge. This article

distilleries has also been found, but these were staple industries rather than war-related. Perhaps as a result of the need for better transportation during the war, a stock company was organized to build a toll bridge at Washington, North Carolina, which bridge was eventually completed; while another company attempted to raise money for a canal against the "horrid languor and inertness here [New Bern] which almost forbid exertion—," as Gaston wrote to a friend in 1814.[16] It is difficult to find any real establishment of industry that actually resulted from the war.

Free "men of colour" made some progress toward greater equality during the war: whereas initially they were not allowed to enlist in the militia except as musicians, by the Militia Act of 1814 they were allowed to be enrolled provided that their color was indicated. Three free Negroes petitioned to be allowed to enlist from Lenoir County; three or four appeared at Fort Hampton for service under Major Tisdale but were sent home; and one white man who paid a "dark skinned" man to be his substitute learned that the latter had been rejected and the white man held liable for service. It does not appear that a large number of free Negroes were in military service from North Carolina. Two free men of color were killed in an accident when Gunboat No. 146 blew up, thus indicating that a few free blacks also served in the navy.[17]

The greatest role, however, that blacks played in the War of 1812 was in the creation of fear on the part of the white man. Always present was the fear of insurrection by the slaves. When arms were originally placed in the United States arsenal at Fayetteville in 1790, it was for the purpose of suppressing "insurrection among the Blacks." Major General Brown requested cavalry at Fort Johnston to be available in case of a slave uprising. Following the arrival of arms for the

---

pinpointed Warren and Halifax counties. A preliminary search of the deed indexes for Halifax County has not yet proven a connection between David Penn and Jones Lee.

16. Raleigh *Minerva*, 9 Oct. 1812; *Carolina Federal Republican*, 13 Feb. 1813; William Gaston to John F. Burgwyn, 19 June 1814, Gaston Papers, SHC.

17. *Laws of North Carolina, 1812*, chap. 1, p. 3; ibid., *1814*, chap. 1, p. 3; *N.C. Senate Journal, 1814*, p. 5; Nathan Tisdale to Calvin Jones, 8 Sept. 1812, Hawkins Letterbook 18, p. 306; affidavit by Jacob Vandegriff, 27 Sept. 1814, Hawkins Papers; *Raleigh Register*, 9 Sept. 1814.

southern counties, John Gray Blount requested powder and ball from the governor so that there would be no need to fear insurrection. The legislature of 1813 reflecting these fears required the highest militia officer in a county where an insurrection might occur to take immediate steps to suppress it, and to send an express without delay to the governor.[18]

Taking advantage of these fears, the British sought to turn them to their own use. Discovering that runaway Negroes were "resorting to his Majesty's ships," Admiral Warren asked for instructions as to their "disposal." The best method appeared to be arming them and using them in the war. Warren wrote to the admiralty that the "Black population of these Countries, evince upon every occasion, the strongest predilection for the cause of Great Britain, and a most ardent desire to join any Troops or Seamen acting in the Country." He had some sixty or seventy escapees serving in his squadron, he informed the Admiralty, some of whom reported that parties of Negroes were exercising with arms in the night on shore and alarming the whites thereby. Cockburn's proclamation that he intended to raise a corps of Colonial Marines from the "People of Colour" who escaped from the Americans heightened the fears, as did Cochrane's plan to recruit Indians and blacks in Alabama for use against the Americans.[19] The citizens of New Bern declined to hire out their slaves to build a fort on Beacon Island lest the British come and take them off. At least two general alarms of insurrection arose during the summer in which the British landed at Ocracoke. A runaway Negro who was caught in Beaufort in June reported that an uprising was being planned in the west of the county. The White Oak militiamen who were on duty there asked permission to return home to protect their families and property, which they were allowed to do. Another alarm came from Halifax because of letters allegedly found from Virginia Negroes to those in North Carolina advising a general massacre on 21 July. The chain of letters went from Virginia to Edge-

18. John Cameron to William Hawkins, 22 May 1812, Hawkins Letterbook 18, p. 164; Thomas Brown to Hawkins, 14 July 1812, ibid., p. 236; John Gray Blount to Hawkins, 25 May 1813, Hawkins Papers; *Laws of North Carolina, 1813*, chap. 1, p. 3.

19. Admiralty to Sir John B. Warren, 2 Oct. 1813, Adm 2/933, p. 44; Warren to Admiralty, 28 May 1813, Adm 1/503; Proclamation by George Cockburn, 19 May 1814, Adm 1/507.

combe County, to Northampton County, and then to Halifax, although no one actually produced any of the letters. Advice to reactivate the patrol, to keep powder and ball handy, and to require passes for slaves in the Halifax area was issued, under the theory that even if the letters proved to be forgeries, it was better to be prepared than to be sorry. In Plymouth a citizens' meeting was held to take stock of these reports and to organize a search throughout the county for concealed arms, ammunition, and the like. The warning was passed on from Plymouth to John Gray Blount at Washington.[20] The fears were groundless, for no insurrection broke out, although they are indicative of the constant awareness of the edge of the volcano on which the slave-owning whites were forever balanced.

In many ways the home front changed little or none from peacetime conditions. The newspapers continued to report horse races, theatrical performances, lotteries, murders, divorces, law suits, earthquakes, all as usual. A ball in Wilmington held in November 1814, during the days of darkest despair, was gay and well attended. The Raleigh Company of the Volunteer Guards held a picnic at John Rex's spring with a "plain but plentiful dinner" and an adequate supply of "homemade liquors." Among the songs raised at the picnic were "Hail Liberty," "Hail Columbia," "Oh Listen to the Voice of Love," and others; music played but not sung included "None But the Brave Deserve the Fair," "Yankee Doodle," "Jefferson's March," "Oh Ça Ira," "Bold Be the Rebel's Cast," and "The Spinning Wheel." Independence Day in 1814 was celebrated with a procession from the courthouse in Raleigh to the state house where an ode was sung and the Declaration of Independence read to the assembled crowd. Dinner at Mrs. Casso's at two o'clock and a ball in the evening crowned the festivities.[21] Violence occurred, also as usual. When four young men in Wilmington who were swimming in the river were allegedly attacked by "ruffians" from the United States gunboat, the captain of the gunboat was figuratively drawn and

20. William Croom to William Miller, 26 Dec. 1814, Miller Letterbook 21, p. 31; Matthew Norris to — [Hawkins?], 18 June 1813, Hawkins Papers; Raleigh *Minerva*, 25 July 1813; Ben B. Hunter to John Gray Blount, 26 July 1813, Blount Papers.

21. Myer Myers to Samuel Mordecai, — Nov. 1814, Mordecai Papers; Raleigh *Minerva*, 10 July 1812, 8 July 1814.

quartered although in actuality acquitted of all charges. The imprisonment of sixty-one crew members from the mutineers on the privateer *General Armstrong* led to a notorious murder trial. The mutineers were imprisoned on several vessels in the harbor at Wilmington; a night guard rowed around periodically to check on their safekeeping. During one such evening Sailing Master Evans and Midshipman M'Chessney ordered a rowboat to halt and identify itself; a row followed during which the occupant of the rowboat fired at the naval officers and when M'Chessney returned the fire, the occupant, one Captain John S. Oliver, was killed. Although public opinion at first ran strongly against the navy, testimony at the trial and the conduct of the officers changed the public attitude. Both men were found not guilty.[22] Outbreaks of "roguery" in Rowan County led to the formation of a vigilante group composed of "many of the most respectable gentlemen," who offered ten-dollar rewards for apprehending rogues. Nearly one hundred men joined, putting up five dollars each to provide the reward money.[23] Earthquakes in Raleigh and in Caracas, Venezuela, occurred, although a tremendous and graphically described earthquake in Asheville, preceded by a comet and the aurora borealis, turned out to be a hoax.[24] Israel Pickens's effort to add an amendment to the Constitution dealing with the method of choosing presidential electors failed to pass the House of Representatives by the necessary two-thirds majority.[25] The final event of the war years on the home front was pestilence—an epidemic during the winter of 1814-15 that attacked the infirm, the debilitated, the wearied, and the intoxicated. Dr. James Norcom, who called it a "typhous state," reported that the old, the poor, and the inebriated suffered most, three or four out of each hundred dying from it. The epidemic appeared also in Maryland and Virginia, and the troops returning home from Norfolk in February 1815 carried death back to North Carolina with them.[26]

22. Raleigh *Minerva*, 19 June 1812, 20 Nov. 1812; Gautier Letterbook, 18 Apr. 1813; *National Intelligencer*, 18 Nov. 1813.

23. Raleigh *Minerva*, 8 July 1814, 5 Aug. 1814.

24. *National Intelligencer*, 28 Dec. 1811, 2 May 1812, 28 Jan. 1812, 15 Feb. 1812.

25. *National Intelligencer*, 19 Jan. 1813, 21 Jan. 1813, 22 Dec. 1813, 5 Jan. 1814, 1 Feb. 1814.

26. Raleigh *Minerva*, 10 Mar. 1815.

10 *CONCLUSION*

The articles of peace were signed by the Americans and the British at Ghent on 24 December 1814. The news crossed the Atlantic in January and a circular from Secretary of State Monroe to Governor Miller dated 14 February 1815 officially notified him of the momentous event.[1] Celebrations broke out spontaneously to be followed by more carefully planned ceremonies. In Raleigh the peace produced "so general, so animated a picture of public satisfaction . . . in all ranks," reported the *Raleigh Register*. Cannons were fired, "heart-cheering huzzas," bonfires, a procession and music, and a "general and brilliant illumination" paid tribute to the happy day. On Sunday the Presbyterian clergyman delivered an "appropriate discourse," followed on Wednesday, Washington's birthday, with a ball at Yancey's tavern. The tavern was tastefully decorated with two elegant transparencies, one representing General Washington and the other an eagle with an olive branch hovering over hills, with the word PEACE written beneath it. Concluding the festivities was a public dinner at Mrs. Casso's tavern. In Salem the Moravians sang "a happy offering of praise" at the evening singstunde, followed on 1 March with an illumination. "There was no wind, so burning candles could be used in the open air in front of

1. "Circular," 14 Feb. 1815, Miller Letterbook 21, p. 101.

the houses and on the Square before the principle buildings. In some windows the word *Peace* gleamed happily in German and in English." Musical as the Moravians were, they did not neglect to have the musicians play "appropriate melodies on the wind instruments, as they marched all over town," concluding in front of the chief buildings by singing "Now thank we all our God" in "a true spirit of brotherly love and genuine thankfulness to the Lord." Later, a special ode was composed and sung at the Peace Festival on 13 April. Bethabara, another Moravian village, marked the occasion by an evening meeting. After a short address, "then, accompanied by the trombone, our hearts and lips brought to our merciful and gracious Lord a due thank-offering of praise, for the unexpectedly soon and greatly desired end of the distress and misery of war in our dear fatherland."[2]

Letters to the governor and other politicians congratulated them upon the restoration of peace, expressing views similar to those of such national figures as Madison, Calhoun, Gallatin, Coggeshall, and Monroe. Pickens told Thomas Lenoir, his brother-in-law, that "a national character seems to be impressed on the republick which was not before; we are now ranked among the first-rate powers, formerly we did not rank ourselves as more than a 2nd rate power. We looked to the *changes in Europe*, for peace, & security in the enjoyment of our rights. Now we look at home for the enforcement of them." Rejoicing at the news of the victory at New Orleans, Pickens told Lenoir, "We have met England single handed . . . We have *always* beaten both her land & sea forces man to man & gun to gun. Such a character as we have now through Europe & even with our enemy will be worth ten fold what the war has cost us in the future peace which it will ensure us." A particularly interesting letter was written by J. J. Little of Littleton:

Tell them I congratulate them and all our republican brethren throughout the United States that *Peace* is once more restored to our beloved Country, and that an honourable one, for I do contend taking all the Circumstances into view, considering that we had been for thirty years at peace during which time our military science

2. *Raleigh Register*, 24 Feb. 1815; *Moravian Records*, 7:3,255, 3,256, 3,251, 3,252, 3,258, 3,275.

and even the military pride of the country had become almost extinct, that we had one of the most powerfull nations by sea and land to contend with, and that single handed and that we had a host of traitors at home who were doing everything in their power to embarras the government and counteract it in all its measures, that the peace lately concluded was highly honourable to our government and even if it has not been quite as favourable Genl. Jacksons victory at New Orleans gave such an excellent finishing stroke, that it coud not be otherwise than glorious *that*, is a better security against future encroachments on our rights than parchment, I think the war was a most glorious one as well for the administration who declared and conducted it as for our heroes by sea and land who fought our battles and have cover'd themselves with never fading laurels I think it has been worth more than an age of dishonourable and submissive peace, indeed I think it has guarranteed to this Country half a century of peace, it has united the Conflicting opinions of our patriots and statesmen relative to the expediency and policy of having a respectable navy it has effectually silenced or at least ought so to do, [illegible]— amous against our Republican form of government and [illegible] shewn that it is as firm as persevering and energetic in war, as it is mild and moderate in peace and finally it has shewn the world that a set of free men under a free government contending for their rights and privilidges against a set of tyrants and despots are invincible.[3]

Although this is an impossibly long sentence, it embodies most of the results of the War of 1812 as seen from today's vantage point. The feeling of independence from Europe and from England, the creation of new national heroes, pride in the republican form of government, the growth of a new nationalism, and the political unity of the Era of Good Feelings under the National Republican party may all be seen here in the views of this North Carolinian.

Only two sour notes have been found, both from Federalists. Ebenezer Pettigrew criticized the citizens of Edenton for their lack of interest and their ignorance of national affairs.

3. Israel Pickens to William Lenoir, 2 Jan. 1815, 13 Feb. 1815, Lenoir Papers; J. J. Little to ———, 31 Mar. 1815, John Vann Papers, 1765-1888, Box 1, NC Archives; Archibald D. Murphey congratulated Governor William Miller, 16 Mar. 1815 (*Murphey Papers*, 1:80). Similar expressions may be found in *Madison Writings*, 1:602; speech by Calhoun in *National Intelligencer*, 26 Mar. 1815; *Gallatin Writings*, 1:651-52, 700, 705; Coggeshall, *American Privateers*, p. 398; *Monroe Writings*, 5:322, 331.

"I was last week in Edenton," he wrote his father-in-law, "the peace has not yet awoke the inhabitants from their Lethargy I suppose about august they will begin to think what they will be at next." The *Minerva*, of course, castigated it as a mere truce or cessation of hostilities, not a peace treaty at all. The editor hoped that it had doomed the reputation of the Republicans and he foresaw victory at the next election for the Federalists on the basis of an insignificant fizzling end to the war.[4]

As rapidly as possible the military demobilized. At Norfolk a general order directed that "hostilities are to cease immediately between the troops of the U.S. and those of Great Britain." All recruiting stopped and the detached militia on its way to the rendezvous at Wadesboro for southwestern service was sent home. General Pinckney contacted Admiral Cockburn for a mutual cessation of hostilities, which Cockburn received with "real pleasure" and concurred in. Cockburn, however, did not evacuate his headquarters on Cumberland Island in Charleston harbor until he received a copy of the treaty. When this came, Pinckney discharged the militia in order that it might return home in time for the spring planting. He himself was officially relieved by General Andrew Jackson and the troops under his immediate command were taken over by Colonel Jack of the Georgia district. With a wish to President Madison that the remainder of his administration would be "prosperous and happy," Pinckney returned to his plantation.[5]

The effects of the war on North Carolina were subtle. While it is generally held that the war destroyed the Federalist party, in North Carolina it had been weak since the late 1790s and was decidedly in the minority. As for destroying what there was left of it, this appears not to have been the case. In the election following the war, Federalists Gaston and Culpepper, both outspoken against the war, were reelected for

4. Ebenezer Pettigrew to William Shepard, 14 Apr. 1815, Pettigrew Papers, SHC; Raleigh *Minerva*, 7 Apr. 1815.

5. Order, 18 Feb. 1815, N.C. Militia Papers, 5th Regiment; *Raleigh Register*, 24 Feb. 1815; Thomas Pinckney to Secretary of War, 23 Feb. 1815, RG 107, M 221; General Order, ibid.; George Cockburn to Pinckney, copy, 1 Mar. 1815, ibid.; Pinckney to Secretary of War, 11 Mar. 1815, 30 May 1815, 29 June 1815, ibid.

another term. Pearson, also very outspoken, was defeated, the only defeat for a Federalist in the state. Kennedy, a Federalist who had supported the administration and voted for war measures, was also defeated, but Stanford, antiwar Republican, was reelected. It must be concluded that these election results were based on the personalities of the men rather than on their attitudes toward the war. Rewards came to two members of the North Carolina congressional delegation: Macon was made United States senator and served two terms; Jesse Franklin was elected governor. The outstanding men in the delegation, other than Gaston and Macon, moved from the state and went southwest to Alabama, Mississippi, or Tennessee, as did King, Pickens, and Murfree. This drain of men of ability was apparent throughout the next two decades, as both blacks and whites by the hundreds and thousands left the state taking with them their talent, their initiative, their wealth, and their labor.

Industry was not promoted, although a few men such as Archibald Debow Murphey attempted to encourage its growth. A sudden increase in commerce in the year following the end of the war failed to continue. Economically, the war neither helped nor hurt the state, inasmuch as direct results are concerned. Indirectly, however, North Carolina was hurt because the opening of the Southwest, free from Indian and British menace, and shortly to be free from Spanish influence also, lured away too many of the best young people. For the next twenty years, the state sank deeply into the doldrums and only too well deserved its nickname of the "Rip Van Winkle" state.

BIBLIOGRAPHY

MANUSCRIPTS

Chapel Hill, N.C. North Carolina Collection, University of North
    Carolina Library.
    Burns, Annie Walker, comp. Abstract of Pensions of North
        Carolina Soldiers of the Revolution, War of 1812, and Indian
        Wars. 10 vols. Typescript.
Chapel Hill, N.C. Southern Historical Collection, University of
    North Carolina Library.
    William Gaston Papers.
    Thomas N. Gautier Letterbook, 1808-1813.
    William S. Hamilton Papers.
    Calvin Jones Family Papers. Microfilm from original in the
        State Department of Archives and History, Nashville, Tenn.
    Calvin Jones Papers.
    Lenoir Family Papers.
    Mordecai Papers, 1649, 1783-1817.
    North Carolina Militia Papers, 5th Regiment.
    Pettigrew Papers.
    James Stuart Journal, 1814.
East Point, Ga. National Archives and Record Service, Regional
    Archives Branch, Federal Records Center.
    Record Group 21. Records of the United States District and
        Circuit Courts for the Eastern District of North Carolina,
        1801-1816. Microfilm in possession of the author.

London. Public Record Office.

Admiralty 1/502-507. Letters Received by the British Admiralty from Admirals on the North American Station, 1808-1815. Microfilm in possession of the author.

Admiralty 2/932-933. Letters Sent by the British Admiralty, 1808-1815. Photostats in the Library of Congress, Washington, D.C.

Admiralty T 88/1. Miscellaneous Records of the Admiralty: Vouchers to the Account of the Commissioners for American Ships and Cargoes Condemned as Prize; Restitutions and Receipts for the Proceeds in the Cases of Certain Vessels. Microfilm in possession of the author.

Raleigh, N.C. State Department of Archives and History.

John Gray Blount Papers.

Josiah Collins Papers.

William R. Davie Papers.

William Gaston Papers.

Joseph Graham Papers, 1780-1836.

Wood Jones Hamlin Papers.

Governor William Hawkins Papers, 1811-1814.

William Hollister Account Books, 1808-1818.

Charles E. Johnson Collection.

Nathaniel Macon Papers.

Michaux-Randolph Papers.

Pattie Mordecai Collection, 1796-1876.

Archibald D. Murphey Papers.

North Carolina, Buncombe County, Clerk of the Superior Court, War of 1812 Claims of Service, April 1855.

North Carolina, Craven County, Estate Records (Johnson).

North Carolina, Executive, Governor's Warrant Book, 1815.

North Carolina, Executive, Letterbooks of Governor William Hawkins, 1811-1814.

North Carolina, Executive, Letterbooks of Governor William Miller, 1814-1815.

North Carolina, Military Collection, War of 1812, Account Books, 1813-1821.

North Carolina, Wake County, Court Minutes, 1814.

Pettigrew Papers.

Quaker Church of Rich Square, Northampton County, North Carolina, Monthly Meetings Minutes, Men, 1760-1943.

William Rombough's Account Book, Edenton, North Carolina, 1793-1810.

Richard Stanford Papers, 1803-1901.

John Steele Papers.

Montford Stokes Papers.
Untitled Private Collection 750.1.
John Vann Papers, 1765-1888.
Washington, D.C. Library of Congress.
    J. M. Garnett, Jr. Manuscripts. Xerox of selected letters to Richard Stanford in possession of the author.
    Joseph Nicholson Papers. Microfilm of selected letters from Nathaniel Macon in possession of the author.
Washington, D.C. National Archives.
    Record Group 45. Naval Records Collection of the Office of Naval Records and Library, Microcopy 124, 149, 625. Xerox of selected documents pertaining to Johnston Blakeley in possession of the author.
    Record Group 59. Records of Impressed Seamen: Seamen's Register of Certificates, 1808-16, Entry 861; Miscellaneous Lists and Papers, 1796-1814, Entry 862; Letter from P. Irving, 1814. Microfilm in possession of the author.
    Record Group 94. Records of the Adjutant General's Office: Letters Sent by the Office of the Adjutant General, Microcopy 565; Letters Received by the Office of the Adjutant General, Microcopy 566. Microfilm of selected reels in possession of the author.
    Record Group 107. Records of the Office of the Secretary of War: Letters Received by the Secretary of War, Microcopy 221. Microfilm and xerox in possession of the author.

NEWSPAPERS

The American, Fayetteville, N.C.
The Carolina Federal Republican, New Bern, N.C.
The Carolinian, New Bern, N.C.
The Edenton Gazette, Edenton, N.C.
The Hornet's Nest, Murfreesborough, N.C.
The Minerva and *The Raleigh Minerva*, Raleigh, N.C.
The National Intelligencer, Washington, D.C.
Niles' *Weekly Register*, Baltimore, Md.
The Raleigh Register, Raleigh, N.C.
The Star, Raleigh, N.C.
The Wilmington Gazette, Wilmington, N.C.

PUBLIC DOCUMENTS

North Carolina.
  Adjutant General.
    Muster Rolls of the Soldiers of the War of 1812: Detached

from the Militia of North Carolina. Raleigh: Ch. C. Raboteau,
1851.
General Assembly.
Laws of North Carolina, 1809-1816.
*Report of the Select Committee on the Claims of the State
upon the General Government.* Raleigh: Lawrence & Lemay,
1833.
General Assembly, House of Commons.
*Journals of the House of Commons of the State of North
Carolina, 1812-1817.*
General Assembly, Senate.
*Journals of the Senate of the State of North Carolina, 1812-
1817.*
United States.
Congress.
American State Papers. Washington, D.C.: Gales & Seaton,
1832-61.
Annals of Congress, 1789-1824. Washington, D.C.: Gales &
Seaton, 1834-56.
*Congressional Reports Relating to North Carolinians in the
War of 1812.* Bound in one volume, North Carolina Col-
lection, University of North Carolina Library, Chapel Hill,
N.C.
House of Representatives.
Biographical Directory of the American Congress, 1774-1949.
H. Doc. 607, 81st Congress, 2d session, 1950.
Committee on Claims, *H. Report 96,* 64th Congress, 1st session,
1915.
*A Report of the Engineer Department in Relation to a Survey
of the Waters of Virginia and North Carolina,* H. Doc. 125,
19th Congress, 1st session, 1825.
Marshall's Office.
Circular. Raleigh: n.p., 1812.
Senate.
Executive Document 84, 47th Congress, 2d session, 1882.
Miscellaneous Document 76, 42d Congress, 3d session, 1872-73.

GENERAL SOURCES

Adams, Henry. *A History of the United States during the Admin-
istrations of Jefferson and Madison.* 9 vols. New York: Charles
Scribner's Sons, 1918.
*An Address of Members of the House of Representatives of the
Congress of the United States on the Subject of the War with*

Great Britain. Raleigh: Lucas & A. H. Boylan, at the Minerva Press, 1812.

Anderson, George A. *Bartlett Yancey.* James Sprunt Historical Publications, vol. 10, no. 2. Chapel Hill: University of North Carolina Press, 1911.

Armytage, Frances. *The Free Port System in the British West Indies.* New York: Longmans, Green & Co., 1953.

Ashe, Samuel A'Court, Weeks, Stephen B., and Van Noppen, Charles L., eds. *Biographical History of North Carolina.* 8 vols. Greensboro: L. Van Noppen, 1908.

Barlow, William Ray. "Congress during the War of 1812." Ph.D. dissertation, Ohio State University, 1961.

Bassett, John Spencer. *The Life of Andrew Jackson.* 2 vols. New York: Macmillan Co., 1916.

Battle, Kemp Plummer. *History of the University of North Carolina from Its Beginnings to the Death of President Swain, 1789-1868.* 2 vols. Raleigh: Edwards & Broughton, 1907-12.

———. "A North Carolina Naval Hero and His Daughter." *North Carolina Booklet* 1 (January 1901): 1-15.

Bayard, James A. "The Papers of James A. Bayard, 1796-1815." Edited by Elizabeth Donnan. In *Annual Report of the American Historical Association for the Year 1913.* Vol. 2. Washington, D.C.: Government Printing Office, 1915.

Branson, L. *The North Carolina Business Directory.* Raleigh: n.p., 1872.

Driggs, Willis G. *Henry Potter, 1766-1857.* Raleigh: Edwards & Broughton Co., 1953.

Brockenbrough, J. W., ed. *Report of Cases Decided by Hon. John Marshall in the Circuit Court of the United States for the District of Virginia and North Carolina, 1802-1833.* 2 vols. Philadelphia: James Kay, Jun., & Bro., 1837.

Brown, John P. *Old Frontiers.* Kingsport, Tenn.: Southern Publishers, 1938.

Brown, Roger II. *The Republic in Peril: 1812.* New York: Columbia University Press, 1964.

Bruce, William Cabell. *John Randolph of Roanoke, 1773-1833.* 2 vols. New York: G. P. Putnam's Sons, 1922.

Burns, Walter Francis. *Captain Otway Burns, Patriot, Privateer and Legislator.* New York: n.p., 1905.

Burt, A. L. *The United States, Great Britain and British North America from the Revolution to the Establishment of Peace after the War of 1812.* New Haven: Yale University Press, 1940.

Calhoun, John C. *The Papers of John C. Calhoun.* Edited by Robert L. Meriwether. Vol. 1. Columbia: South Caroliniana Society, 1959.

Clark, Allen Culling. *Life and Letters of Dolly Madison.* Washington, D.C.: W. F. Roberts Co., 1914.

Clauder, Anna Cornelia. *American Commerce as Affected by the Wars of the French Revolution and Napoleon, 1793-1812.* Philadelphia: University of Pennsylvania Press, 1932.

Clay, Henry. *The Papers of Henry Clay.* Edited by James F. Hopkins. Vol. 1. Lexington: University of Kentucky Press, 1959.

Coggeshall, George. *History of the American Privateers, and Letters-of-Marque, during our War with England in the Years 1812, '13 and '14.* 2d ed. New York: Published by and for the author, 1856.

Coles, Harry L. *The War of 1812.* Chicago History of American Civilization, edited by Daniel J. Boorstin. Chicago: University of Chicago Press, 1965.

Connor, R. D. W. "Captain Blakel[e]y in the War of 1812." *North Carolina Review* (Literary and Historical Section of the *News and Observer* [Raleigh]), 6 April 1913.

———, ed. *A Manual of North Carolina.* Raleigh: Uzzell Printers, 1913.

Cruikshank, Capt. E., ed. *Documentary History of the Campaign on the Niagara Frontier in 1814.* 9 vols. Welland, Ontario: Lundy's Lane Historical Society, 1896-1908.

Cullum, George W. *Biographical Register of the Officers and Graduates of the U.S. Military Academy at West Point, N.Y.* New York: D. Van Nostrand Co., 1868.

Dodd, William E. *The Life of Nathaniel Macon.* 1908. Reprint. New York: B. Franklin, 1970.

Dodson, John. *Reports of Cases Argued and Determined in the High Court of Admiralty: Commencing with the Judgments of the Right Hon. Sir William Scott, Trinity Term 1811.* London: A. Strahan, 1815.

Duane, William. *Handbook for Infantry.* Philadelphia: For the author, 1812.

Edwards, Thomas. *Reports of Cases Argued and Determined in the High Court of Admiralty: Commencing with the Judgments of the Right Hon. Sir William Scott, Easter Term 1808.* London: A. Strahan, 1812.

Elliott, Charles Winslow. *Winfield Scott: The Soldier and the Man.* New York: Macmillan Co., 1937.

Firth, Edith G., ed. *The Town of York, 1793-1815: A Collection of Documents of Early Toronto.* Toronto: University of Toronto Press, 1962.

Fries, Adelaide, ed. *Records of the Moravians in North Carolina.*

Vol. 7. Raleigh: State Department of Archives and History, 1947.

Gallatin, Albert. *The Writings of Albert Gallatin.* Edited by Henry Adams. 1872. Reprint. New York: Antiquarian Press, 1960.

Garland, Hugh A. *The Life of John Randolph of Roanoke.* 2 vols. in 1. New York: D. Appleton & Co., 1860.

Gaston, William. *Circular.* Washington: n.p., 1815. North Carolina Collection, University of North Carolina Library, Chapel Hill.

Gilleland, J. C. *History of the Late War, between the United States and Great Britain.* Baltimore: Schaeffer & Maund, 1817.

Gray, Alexander. *To the Free Citizens of Rowan, Chatham, and Randolph.* Salisbury, N.C.: Coupee and Crider, 1813.

Hamilton, J. G. de Roulhac. *The Political and Professional Career of Bartlett Yancey.* James Sprunt Historical Publications, vol. 10, no. 2. Chapel Hill: University of North Carolina Press, 1911.

———. *William Richardson Davie: A Memoir.* James Sprunt Historical Monograph, no. 7. Chapel Hill: University of North Carolina Press, 1907.

Haywood, Marshall Delancey. *Builders of the Old North State.* Edited by Sarah McCulloh Lemmon. Raleigh: Litho Industries, 1968.

Heitman, Francis. *Historical Register and Dictionary of the United States Army, from Its Organization, September 29, 1789, to March 2, 1903.* 2 vols. Washington, D.C.: Government Printing Office, 1916.

Herrman, Margaret Edgar. "Beaufort, North Carolina: 1800-1830." Master's thesis, University of North Carolina, 1970.

Horsman, Reginald. *The Causes of the War of 1812.* Philadelphia: University of Pennsylvania Press, 1962.

Hunt, Gaillard. "Joseph Cales on the War Manifesto of 1812." *American Historical Review* 13 (1907-8):303-10.

Ingersoll, Charles Jared. *Historical Sketch of the Second War between the United States of America, and Great Britain, Declared by Act of Congress, the 18th of June, 1812, and Concluded by Peace, the 15th of February, 1815.* 3 vols. Philadelphia: Lea and Blanchard, 1845.

Jacobs, James R., and Tucker, Glenn. *The War of 1812: A Compact History.* New York: Hawthorn Books, 1969.

Johnson, William. "Biographical Sketch of Capt. Johnston Blakel[e]y." *North-Carolina University Magazine* 3 (February 1854):1-16.

Kaplan, Lawrence S. "France and Madison's Decision for War." *Mississippi Valley Historical Review* 50 (1964):652-71.

Kreidberg, Marvin, and Henry, Merton G. *History of Military*

Mobilization in the United States Army, 1775-1945. Washington, D.C.: Department of the Army, 1955.

Latimer, Margaret Kinard. "South Carolina—A Protagonist of the War of 1812." *American Historical Review* 61 (1955-56):914-29.

Lemmon, Sarah McCulloh. *North Carolina and the War of 1812.* Raleigh: State Department of Archives and History, 1971.

——, ed. *The Pettigrew Papers.* Vol. 1, *1686-1818.* Raleigh: State Department of Archives and History, 1971.

Letters to Bartlett Yancey. James Sprunt Historical Publications, vol. 10, no. 2. Chapel Hill: University of North Carolina Press, 1911.

Lossing, Benson J. *The Pictorial Field Book of the War of 1812.* New York: Harper & Brothers, 1869.

McIver, George W. "North Carolinians at West Point before the Civil War." *North Carolina Historical Review* 7 (1930):15-45.

Maclay, Edgar Stanton. "The Exploits of Otway Burns, Privateersman and Statesman." *United States Naval Institute Proceedings* 42 (May-June 1916): 873-911.

MacRae, James C. "The Fayetteville Independent Light Infantry Company." *North Carolina Booklet* 7 (April 1908):248-66.

Madison, James. *Letters and Other Writings of James Madison, Fourth President of the United States.* Published by order of Congress. 4 vols. Philadelphia: J. B. Lippincott Co., 1867.

Mahan, Alfred Thayer. *Sea Power in Its Relations to the War of 1812.* 2 vols. London: Sampson Low, Marston & Co., 1905.

Mahon, John K. "The Carolina Brigade Sent against the Creek Indians in 1814." *North Carolina Historical Review* 28 (1951): 421-25.

Malone, Henry T. "Cherokee-White Relations on the Southern Frontier in the Early Nineteenth Century." *North Carolina Historical Review* 14 (1937):1-14.

Martell, J. S. "A Side Light on Federalist Strategy during the War of 1812." *American Historical Review* 43 (1937-38):553-66.

Masterson, William H. *William Blount.* Baton Rouge: Louisiana State University Press, 1954.

Monroe, James. *The Writings of James Monroe.* Edited by Stanislaus Murray Hamilton. Vol. 5. New York: G. P. Putnam's Sons, 1901.

Murphey, Archibald Debow. *The Papers of Archibald Debow Murphey.* Edited by William Henry Hoyt. 2 vols. Raleigh: E. M. Uzzell & Co., 1914.

——. *Statistical Tables of the Population, Agriculture, Commerce, and Finances, of North Carolina.* Raleigh: Tho. Henderson, Jun., 1816.

———. *To the Freemen of Orange County.* Raleigh: T. Henderson, 1813.

North Carolina Historical Commission. "The British Invasion of North Carolina, 1813." *Uplift* 29 (1941):20-21.

North Carolina Magazine 1, no. 3 (October 1813). North Carolina Collection, University of North Carolina Library, Chapel Hill.

"Otway Burns and the Snap Dragon." *North Carolina University Magazine,* 2d ser. 4 (1855):407-67; 5 (1856):126-31, 205-8.

Pancake, John S. "The 'Invisibles': A Chapter in the Opposition to President Madison." *Journal of Southern History* 21 (1955):17-37.

Parton, James. *Life of Andrew Jackson.* 3 vols. Boston: Houghton Mifflin Co., 1887-88.

Pearson, Joseph. *Circular.* Washington: n.p., 1815.

Perkins, Bradford. *Prologue to War: England and the United States, 1805-1812.* Berkeley: University of California Press, 1961.

Pickens, Israel. *Circular to the Citizens of Burke, Rutherford, Lincoln, Buncombe, and Haywood.* Washington, D.C.: n.p., 1812.

———. *Letter to His Constituents.* Washington, D.C.: n.p., 1813.

Pitkin, Timothy. *A Statistical View of the Commerce of the United States of America: Including also an Account of Banks, Manufactures and Internal Trade and Improvements* . . . New Haven: Durrie & Peck, 1835.

Preston, William C. *The Reminiscence of William C. Preston.* Edited by Minnie Clare Yarborough. Chapel Hill: University of North Carolina Press, 1933.

Ravenel, Harriott Horry Rutledge. *Life and Times of William Lowndes of South Carolina, 1782-1822.* Boston: Houghton Mifflin Co., 1901.

"A Rendezvous for the Third Regiment of Riflemen," *Circular.* n.p.: 1814. North Carolina Collection, University of North Carolina Library, Chapel Hill.

Risjord, Norman K. "1812: Conservatives, War Hawks, and the Nation's Honor." *William and Mary Quarterly,* 3d ser. 18 (1961): 196-210.

Robinson, Blackwell P. *William R. Davie.* Chapel Hill: University of North Carolina Press, 1957.

Robinson, Chr. *Reports of Cases Argued and Determined in the High Court of Admiralty: Commencing with the Judgments of the Right Hon. Sir William Scott, Michaelmas Term 1798.* Vol. 5. London: A. Strahan, 1806; Vol. 6. New York: Isaac Riley, 1810.

Schauinger, Joseph Herman. *William Gaston, Carolinian.* Milwaukee: Bruce Publishing Co., 1949.

Sears, Louis Martin. *Jefferson and the Embargo*. Durham, N.C.: Duke University Press, 1927.

Seybert, Adam. *Statistical Annals . . . of the United States of America*. Philadelphia: Thomas Dobson & Son, 1818.

Stanly, John. *Speech in the North Carolina House of Commons, December 1815*. Privately printed, 1816. North Carolina Collection, University of North Carolina Library, Chapel Hill.

Starkey, Marion. *The Cherokee Nation*. New York: Alfred A. Knopf, 1946.

Steele, John. *The Papers of John Steele*. Edited by Henry McGilbert Wagstaff. 2 vols. Raleigh: Edwards & Broughton Printing Co., 1924.

Talmadge, John E. "Georgia's Federalist Press and the War of 1812." *Journal of Southern History* 19 (1953):488-500.

Taylor, Melonie Johnson. "David Stone: A Political Biography." Master's thesis, East Carolina University, 1968.

Tucker, Glenn. *Poltroons and Patriots*. 2 vols. New York: Bobbs-Merrill Co., 1954.

Wagner, Edward James, II. "State-Federal Relations during the War of 1812." Ph.D. dissertation, Ohio State University, 1963.

Wagstaff, Henry McGilbert. *Federalism in North Carolina*. James Sprunt Historical Publications, vol. 9, no. 2. Chapel Hill: University of North Carolina Press, 1910.

Webster, Daniel. *The Private Correspondence of Daniel Webster*. Edited by Fletcher Webster. 2 vols. Boston: Little, Brown & Co., 1857.

Williams, Robert. *An Order* [from the Adjutant General's Office]. n.p.: 1819.

Williams, Stephen K., ed. *Cases Argued and Decided in the Supreme Court of the United States*. Lawyers' Edition. Book 4. Rochester: Lawyers Co-operative Publishing Co., 1926.

Wiltse, Charles M. "The Authorship of the War Report of 1812." *American Historical Review* 49 (1943-44):253-59.

Wood, William, ed. *Select British Documents of the Canadian War of 1812*. 3 vols. in 4. Toronto: University of Toronto Press, 1920-28.

Zimmerman, James Fulton. *Impressment of American Seamen*. Studies in History, Economics and Public Law 118, no. 1. New York: Columbia University Press, 1925.

INDEX

A

Adams, John, 87, 174
Adjutant general, 34, 36, 45, 46, 47, 48, 53, 58, 59, 61, 69, 76, 189. *See also* Cushing, Thomas
Alabama, 52, 94, 164, 167, 197
Alabama River, 29, 115
Albemarle Sound, 128, 148
Alston, Willis, 18, 20-21, 22, 172, 174, 175, 179; sketch of, 160 63
American Revolution, 84, 99, 168. *See also* Revolutionary War
Anson Court House, 191-92
Armstrong, John, 66, 68, 102, 103. *See also* Secretary of war
Arrington, William, 83
Asheville, 9, 50, 199
Atkinson, Henry, 56; sketch of, 63-64
Atkinson, Richard, 112, 141n
Augusta, Ga., 160, 195

B

Baltimore, 61, 103, 149, 157, 158, 192, 193
Banks, 25, 28, 33, 48, 175
Banks, Thomas, 135
Bauer, (Lieutenant), 129
Bayner, Richard, 42n
Beacon Island, 88, 89, 91, 121, 137, 139, 197
Beaufort, N.C., 11n, 36, 41, 43, 44, 120, 121, 122, 128, 129, 135-36, 148, 157, 158, 197
Beaufort, S.C., 39, 40, 153
Beaufort County, 123
Beasley, John, 87, 137
Bell, Brickhouse, 129, 149
Bell, Egbert H., 34, 71n
Bermuda, 127, 143, 144, 147
Bigby, Archibald, 50
Blackledge, William, 15-28 *passim*, 148, 169-79 *passim*, 182; sketch of, 163
Blacks. *See* Negroes
Bladen County, 122
Blakeley, Johnston, 143, 149-54; sketch of, 72-73
Blockade, 3, 6, 13, 21; of U.S., 11, 127, 128, 140-54 *passim*, 192, 193
Blount, John Gray, 43-44, 120, 126, 147, 163, 186, 197, 198
Blount, John Gray, Jr., 31n, 48, 64, **104**
Blount, Thomas, 163, 172
Blount, Thomas H., 139n, 149
Blount, William, 12n
Blount, William A., 51, 64
Bonner, John, 42n
Bodenhamer, William, 182
Boylan, William, 180, 184
Brandon, A. H., 52
Bridges, George R., 75n
Brite, Jeremiah, 126